THE
Not Quite
PRIME
MINISTERS

THE
Not Quite
PRIME
MINISTERS

LEADERS OF THE OPPOSITION
1783–2020

To James,

NIGEL FLETCHER

The best publisher!

\B^b\
Biteback Publishing

First published in Great Britain in 2023 by
Biteback Publishing Ltd, London
Copyright © Nigel Fletcher 2023

Nigel Fletcher has asserted his right under the Copyright, Designs and Patents Act 1988
to be identified as the author of this work.

ISBN 978-1-78590-810-1

10 9 8 7 6 5 4 3 2 1

A CIP catalogue record for this book is available from the British Library.

Set in Adobe Caslon Pro

Printed and bound in Great Britain by
CPI Group (UK) Ltd, Croydon CR0 4YY

FSC
www.fsc.org
MIX
Paper | Supporting
responsible forestry
FSC® C171272

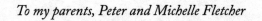

To my parents, Peter and Michelle Fletcher

Contents

Foreword *by Matt Chorley*   ix

Introduction   xiii

1   Charles James Fox   1
2   George Ponsonby   19
3   George Tierney   29
4   Henry Petty-Fitzmaurice, 3rd Marquess of Lansdowne   37
5   John Spencer, Viscount Althorp   42
6   Lord George Bentinck   48
7   Charles Manners, Marquess of Granby   55
8   John Charles Herries   59
9   Granville Leveson-Gower, 2nd Earl Granville   65
10   James Harris, 3rd Earl of Malmesbury   73
11   Hugh Cairns, 1st Baron Cairns   80
12   Charles Gordon-Lennox, 6th Duke of Richmond   88
13   Spencer Cavendish, Marquess of Hartington   95
14   Sir Stafford Northcote   104
15   Sir Michael Hicks Beach   111
16   John Wodehouse, 1st Earl of Kimberley   116
17   Sir William Harcourt   121

18 John Spencer, 5th Earl Spencer   128
19 George Robinson, 1st Marquess of Ripon   133
20 Henry Petty-Fitzmaurice, 5th Marquess of Lansdowne   137
21 Joseph Chamberlain   143
22 Sir Edward Carson   150
23 William Adamson   156
24 Sir Donald Maclean   162
25 Arthur Henderson   168
26 George Lansbury   175
27 James Maxton   183
28 Hastings Lees-Smith   188
29 Frederick Pethick-Lawrence   193
30 Arthur Greenwood   199
31 Herbert Morrison   205
32 Hugh Gaitskell   213
33 George Brown   223
34 Robert Carr   229
35 Michael Foot   232
36 Neil Kinnock   241
37 John Smith   250
38 Margaret Beckett   257
39 William Hague   264
40 Iain Duncan Smith   274
41 Michael Howard   281
42 Harriet Harman   291
43 Ed Miliband   297
44 Jeremy Corbyn   306

Epilogue   323
Notes   327
Acknowledgements   337
Index   339

Foreword

by Matt Chorley

Yvonne Fair is an unlikely political commentator. The Motown singer enjoyed only modest commercial success in the 1960s and 1970s. Her one hit – 'It Should Have Been Me', a cover of a song written for Kim Weston – reached number 5 in the UK charts in 1975, telling of the pain of being overlooked for another. It would be almost half a century before it became the unlikely soundtrack to an exploration of the losers who were jilted at the electoral altar when the British public picked someone else.

Whilst today's crop of politicians (and political commentators) like to think that everything is new, that their skills are unique, that their achievements and failures are unprecedented, the truth is that much of what happens today has occurred before. As a result, some of the greatest political leaders have been those with a strong sense of history, who wanted to learn from the mistakes of those that went before them.

It is why my mid-morning political show on Times Radio leans heavily on history to explain what is happening today. Having spotted that 2021 marked 300 years since Robert Walpole became our first Prime Minister, I launched a weekly feature with the historian and journalist Andrew Gimson, where each Monday we would spend ten minutes going through the lives of one of the occupants of No. 10. It was a brilliant way to not just learn more about the big ones – Pitt, Gladstone, Churchill, Thatcher – but to give the same prominence to the less-known PMs: Goderich, Rosebery, MacDonald. With fifty-five in total (at least at the time), it fitted almost perfectly into a year.

So, when 2022 was dawning, I was keen to explore the other side. Those who sought the highest office but came up short. Nobody can be said to have got closer to power than a Leader of the Opposition who never made it into No. 10.

There was no better choice for the feature than Nigel Fletcher, whom I have known for many years as the co-founder of the Centre for Opposition Studies. His knowledge comes not just from history books but from his own experience as an adviser to the Conservatives in their wilderness years and even as Leader of the Opposition himself as a councillor in the Royal Borough of Greenwich. He combined his detailed research with an eye for the absurd, often spotting poignant parallels with the politics of today. It was a perfect example of my show's motto: politics without the boring bits.

What is striking about the collection he has put together is that right from its emergence as part of our batty constitution, the role of Leader of the Opposition has been mostly a tiresome, thankless task. More often than not, it has involved picking up the pieces from defeat, rather than marching to glorious victory.

Since the 1911 Parliament Act, which gave the Commons (and the party leaders who sat there) pre-eminence over the Lords, there have been thirty-five Leaders of the Opposition. Just fourteen made it to become Prime Minister. The rest lost or were removed from office by their colleagues or the Grim Reaper before they got the chance to make their case to the country.

Yet anyone with hopes of defying the odds and crossing the floor to form a government (yes, I'm looking at you Keir) would do well to study Nigel's history of those who went before them. The lessons are many and varied: don't challenge the PM to a pistols-at-dawn duel, do look after your health, don't lose your own seat, do grab it if the chance to be PM comes, don't wear a baseball cap.

For some, like George Ponsonby or Jeremy Corbyn, being the nearly man was the pinnacle of their political lives. For others, like Joseph Chamberlain or William Hague, their careers are better known for what they did before and after.

All of them, however, will have had reason to gaze across the despatch box and wonder what they might do if they were on the other side. To bemoan the circumstances that prevented them from reaching the highest office. And, even later in life, to wonder what might have been. To think: it should have been me.

Introduction

History, as the old adage goes, is written by the winners. But it is also written predominantly *about* them, too. Those who make it to the top of politics in the UK and enter 10 Downing Street are assured of a place in history, however unimpressive or brief their premiership turns out to be. Whilst they might find themselves hugely overshadowed by the achievements of others, they can still claim the achievement of having secured the ultimate prize. In the words of Liz Truss, who set a new record for the shortest tenure in the job, 'At least I've been Prime Minister.'

The interest in the office has led to multiple libraries' worth of books on the subject, from studies of its holders to earnest academic tomes on every aspect of the role. We have musings on different prime ministerial leadership styles, the geography of power in No. 10, the role of advisers, and the mental and physical health of leaders over time. Full-length biographies on individual Prime Ministers have been supplemented by numerous anthologies bringing together biographical sketches of all or some of them. Most of these books are fascinating, and I am as partial to consuming this vast literature as any other political and historical addict. But look across to the other side of the political equation and it is a very different story.

Despite usually being portrayed as the UK's alternative Prime Minister, a search for books on Leaders of the Opposition turns up a dramatically reduced list of results, if any at all. As someone who finds political opposition a fascinating subject, this is a source of constant frustration to me, and I have tried to do what I can to provoke greater interest. This has involved co-founding the Centre for Opposition Studies (with my friend and colleague Professor Mohammed Abdel Haq), organising numerous events and conferences on the topic and generally sounding off about it whenever given a platform, microphone or any form of audience. Despite my best efforts, opposition remains somewhat in the shadows.

I was therefore delighted when Matt Chorley from Times Radio suggested to me at the start of 2022 that I join him on his show each week to talk about a different Leader of the Opposition. The previous year, Andrew Gimson had done the same with Prime Ministers, and this seemed a neat variation on the theme. I started compiling a list, keeping to Matt's primary rule that the leaders must only be those who failed in the end to become Prime Minister, to avoid repetition of those who had been covered in Gimson's list. In this contest, winning was a disqualification.

The first question was how far back in history to go. Like everything about the British constitution, the role of Leader of the Opposition evolved over time, and there is no definitive point of origin. As you go back into the mists of time, party structures become less distinct, and it is progressively harder to identify a single figure as being the pre-eminent oppositionist amongst the shifting mess of personalities and factions jostling for position. Until Robert Walpole, it was not even clear who was the leader of the government, and the situation on the other side of the House was even more confused.

I therefore chose to start with a prominent figure who made his name in opposition during the latter part of the eighteenth century and who was certainly a contender to become Prime Minister during his tenure. Charles James Fox has a better claim than most to be considered the first Leader of the Opposition, despite that job not having yet solidified into its modern form. He is also a major figure in parliamentary history and a colourful character in his own right, so his life and career would certainly make for an interesting and entertaining start to the list.

The existence of two houses of Parliament provided another complicating factor, as throughout the eighteenth and nineteenth centuries, Prime Ministers could be appointed from either of them. Parties had leaders in both houses, and it was often difficult to determine which of the two was the real alternative Prime Minister. Sometimes it turned out to be neither of them, though they usually had the strongest claim. I therefore included opposition leaders from both the Commons and the Lords up until 1911, when the Parliament Act relegated the upper House to a clearly subservient position and since when Prime Ministers have only come from the Commons.

Also included on the list were a number of individuals whose status as Leader of the Opposition was contested or not properly acknowledged at the time but who nevertheless either met the accepted definition of the role or fulfilled its duties. During at least two periods in the twentieth century there was some ambiguity about who should be recognised as Leader of the Opposition, with rival claimants to the title. As a result, names such as William Adamson and James Maxton, which had been omitted from certain other online lists, appeared on my nerdy spreadsheet. For the sake of completeness, I also included all those who led the main opposition party, regardless of how short their tenure. Thus, the list encompassed not only acting Labour leaders George Brown, Margaret Beckett and Harriet Harman but also the

Conservative Robert Carr, who took on the duties of the job for just a week in 1975 after Edward Heath stood down.

Playing by these rules, I ended up with a list of forty-four Leaders of the Opposition, which, after accounting for a handful of breaks during the year, would take us from mid-January to just before Christmas 2022. Every week, I settled into a routine of researching the next leader on the list, in readiness for the time shortly before noon on Monday when I would set up the microphone at my desk and join Matt on his show for between five and ten minutes, regurgitating a stream of biographical facts until the midday news bulletin cut me off.

To introduce the slot, Matt wanted an appropriate piece of music, but after putting out an appeal on Twitter for the best songs, we decided there were just too many good ones to narrow it down. This was the origin of what became known (at least to us) as the best political music montage on the radio, with a megamix encompassing Beck's 'Loser', D:Ream's 'Things Can Only Get Better' and ending with the superb 'It Should Have Been Me' by Yvonne Fair. For the whole year this heralded my weekly countdown of leaders, and since then my Monday mornings have felt somewhat empty without my personal theme music to perk them up.

It was great fun to be part of the show, whose mantra is to offer listeners 'politics without the boring bits', and I duly tried to enliven my brief biographical sketches with fun facts and pub quiz trivia. Duels with pistols, questionable nicknames and links to classic children's TV shows all got a mention at various times. The feature seemed to be getting good feedback and reached a wider audience when the whole series was released as a set of omnibus episodes of the *Red Box Politics Podcast*.

There was, however, a limit to how much we could discuss on air, and I began thinking about what to do with the sets of notes I had compiled throughout the year. Matt was amongst those who suggested I consider turning them into a book, and I was delighted when the idea found favour with the team at Biteback Publishing. And so began the task of compiling the volume you now have in your hands.

I say 'compiling', but it swiftly became clear that my brief notes really only scratched the surface of the leaders and their lives, and I would need to go back to the sources I had previously consulted, as well as a number of others. For some of the leaders there exist full published biographies, but for others the material was more scant. I am indebted to the *Oxford Dictionary of National Biography*, which provided a great starting point for many of the entries, particularly towards the beginning of the period. The 'History of Parliament' project was also very helpful for some of them. But I decided to add another major source of material to my research, which seemed appropriate given the origins of this project. This was the archive of *The Times* newspaper, available to online subscribers as well as via certain academic databases.

With newspapers going back to 1785, this superb resource neatly spanned the whole of the period I needed to cover and provided a wonderful insight into how each leader was perceived during their time and how they were remembered afterwards. In fact, the obituaries were a particularly rich source of material, and I soon found that many of them pulled no punches in making frank and harsh judgements about the recently departed, damning them with faint praise or worse. I have drawn extensively from these but have also tried to use coverage of other notable incidents during their lives as well. Piloting my computer back through the centuries to specific days in history was an absolute joy, and I can highly recommend this form of virtual time travel. If you want to try it for yourself, access to 200 years of the archive from 1785 to 1985 is included in the price of an online subscription to *The Times* and to my mind justifies the cost on its own.

It is, however, quite a sobering experience to read a succession of death notices and obituaries in a fairly short space of time, particularly after having researched the subjects' lives and careers and seen them as fully rounded people, rather than just names on a list. It was sometimes a tragic trajectory: early promise, political advancement, onwards towards the ultimate prize, only to see that ambition thwarted in some way, leading to disappointment in later life before they succumbed to inevitable decline and death. But whilst that is the pattern we might typically expect from a book on 'failed' leaders, in truth their experiences varied considerably. Whilst some of them did indeed set their hearts on becoming Prime Minister and will for ever be marked by their failure to achieve that objective, others were never remotely in contention for that office and knew they were merely minding the shop in opposition. Others had highly distinguished careers in the great offices of state and were, by any objective measure, successful and consequential figures, whose period as Leader of the Opposition was often a brief and unremarkable interlude.

In writing their entries for this book, I faced the perennial challenge of how to condense full and complex lives into an average of just 2,000 words per person. Clearly any such exercise had to be selective, but I didn't want to restrict myself to just writing about their tenures as leader. What I thought was most interesting was to give a sense of how they ended up in the job, where they came from and the type of person they were. If they later went on to greater glories, that was also worth noting, but it was their backstory that I thought needed to be told in the first instance. Inevitably, this too had to be done in broad terms, and I apologise in advance to the scores of historians with greater expertise on each of the individual leaders, who will no doubt consider that I have left out some vital piece of the story or oversimplified the politics of the age.

What I cannot apologise for, however, is the degree of triviality and irreverence that often emerges in some of the stories I have chosen to include. One of the reasons I was so pleased to join Matt's show in the first place was that I had already come to enjoy its splendid mix of serious political commentary and unashamed silliness. There is already enough dullness in politics and sadness in the world, so the occasional bit of light relief is essential to save us all from despair. Matt and his team do a great job on that score, and I have tried to bring some of that spirit into what follows. Silliness is a vastly underrated component of life, and my only regret is that there isn't even more of it in the book.

Of the more serious themes that emerge, I think the most striking is the supreme importance of luck and chance in the fortunes of leading politicians. We talk about 'accidents of history' as though they are somehow exceptional, but the truth is that history is just one long accident. This is particularly noticeable in politics, where the fates of particular individuals can have a significant measurable effect on the course of events. Whilst it is tempting to see personal qualities and political acumen as the biggest factors in determining whether someone makes it to No. 10, this denies the sheer bloody-minded randomness of events. Untimely deaths and illnesses, resignations and electoral losses have all intervened at various times to obstruct the ambitions of would-be Prime Ministers and to put others in their place. The gap between success and failure is often much narrower than many would care to admit.

Whether or not Leaders of the Opposition stand much chance of being Prime Minister, they are nevertheless defined by their relationship with that office. They stand in the shadow of 10 Downing Street, whose occupant is the focus of all their political activity for however long they are doing the job. They can never be allowed to forget that their opponent is in power and they are not.

But opposition in Parliament is in itself a worthy and necessary duty, and its toleration within the political system is an important democratic principle. Providing the country with a licensed critic of the government, and demonstrating that an alternative to them exists, is a potent constitutional statement, however thankless the task might seem. Many of the people on this list could easily have ended up in No. 10, whilst for others, the prospect was little more than a theoretical possibility. But in the roller coaster world of politics, even making it to the leadership of the opposition is an achievement worth noting. Certainly, all of those whose lives are covered in these pages achieved some degree of success in their careers or fulfilment in their personal lives. There is much more to them than not quite becoming Prime Minister.

Charles James Fox

Whig, Leader of the Opposition 1783–1806

Charles James Fox was a big figure. In the history books, as in life, he looms large, a substantial presence in every sense. Unusually for someone who did not become Prime Minister, his name is more familiar to many historians than some of those who did. Having commanded the floor of the old House of Commons in the late eighteenth and early nineteenth centuries, his imposing physical presence remains there, immortalised in marble with his right hand raised mid-speech, as one of the statues lining what is now St Stephen's Hall in the Palace of Westminster, the site of the old chamber. There he faces his old adversary William Pitt the Younger, their political rivalry frozen in time.

Completed in 1856, fifty years after his death, it is not the most flattering of statues. His coat is held together at his chest by a single button, which strains to contain the ample stomach pushing his waistcoat out beneath. His size had been a signature target for cartoonists of his age such as James Gillray, but even the more formal pictures showed off his bulging waistline, with a 1782 portrait by Joshua Reynolds showing his coat similarly parted. These visual representations captured a key aspect of his character, as someone whose private excesses and enjoyment of life's material pleasures were notorious. But he was also a huge figure in the politics of the age, and it is this which has kept his name echoing down the centuries.

He was born on 24 January 1749 in London, the second son of Henry Fox (later 1st Baron Holland). His mother was Lady Caroline Lennox, daughter of the 2nd Duke of Richmond, whose father was the illegitimate son of King Charles II and his mistress Louise de Kérouaille, Duchess of Portsmouth. Fox was therefore the biological great-great-grandson of the 'merry monarch', whose colourful private life he was in many ways destined to emulate.

His family links to the Stuart royal line were not confined to these maternal genes, however. His paternal grandfather Sir Stephen Fox had been a pageboy to Charles I at the time of his execution 100 years earlier, and it is no coincidence that he was himself given the very Stuart names Charles and James. That someone with such a royalist pedigree should have spent most of his political life criticising a king is something of an historical irony, though of course the Hanoverian George III was from a different royal line.

The baby Charles seems initially not to have impressed his father, who described him as 'weakly' and observed, 'His skin hangs all shrivell'd about him, his eyes stare, he has a black head of hair, and 'tis incredible how like a monkey he look'd before he was dressed.'[1] Despite this inauspicious start, father and son soon developed a close relationship, with Henry finding the young boy 'infinitely engaging & clever' and greatly enjoying spending time with him.

Throughout his childhood, Charles was constantly indulged by his father, in whose eyes he could do no wrong. It was said the elder Fox once forgot a promise to his son that he could watch a wall being demolished and ordered it to be rebuilt purely so Charles could watch it being knocked down again. Similar stories began circulating in

London society, including the occasion when Charles walked into his father's room whilst he was working, picked up one of his papers, declared that he didn't like it and threw it onto the fire. Instead of punishing this insolence, his father quietly wrote it out again.

His relationship with his mother was more distant, though even she recognised his precocious intelligence and praised how 'infinitely engaging' he was, entering into his parents' conversations, reading with them and being 'in every respect the most agreeable companion'. Despite this, she recognised that his excessive self-confidence might not endear him to others, writing to her sister, 'These same qualities, so pleasing to us, often make him troublesome to other people. He will know everything ... and is too apt to give his opinion about everything.'[2] This astute observation certainly pointed towards a career in politics.

He was educated at Eton, where he made a number of lifelong friends who he called 'the gang'. His achievements as a Latin scholar impressed his tutors, but it was another form of education that was perhaps to have a greater effect on his later life. At the age of just fourteen he was taken to Paris by his father, given a large amount of money and allowed to indulge himself for the first time in the pleasurable vices of gambling and sex. Returning to Eton somewhat more worldly, he was asked to leave the college early the following year, having been judged to be 'too witty' and 'a little too wicked' to stay on.[3]

Instead, he went up to Oxford, where he studied mathematics and classics but left without a degree. He was soon back in Paris, where he stayed a while before embarking on a grand tour of Europe that took in Italy and Switzerland. It was in these early years that he developed his love of French fashion and became friends with many of the country's leading society figures. Travelling with his gang of Etonian friends, he met intellectual figures including Voltaire, partied with the

Duc d'Orléans and bedded a succession of mistresses and prostitutes, cheerfully writing home to his friends about the collection of 'poxes and claps' he picked up along the way.[4]

Having been a precocious child, it was fitting that his entry into Parliament should have been equally premature. He was elected in 1768 at the age of nineteen, which was technically too young for him to have been legally eligible, though this does not seem to have impeded him. His seat of Midhurst had been secured for him by his father, whose own political career had come to an end three years earlier when, shortly after accepting a peerage as Lord Holland, he was forced from his post as Paymaster of the Forces. In those days it was not unusual for holders of such public offices to use them to line their own pockets, but Holland was viewed as having done so excessively, embezzling large sums of public money to make himself a fortune.

Having been a much-indulged son, Fox spent much of his political career repaying the favour by publicly defending his father's honour – a rather thankless task, given the circumstances. As well as deflecting questions about financial propriety, anther long-running battle he took up was on the question of his parents' marriage. They had eloped, with the wedding being against the wishes of the bride's parents, the Duke and Duchess of Richmond. In 1753 Lord Hardwicke had brought forward legislation which became the Clandestine Marriages Act, designed to help aristocratic parents prevent such romantic scandals, and Henry Fox had understandably taken the measure as a personal affront.

Nearly twenty years later, as an offspring of that marriage, Charles James Fox sought to remove the taint from his parentage by proposing a repeal of Hardwicke's Act. He had by this time developed a reputation as a talented orator, making frequent contributions in the chamber, which marked him out as a young man of great ability. These skills were all the more impressive given he spent a large part of his time gambling, betting on horses and drinking. The circumstances in which he introduced his marriages bill in 1772 were a prime example, as one of his biographers vividly described:

On the 7th of April Fox's bill for the repeal of Lord Hardwicke's Act came on for discussion. The day before Fox had been at Newmarket, losing heavily as usual on the turf. On his way back to town to introduce his first important measure into Parliament – a bill which was to alter the social arrangements of the country, and remove a stigma from his family – he fell in with some friends at Hocherel. Characteristically enough, he spent the night drinking with them instead of preparing for the struggle of the morrow, and arrived on the next day at the House without having been to bed at all, without having prepared his speech, and without even having drafted his bill. Nothing but the most consummate talent could have saved him.[5]

Luckily for him, he possessed such talent and produced a masterful performance. He briefly introduced his bill, then sat down to allow the Prime Minister Lord North and Edmund Burke to make their case against it. According to Horace Walpole, who witnessed the scene, Fox seemed barely to have listened to them but then rose and 'with amazing spirit and memory' ridiculed and refuted their arguments and won the day. As Walpole commented, 'This was genius.'[6]

It was a short-lived triumph, however. Having won its first reading by a majority of one, the bill came up again the following month for debate. Fox was absent, the call of the racecourse having once again been too much to resist, and by the time he had hurried back from Newmarket, the bill had been thrown out by a large majority. This episode neatly illustrates the tension between his reputation as a brilliant parliamentarian and his equally prominent reputation for indulging his private vices. In the following two years his father had to bail him out financially, paying off gambling debts that had reached the staggering figure of £120,000 (over £14 million in 2023 prices).

He was also getting a reputation for capricious behaviour in politics. He had accepted junior office in Lord North's government as a member of the Board of Admiralty in 1770 but resigned two years later in protest of the passing of the Royal Marriages Act, which he saw as another slight against his parents. North then appointed Fox to the Treasury board in late 1772, where he was reported to have worked diligently over the following year before a sudden outbreak of cavalier behaviour led to his being dismissed. The row blew up over the obscure issue of a pamphlet which had been published impugning the impartiality of the Speaker of the House of Commons. The printer was summoned before the House to apologise, but Fox was not content to let the matter rest there and publicly berated North for not pursuing the matter more strongly.

This attack on the Prime Minister by a 25-year-old junior colleague was considered outrageous by King George III, who furiously instructed that the young upstart be sacked. Lord North duly wrote Fox a letter informing him of his dismissal from office with the delicious words, 'Sir, his Majesty has thought proper to order a new commission of the Treasury to be made out, in which I do not perceive your name.'[7]

Such was the dry wit of this note that Fox initially thought it was a practical joke by his friends. Once he realised the truth, he made his displeasure clear in person to the king, making a cutting remark about his dismissal when they met in passing at court the next day. The king, making dismissive small talk, reportedly asked whether he was 'out today', to which Fox replied, 'No, but I was yesterday thanks to your

Majesty.'⁸ The enmity between the two men would last for the rest of their lives and have serious consequences for the politics of the age.

After these early brief periods in government, Fox remained firmly in opposition for much of the next decade, during which time his political views matured and became more radical. During the American War of Independence Fox aligned himself with the revolutionary Americans, which provided a substantive issue on which he could attack Lord North's government – a task he set about with relish. He also started to see parallels between the fight for representative democracy in the United States and what he saw as the undemocratic exercise of power and influence by George III and his ministers in Great Britain. Such attitudes saw him painted as unpatriotic or even treasonous, but his scathing performances in the Commons in which he attacked ministers for the conduct of the war came to be dreaded by those in government.

Nineteenth-century biographer Henry Offley Wakeman called Fox 'the first of parliamentary gladiators', and believed, 'His unfailing spirits, his universal popularity, his iron nerves, his unrivalled power as a debater, all marked him out as the real leader of the Opposition in the House of Commons.' It was during the debates on the American Revolutionary War, he said, that Fox perfected 'the gifts of quick retort, ready wit, clear statement and dashing attack'.⁹

Nor was his activism restricted to the power of his oratory. On occasion his political battles became very much more physical. In the spring of 1779, Fox and other leading Whigs took up the cause of a senior naval officer – Admiral Keppel, a member of one of the great Whig families – who was being court-martialled for refusing to engage a French fleet in the Channel. Fox and his colleagues believed the trial was politically motivated, and when the verdict of Keppel's acquittal came through they organised a triumphant riot, encouraging a mob of supporters to march to the Admiralty and smash windows, which forced the First Lord of the Admiralty and others to flee in panic. In a sign of the fashion for political dissent to be brewed alongside caffein-ated beverages, Fox was said to have plotted the violent demonstration from a coffee house in St James's called Betty's.

The mixing of politics with violence during this time threatened to end Fox's career in a most dramatic way. In November of the same year, a supporter of Lord North called William Adam accused Fox of having libelled him, an accusation which the latter denied. This being the eighteenth century, there was only one way for their honour to be satisfied. On 29 November the two men met at 8 a.m. in Hyde Park to fight a duel. They both fired their pistols twice, and Fox was hit in the stomach but 'only slightly'. He later joked that he would have been killed if his opponent had not charged his pistol with substandard government gunpowder.[10]

It was characteristic of Fox that he should treat such a near-death experience so casually. A few years later the mounting debts caused by his gambling led to an order for all his goods to be sold. Horace Walpole happened to be passing his house at the time and reported that as his home was stripped bare, Fox came out and talked to him nonchalantly about a bill before Parliament as if nothing out of the ordinary was happening.

Having perfected his skills in opposition, Fox had become one of the leading political figures of the day. In 1780 he became the MP for the high-profile Westminster constituency and completed his move to a populist Whig 'man of the people', supporting protest movements against the government and appearing on platforms alongside noted radicals such as John Wilkes. Despite these anti-establishment cre-dentials, he was soon transported back to the heart of government.

When Lord North resigned from office in 1782, his replacement, the Marquess of Rockingham, appointed Fox as Foreign Secretary. However, his tenure in high office was cut short when Rockingham died just a few months later. George III informed his ministers that he would appoint the Earl of Shelburne as his new Prime Minister, a decision to which Fox reacted angrily, speaking to the king 'in a strong way' and resigning his seals of office. He then went out for dinner at Brooks's and stayed there drinking until 4 a.m., when he moved onto White's. In an ominous sign of the political divisions within the royal family, Fox's dining companion that night was his friend the Prince of Wales.

Fox's opposition to Shelburne put him into an unlikely alliance with Lord North, who also opposed the new government's approach to finalising peace with America. They united their supporters with the aim of bringing about the downfall of the government and eventually succeeded in doing so. When Shelburne resigned, the king tried in vain to find an alternative to Fox and North but was eventually forced to accept what became known as the Fox–North coalition, nominally headed by the Duke of Portland. Not only did George III get no choice over his Prime Minister, but Fox and North gave him no say whatsoever over the composition of the government, instead presenting him with complete lists of ministers, with North serving as Home Secretary and Fox returning as Foreign Secretary. This represented a significant curtailing of the royal prerogative and was such a humiliating personal defeat for the king that he talked seriously about abdicating the throne.

Instead, George III determined to obstruct the coalition however he could. It lasted from March to December 1783, when it was defeated in the House of Lords on the East India Bill, which sought to increase government control of the East India Company. The measure had been approved by a large majority in the House of Commons, but the king pressured peers to vote against it in the House of Lords, telling them that any who voted with the government would be considered his enemies. When the bill was defeated he dismissed the government, sending messengers that very night to demand Fox and North hand over their seals of office. In their place he appointed William Pitt the (very much) Younger as Tory Prime Minister at the age of just twenty-four.

Fox was outraged by this further abuse of the royal prerogative over a measure which had the clear support of the Commons. But he also took satisfaction in the fact that the king's behaviour would now be seen as plainly unconstitutional and that his own supporters in the Commons would not put up with it. Certainly, many Whigs considered the appointment of Pitt a laughable act of desperation, with no other politician willing to attempt to govern without support in the Commons. They dubbed his government the 'mince pie administration', as they predicted it would not last beyond the end of Christmas.

Throughout the beginning of the new year, Pitt attempted to persuade Fox to take office alongside him but was firmly and publicly rejected. Instead, Fox ramped up the rhetoric about the abuse of royal power and used his parliamentary majority to bring government to a standstill. However, as the weeks wore on, his majority slowly diminished as traditionalist-minded MPs became alarmed at the ongoing constitutional crisis and moved to back the government. Then, in March 1784, the king dissolved Parliament, despite it having three years left to run, and plunged the country into an acrimonious election to settle the matter.

In a vitriolic and dirty campaign, the king used all the influence of the Crown to help return a majority for Pitt's government. Fox feared he might lose his Westminster constituency, such was the intense campaigning. Whilst he avoided that indignity, he was roundly defeated across the country in a result that was seen as a vindication of George III's belief in his right to choose his own ministers. The 'mince pie administration' of William Pitt that had been predicted to last a matter of days in the event lasted for seventeen years.

As a result, Fox himself was cast back into opposition, where he remained for twenty-two long years. Later Leaders of the Opposition might consider that sentence to be a cruel and unusual punishment, and it certainly dwarfs the very brief periods that some served in the role. But it must be remembered that there was at this time no formalised role for a Leader of the Opposition in the modern sense. Fox was out of office, and personally opposed to Pitt's government (and indeed to the king himself), but the extent to which he chose to exert himself in the duties of scrutinising and challenging the government ebbed and flowed over the years. For a time it seemed his political career might be over, but the events that would take place a few years later brought him back into contention.

First was the impeachment of Warren Hastings, the former governor of Bengal, who was accused of mismanagement and corruption whilst in India. Fox was appointed as one of the managers of the trial, and in its early weeks in 1788 sought to link the allegations to the purposes behind his East India Bill of four years ago, which had led to the fall of the coalition government. His interest was less in the individual charges against Hastings and much more in seeking retrospective vindication for the measures he had proposed in government. It was left to Edmund Burke to do most of the hard work on the trial, which would eventually last for seven years. Having played a prominent role at the start, Fox's interest dwindled as the proceedings ground on, and he had concluded that it was a wasted effort long before Hastings was eventually acquitted.

Meanwhile, in the same year the trial started, the bitter feud between Fox and King George III had taken a dramatic turn when, in October, the king was incapacitated by some form of mental illness. The events of what became known as the Regency Crisis are today most familiar to audiences of Alan Bennett's 1991 play *The Madness of George III* and the film version made three years later. The play charts the dramatic months during which it seemed the king would be permanently unable to fulfil his duties and showed the Prince of Wales plotting with Fox to have a regency declared, after which the prince would remove Pitt from office and replace him with Fox and his colleagues.

Whilst this fictionalised account captures something of the drama and political intrigue of the time, it rather overstates Fox's role. In fact, when the king was first taken ill Fox was overseas, on a tour of France and Italy, and did not return for several weeks. When he did, he was reported to be ill and his attendance at party meetings and debates was sporadic. As the crisis continued into the new year in 1789, Fox left London for a month and his attempts to control the Whig response by post were not wholly effective. Despite these absences, he had set out his clear views on the matter in December, arguing that if the king was incapable, the constitution should behave as though he were dead and the Prince of Wales should automatically exercise the full powers of the Crown. He strenuously opposed Parliament placing restrictions on those powers, an argument which seemed rather at odds with his impassioned defence of Parliament's rights five years earlier.

Had the king remained incapacitated, a regency would have been declared and Fox would have been returned to office. Indeed, he and his colleagues had occupied themselves during the crisis drawing up lists of Cabinet appointments, whilst assuring the Prince of Wales that his accession as Prince Regent was imminent. But it was not to be. The king recovered and the Regency Bill was abandoned. After coming so close to winning back power and avenging the humiliation of five years earlier, Fox was once again cast back into the political wilderness by his nemesis, the king.

Returning to opposition, Fox immediately faced the problem of holding the Whig Party together as opinion divided on one of the major issues of the day. Ironically, this particular division also centred on the proper role of the Crown in the constitution, but in this case it was the French Crown, with the debate being about how to respond to the French Revolution of 1789. Fox himself had reacted to the storming of the Bastille by writing excitedly to a friend that it was 'the greatest Event that has ever happened in the world', and he continued to view developments across the Channel as an exciting advance towards a more progressive constitutional monarchy.[11] In this he was at odds with his former mentor Edmund Burke, who viewed the revolution as a disaster and angrily denounced Fox's views. The breakdown of relations between the two men over the issue was complete and they never spoke again.

The split with Burke was symptomatic of Fox's inability to unite the Whigs during this time. As the French Revolution turned increasingly bloody with the execution of King Louis XVI in 1793, Fox was appalled by the violence but continued to view the original objectives of the revolutionaries sympathetically and the new French Republic as a lesser evil than despotic monarchy. Such views became increasingly controversial as Britain went to war against revolutionary France and the fracturing of the Whig Party continued, with more and more of Fox's former allies deserting him and giving their support to the government at what they considered to be a time of national crisis.

From 1794 onwards, Fox could barely be said to be leading a party at all, with his supporters reduced to a small band of friends. It was hardly an organised opposition, let alone an alternative government.

He occupied himself for the next few years with vocal opposition to the Pitt government's introduction of controversial measures such as the Treason Bill and the Seditious Meetings Bill, which sought to ban or restrict unauthorised political meetings and public debates. Fox considered these proposals to be an unjustified assault on civil liberties and evidence of the country sliding towards despotism. There was even a direct link to George III himself in the origins of the legislation. The king's carriage had been attacked as he drove to the opening of Parliament in November 1795, with stones thrown from the crowd. Parliamentary outrage at the incident and claims that the event was part of a wider plot provided Pitt with the excuse to introduce the 'emergency' measures.

Fox's speeches against the legislation were a reminder of the power of his oratory in the Commons, even if his band of supporters was diminished. He outlined a clear and compelling argument that clamping down on free speech and political protest would only increase the chances of violent revolution, such as had occurred in France. As he put it:

Look to France before the period of her revolution. Was it the facility of public meetings, or the freedom of discussion granted to the subject, that tended to produce that great change? On the contrary, was it not the absolute prerogative of the King? Was it not the arbitrary power lodged in Ministers? ... In countries where men may openly state their grievances and boldly claim redress, the effect of their complaints and remonstrances may, indeed, for a time be obstructed by the operation of ministerial corruption and intrigue; but perseverance must ultimately be effectual at procuring them relief. But if you take away all legal means of obtaining that object, if you silence remonstrance and stifle complaint, you then leave no other alternative but force and violence.[12]

It is a powerful argument for political freedom of speech and a warning of the consequences if peaceful opposition is restricted. He extended his campaign against the measures beyond Parliament, calling directly for people to protest against them: 'I do hope that the bill will produce an alarm; that while we have the power of assembling, the people will assemble.'[13] He spoke at a public meeting attended by thousands of people and called on them to petition Parliament against the bills. He became increasingly vocal in his campaigning and was less cautious about being associated with radical political causes and extra-parliamentary protest. But the unsuccessful campaign was a last hurrah for his career as a major opposition leader. Disenchanted by his inability to prevent such measures passing, he decided to boycott Parliament completely, beginning in 1797. He sold his London house and moved permanently to St Ann's Hill in Surrey.

Fox's 'secession' from Parliament was not a final departure. He remained an MP and continued to offer advice to other Foxites, who still looked to him as their leader in the absence of a clear replacement. He occasionally attended dinners and gave support to prominent radicals and reformers. At one dinner in 1798 he was recorded to have drunk a toast to 'our sovereign, the People' – an act of perceived disloyalty to the Crown that saw him removed from the list of Privy Counsellors. He had pushed the boundaries of 'loyal opposition' too far.

For four years he remained largely absent from Westminster, and it was only the resignation of Pitt in 1801 that prompted him to return to the political fray. A few years later, in 1804, he entered a surprising political alliance with Pitt's former Foreign Secretary, Lord Grenville, who had chosen not to rejoin Pitt's government. When Pitt died in office in 1806, Grenville became Prime Minister of a coalition with Fox and his supporters, which has become known as the Ministry of All the Talents. Fox was appointed Foreign Secretary, more than two decades after he had last held the job.

The king, however, continued to loathe him, declaring just a few weeks earlier that he would not 'suffer' him to sit 'in any Cabinet'.[14] Despite this, Grenville would not permit a royal veto of the appointment, and Fox returned to the Cabinet, having first been sworn back into the Privy Council, from which the king had excluded him eight years earlier. The displeasure this must have caused George III was perhaps one of the reasons Fox agreed to return, as he had by this point lost his appetite for power and accepted office more from a sense of duty to his followers than any great desire to rule.

He was also by this point very ill and became increasingly so over the summer. He died at a quarter to six on the evening of Saturday 13 September 1806 at the Duke of Devonshire's Chiswick House, which had been lent to him for his last weeks. The report in *The Times* the following Monday recorded that 'his last hours were not disturbed by any bodily suffering'.[15] It then went on to offer a long and glowing appreciation of his life, which contained superlative praise of his abilities, particularly as an orator:

> Of his eloquence and debating powers, it is not easy to speak in terms that can convey an adequate idea of them. His speeches may be considered as among the finest examples of argumentation, abounding in pointed observations and just conclusions, cloaked in forcible expression, and delivered with manly boldness: The leading characteristic of his oratory was a ready and, as it were, intuitive power of analysis, which he possessed beyond any man now living;

and it would not exceed the truth, perhaps, if it were added, equal to any man that has ever lived.

As to his political conduct, we shall not attempt to enlarge upon a subject of such wide extent, of such complicated parts, and abounding in concerns of so much weight and importance. A large volume would scarce be sufficient to contain it; and to attempt to reduce it to a column, would be to disgrace the subject, and disgust the reader. To the Historians we shall leave that difficult and laborious task. To that department, alas! Mr Fox himself is now consigned.[16]

I can only agree with the final sentiment, and I hope my attempt to reduce the subject to this chapter does not 'disgust the reader', particularly if that reader is one of the many historians who have indeed undertaken the 'difficult and laborious' task of properly chronicling the life of Charles James Fox. He continues to fascinate scholars of parliamentary history to an extent that is highly unusual for someone who never made it to 10 Downing Street. There are of course many details of his life and the causes he pursued to which I have been unable to do justice here, but even this partial sketch has occupied much more space than will be given to other leaders in this book. That is an appropriate mark of his significance as an opposition leader.

Why did Fox not make it to become Prime Minister? The single most important factor, we have to conclude, was the lifelong hatred that existed between him and King George III. The origins of that enmity lay in the friendship between Fox and the Prince of Wales (later George IV) and the king's conviction that his son had been led astray into a life of vice. He detested the prince's behaviour and both he and Queen Charlotte blamed Fox for it. This might not have been entirely fair, but the closeness of the two men and their reputation for personal excesses – gambling, drinking and womanising – bound them together in the popular consciousness.

The fact that the king should have the power to block the advancement of a politician he detested both fuelled and justified Fox's attacks on what he saw as the abuse of the royal prerogative. The role of the Crown in the constitution runs as a thread throughout Fox's career, from Britain to America to France. The tension over how vehemently it was possible for him to attack the government whilst remaining loyal to the Crown was a live issue throughout these years. The partisanship of George III would have made it extremely difficult for any opposition leader at this time.

Ironically, it was Fox's closeness to the Prince of Wales that perhaps prevented him being seen as a more dangerous revolutionary. Throughout history, political opposition has often rallied behind the rival court of the heir to the throne, allowing them to attack the monarch's ministers without appearing disloyal to the idea of monarchy. The twenty-year rivalry between Pitt and Fox was in some ways a proxy war between George III and his son, and therefore the Prince of Wales is sometimes credited as being the most important figure in opposition for much of this period. But in truth, Fox's towering presence on the political scene established him as the undisputed Leader of the Opposition, and it was this position, legitimised by the prince's favour, that made him the Prime Minister-in-waiting. Even if, ultimately, that waiting was in vain.

2

George Ponsonby

Whig, Leader of the Opposition 1808–17

'A little-known mediocrity who was related to Lady Grey.' That is the rather devastating phrase with which the historian Archibald S. Foord dismisses the next leader on our list, George Ponsonby.

After more than two decades of the personal battle between William Pitt and Charles James Fox dominating the political debate, their deaths in 1806 were bound to leave something of a vacuum at Westminster. The leaders who followed them, in government and in opposition, struggled to live up to their illustrious predecessors and were perhaps bound to be seen as mediocre by comparison.

After the collapse of the Ministry of All the Talents in April 1807, the Whig opposition was initially led in the House of Commons by Charles Grey, Viscount Howick, who would later (as Earl Grey) become Prime Minister, thereby disqualifying him from our list. It was his elevation to the House of Lords in November 1807 that led to the search for a new Leader of the Opposition in the Commons. An obvious candidate might have been Samuel Whitbread, Grey's brother-in-law, who was an impressive speaker in debate, but considered too radical for the job. Other better-known contenders were also ruled out or declined for one reason or another, so the choice fell on 53-year-old George Ponsonby, who said the job was 'really above my qualifications' but accepted it on the basis that he would do 'more harm by declining than by accepting'. Another colleague gave him the less than ringing endorsement that 'any choice is better than none'.[1]

Who was this reluctant nonentity? Born on 5 March 1755, he was the third son of John Ponsonby, who served as the Speaker of the Irish House of Commons for fifteen years – at the time Ireland was a separate kingdom with its own Parliament, prior to the Act of Union. His mother was Lady Elizabeth Cavendish, daughter of the 3rd Duke of Devonshire. Ponsonby himself was educated first in Dublin, then attended Trinity College, Cambridge, was admitted to Lincoln's Inn at the age of twenty to become a lawyer and was called to the Irish Bar four years later. He was married to Lady Mary Butler, daughter of the Earl of Lanesborough.

He had also followed his father into politics, having been elected to the Irish Parliament in 1778, representing Wicklow. I say 'elected', but this perhaps gives an unduly democratic impression of the process, given the electoral franchise at this time was still rather limited and explicitly barred Catholics from voting. He was then appointed to a number of quite lucrative positions in the Irish government, benefitting from the patronage of successive Lords Lieutenant of Ireland, who were appointees of the British government. One such position was Counsel to the Revenue Commissioners, bestowed upon him in 1782 by the 3rd Duke of Portland, husband of Ponsonby's cousin. This post brought him £1,400 a year – equivalent to about £190,000 in 2023 prices.

Given his Whig connections, he did well to remain in office in Dublin when the Tory government of William Pitt came to power in London, but his fate soon matched that of his Whig counterparts there. During the Regency Crisis he backed an address in the Irish

Parliament calling for the Prince of Wales to be made regent and was dismissed from office in 1789. He therefore entered opposition, becoming a founding member of the Irish Whig Club whilst continuing his practice as a barrister throughout the 1790s. Ponsonby became one of the leading opposition figures in the Irish House of Commons, arguing in favour of ending the ban on Catholics voting in elections and introducing a bill for parliamentary reform. Somewhat surprisingly, he made a brief return to government office in 1795, after the Duke of Portland entered Pitt's government in London and appointed the Whig Earl Fitzwilliam as Lord Lieutenant of Ireland. Ponsonby was offered the post of Attorney General of Ireland, but the administration was suddenly ended the following month when Pitt recalled Fitzwilliam in alarm at his proposals for Catholic emancipation.

Ponsonby spent the following two years attempting in vain to advance the causes of Catholic relief and parliamentary reform, but, increasingly disillusioned by politics, he withdrew from Parliament in protest in 1797, an act that mirrored that of Fox in the British Parliament at the same time. However, he returned after a year in order to fight plans for political union between Ireland and Great Britain, becoming 'the chief conductor of opposition' to the proposed legislation, which would become the Act of Union.[2] He achieved success in delaying the measure in 1799 but was unable to prevent it passing a year later, and subsequently the Irish Parliament was abolished.

He now found himself not just without a parliamentary seat, but without a Parliament. This did not last long, and in 1801, after a hard-fought and expensive campaign, he defeated his opponent by seventy-three votes to be elected as MP for Wicklow in the new Parliament of the United Kingdom. The change in constitutional arrangements was not without incident, as initially his election writ was 'by a blunder … made returnable to the Irish Parliament', voiding the election.[3] After the error was corrected and he was eventually returned to the correct Parliament in a new election, his reputation as a leading Irish Whig went before him, as *The Times* reported at the time: 'Mr Ponsonby, the successful Candidate for the County of Wicklow, is considered as the Leading Member of the Irish Opposition. The greatest expectations are announced by that party, from his eloquence, application and *firmness.*'[4]

These great expectations seemed at first to be fulfilled. In his first months in the new Parliament he threw himself into opposition at Westminster, opposing and acting as a teller in votes against various government measures related to Ireland. He directly tackled Pitt on the floor of the Commons in a debate over foreign affairs, during which Fox himself rose to join the questioning on the points his new colleague had raised. However, this initial burst of activity was not sustained, and after June 1801 he made no contributions to debate for nearly three years, returning frequently to Ireland to continue his legal practice. He did however continue to play an influential role as Fox's leading adviser on Irish matters and an active player in Whig politics.

He was therefore well placed to benefit when the Ministry of All the Talents was formed in 1806 following the death of Pitt. As Fox took office as Foreign Secretary, Ponsonby was made Lord Chancellor of Ireland and joined the Privy Council. It might have been expected that his rise to high office in Ireland would be good news for Catholics there, given his previous support for measures to advance their cause, but his tenure was considered a disappointment in this respect. He made little effort to pursue reform, and soon suggested to Whig leaders in London that he would be prepared to give up the job to return to the House of Commons, from which he had been excluded upon taking office. There was brief consideration of making him Home Secretary but this came to nothing.

After the government fell in 1807 Ponsonby did not contest the general election, so remained out of office and out of Parliament as the Whigs returned to opposition. It was therefore somewhat surprising that he should have emerged as the agreed candidate to replace Earl Grey as Leader of the Opposition in the Commons, given the number of other prominent MPs with far greater energy and skills of oratory. Ponsonby did not even know many of his fellow opposition MPs, nor they him. The reason he emerged, it seems, was that he was the candidate who provoked the 'fewest objections' from across the broad opposition coalition of Foxites and Grenvillites.[5] He was the ultimate compromise candidate, a stop-gap leader who, with Grey joining Lord Grenville in the Lords, would largely defer to direction from those two more senior figures in the upper House. The plan was agreed at a summit meeting on 11 December at the Duke of Bedford's house, attended by Grey, Lord Grenville and his brother Thomas, many of the great and good of the Whig aristocracy, and supporters of the Prince of Wales. In his absence, Ponsonby was elevated to what George Tierney (sarcastically?) called 'the high and lucrative post of leader of the opposition'.[6] The small inconvenience of him not being a member of the House of Commons was remedied the following month when the Duke of Bedford arranged for him to be elected as MP for the pocket borough of Tavistock, in time for the start of the parliamentary session.[*]

In a much-quoted remark, Grenville had told his brother some weeks before that he was hesitant to recommend Ponsonby, arguing that 'a leader of an Opposition cannot be chosen and appointed as a leader of a government party may' and that 'in opposition, people will follow, like hounds ... the man who shows them game.'[7] The choice of

---

[*] So-called 'pocket boroughs' were those seats in the Commons controlled by the patronage of one family, with the MP being essentially their nominee.

simile (which he admits borrowing from Viscount Bolingbroke)* is a particularly fitting one, given that the origin of the term 'whipping' is derived from the 'whippers-in' who bring stray hounds back into the pack. But less well remembered are the next paragraphs, in which he expresses further doubts about the wisdom of the choice:

> Secondly. That if the choice did depend on us, although I incline on the whole to think George Ponsonby would do the best, I do not know enough of him to pledge myself so decidedly to him as I should by such a step as that of making him, by my interference, the leader of our united army; and that I think there is some ground to hesitate between him and Lord Henry Petty.

Whilst he was persuaded to agree to the choice, it remained to be seen whether in leading this particular 'army' Ponsonby was indeed the man to 'show them game'. The signs were not good. His first outing, responding to the king's speech, was distinctly underwhelming. According to Hansard, he 'observed, that his majesty's speech contained such a variety of topics, that it was difficult to express an opinion upon it'. He followed this with a surprising complaint, given the modern habit of complaining about pre-emptive government leaks, that 'had the substance of the speech been known to the public for two or three days before the delivery of it, this difficulty would have been much lessened.'[8]

Another speech a few weeks later went down slightly better, but at the end of February he mismanaged a party dispute and ended up publicly disagreeing with his colleague Samuel Whitbread on the floor of the House, exposing the splits in his ranks. A similar incident

---

* The line recalls a phrase he attributes to Viscount Bolingbroke, who had once written of the Commons that 'they grow like hounds, fond of the man who shows them game'.

occurred again in May. Colleagues despaired, and there was talk of removing him, but the party grandees failed to act. The following year, there were yet more occasions where Ponsonby found himself publicly contradicting Whitbread, who commented witheringly to Grey, 'I confess I should always yield my opinions with less reluctance if I thought Ponsonby had any opinion of his own, but I see no trace of it, either in general plans, or in particular motions.'[9]

During the 1809 session, Ponsonby was warned his party was hopelessly split. There was talk of replacing him with Lord Henry Petty, but this fell down when Petty succeeded to his title as 3rd Marquess of Lansdowne and went to the House of Lords. A clearly exasperated Grenville wrote that 'we must abide by Ponsonby', even if there was no way 'of leading those who have no thought of being led at all'. At the start of the next session, the Speaker of the House of Commons noted in his diary that 'Ponsonby [was] reinstated in the nominal lead of the opposition'.[10]

Having clung on, he remained in place for two dramatic events. First, the final illness of George III saw the Regency Bill proposed, and he played a prominent part in proceedings, criticising the detail of the proposals and the procedures being used to enact them. He also attempted to give the Prince of Wales greater control of royal household appointments, but his motion on this was narrowly defeated. Had the Prince Regent brought the Whigs into power at this time, Ponsonby might have been made Home Secretary – many thought he would have been incapable of leading for the government in the Commons. In the event, the prince kept his Tory ministers in place, and it is even said Ponsonby advised him to do so.

Then, in May 1812, tragedy struck as the Prime Minister, Spencer Perceval, was assassinated on his way into the House of Commons. Ponsonby spoke movingly in tribute to him in the Commons on a motion to provide financial support to the bereaved family, with *The Times* reporting on his speech the next day: 'Though he widely differed from Mr Perceval in political questions, no man entertained a higher opinion of his honour, nor a warmer affection for his person.' In a sign of the unity which breaks out between government and opposition on such tragic occasions, he had begun his remarks with the statement, 'The honour of the House and the country was concerned with show-ing that no variation of principle could prevent an entire participation in the indignant feeling excited by such an atrocity.' His speech was greeted by repeated cries of 'hear, hear' from the Chamber, and after paying further tribute to his fallen opponent's qualities as a 'husband, father, brother and friend', he sat down, as *The Times* put it, 'seemingly greatly affected'.[11]

It was a rare example of a well-received speech from the opposition leader. Despite consistent grumbling from his colleagues, he plodded underwhelmingly on, year after year. On occasion he headed back to Ireland to attend to his interests there, and many felt the opposition was more effective during such times, with George Tierney deputising for him. In 1816 he switched from his English constituency to an Irish one, becoming MP for Wicklow once again, and used the opportunity to urge greater attention by the government to the condition of the Catholic population there. In the 1817 session, like Fox before him, he opposed the draconian introduction by Lord Liverpool's government of a Seditious Meetings Act and refused to join a secret committee on the issue.

On 30 June 1817, he made an intervention on the Irish Grand Jury Presentments Bill. The Chancellor of the Exchequer was about to move a further motion when the House was suddenly adjourned early 'in consequence of the sudden illness of Mr. Ponsonby'.[12] He had collapsed behind the Speaker's Chair, just minutes after finishing his speech. *The Times* described the sad scene the next day:

> Immediately after the motion of adjournment was carried, strangers were excluded from the gallery and the lobbies and passages, in consequence of the sudden indisposition of Mr Ponsonby, who was stricken, as we understood, by some disorder of an apoplectic nature. The Speaker and a number of members remained in the house and in the lobby for a considerable time. Mr Ponsonby was conducted to the room of the Speaker's Secretary, and medical assistance was immediately sent for.[13]

After receiving initial treatment, he was taken back to his house in the Speaker's carriage and Lord Grey and other friends were sent for. He died a week later, on the morning of 8 July. There is a certain tragic irony that five years after Spencer Perceval was mortally injured in the lobby at one end of the Commons Chamber, Ponsonby should himself have been fatally struck down just outside the opposite end. The report of his death in *The Times* is notable for the way it gently but frankly details his shortcomings:

> His talents were more useful than splendid; more suited to the arrangement of affairs, and the detail of business, and the tranquil investigation of truth, than capable of obtaining a command over the understanding of others, of dazzling by their brilliancy, or controlling by their powers. In truth, he was an honest, sincere, steady man: and his eloquence was naturally adapted to the level tenor of his mind. He never aspired to the lofty dignity of a Pitt, and was alike incapable of the quick conception and rapid elocution of a Fox.

He was less fertile in expedients, less perplexing in argument, and less pertinacious in debate than Mr Perceval. The ardent spirits of his own party so far ran beyond him in their attacks, that they almost forgot they fought under his colours; to whom, therefore, he was rather a *point d'appui* after the battle, than a leader in the field.[14]

Despite such hard truths about his performance, Ponsonby's tenure is nevertheless worthy of note. He was the first person to be explicitly chosen as Leader of the Opposition in the Commons, rather than slowly emerging into the role through pre-eminence over time. He presided over a loose coalition of factions but was nevertheless acknowledged as their sole leader in the House, a development that played a significant part in the gradual formalisation of the party system. But above all, for someone put in place as a stopgap compromise leader, he displayed impressive resilience in the face of the constant criticism and ridicule from his own ranks, remaining in post for nearly a decade. As many of his successors would discover, such tenacity in politics is an achievement in itself.

3

George Tierney

Whig, Leader of the Opposition 1818–21

'Mr Tierney, a great Whig authority, used always to say, that the duty of an opposition was very simple – it was, to oppose everything, and propose nothing.'[1] So said Lord Stanley (later the 14th Earl of Derby and three times Prime Minister) in the House of Commons in 1841. The substance of this dictum is often cited and attributed to Stanley himself, whilst its acknowledged author, who had died some eleven years earlier, is somewhat forgotten along with its additional clause – 'and to turn out the government'. For this pithy, if reductive, description of the opposition's role, George Tierney deserves his place in the history of British parliamentary opposition, despite having himself only served as its leader for a few short years.

After the death of George Ponsonby, the Whigs spent a year debating who should replace him as leader in the Commons, or whether they should even have a leader. Having spent much of the previous decade musing about the various people who might do the job better, it is ironic that none seemed keen to take up the challenge themselves when the vacancy arose. As Archibald S. Foord notes, 'All wanted a new Fox to step forward and solve the problem for them,' but no such candidate presented themself.[2] The opposition thus began the 1818 parliamentary session without a designated leader in the lower House, whilst Earl Grey continued the overall leadership of the Whigs from the Lords.

With Grey having failed to resolve the issue, the impetus for action finally came from the party's rank and file members in the Commons. In August 1818, a total of 113 of them signed a letter to Tierney urging him to accept the leadership in the Commons and pledging their support for him. The approach had been agreed at a meeting at Brooks's in July following that year's general election, and the appeal was presented by Lord Duncannon, the party's Chief Whip. After initially resisting, Tierney eventually agreed to take on the job and, as he put it, 'To convert a very good partisan into a very bad leader.' Whereas party leaders of recent times have become all too familiar with plots amongst their backbench colleagues to collect signatures calling for a leader to resign, this was a rare example of the procedure being used for the opposite.

Born in Gibraltar in 1761, Tierney was of Irish ancestry. His father Thomas was a wealthy merchant from Limerick who had gone to the Mediterranean as a prize agent. The young George grew up in England, and was educated at Eton and then Peterhouse, Cambridge, where he studied law. He was called to the Bar at Lincoln's Inn in 1784 but decided not to practice law and to enter politics instead. His electoral fortunes were far from straightforward – he stood unsuccessfully for Wootton Bassett in 1784 as a supporter of William Pitt, but by the time he stood for Colchester four years later he had become a Whig. At that election, both candidates polled the same number of votes, and it took an election committee to award him the seat some months later. He lost it at the election the following year and was defeated again (by his niece's husband) when he stood for Southwark in 1796. Tierney had the result declared void, then lost again at the resulting by-election, before being awarded the seat on petition. There have been easier paths to Parliament, it must be said.

Having struck up a friendship with Charles Grey (later Prime Minister as Earl Grey) during these years, he became active in opposition to Pitt's government and developed a reputation as a radical. He strongly advocated for parliamentary reform and was a vocal supporter of French revolutionary principles. This latter stance saw him portrayed in a contemporary Gillray cartoon as a French executioner.

When Charles James Fox and his supporters quit Parliament for a time, Tierney was left as one of the most prominent figures in opposition to Pitt's Tory government. This led to one of the most dramatic incidents of his career: during a debate in May 1798, Pitt accused him of lacking patriotism for not supporting the government's defence policy. Tierney demanded he withdraw the accusation, and when this was refused he challenged the Prime Minister to a duel with pistols. Observers joked beforehand that it would be a rather unfair contest as Pitt was a very thin man, whilst Tierney was fatter and presented a bigger target (some suggested a chalk outline of Pitt should be drawn on Tierney, with only shots inside it counting). The two men met on Putney Heath at 3 p.m. on Sunday 27 May, accompanied by their 'seconds', and *The Times* described what happened next:

After some ineffectual attempts on the part of their Seconds to prevent further proceedings, the parties took their ground at the distance of 12 paces. A case of pistols was fired at the same moment without effect. A second case was also fired in the same manner, Mr Pitt firing his pistol in the air. The Seconds then jointly interfered,

and insisted that the matter should go no further, it being their decided opinion that sufficient satisfaction had been given, and that
the business was ended with perfect honour to both parties.[3]

Whilst no harm was done to either of them, there was much concern
at the news that the Prime Minister had found himself in such mortal
danger, particularly when the country was at war. *The Times* accompanied its report with the comment that:

> We are sure the Public at large will think, with us, that a life so valu-
> able as Mr Pitt's, and in which the hopes not only of this Nation, but
> of every Cabinet in Europe is concentred, ought not to have been
> risked to gratify the passions of any man.[4]

Tierney had by this point distanced himself from many Foxite Whigs,
and from Fox himself, who never had much time for him. When Pitt
was replaced by Henry Addington as Prime Minister, Tierney began
negotiations for a job in the government, and eventually accepted
office in 1803 as Treasurer of the Navy, which further alienated some of
his Whig colleagues. He resigned with Addington the following year,
and turned down the offer of becoming Secretary for Ireland under
Pitt, who he wished to oppose. When the Ministry of All the Talents
was formed under Lord Grenville there was no place for Tierney's own
talents, largely because of the influence of Fox and his followers. After
Fox died Tierney was eventually brought in, becoming President of the
Board of Control until the coalition fell in April 1807.

At the general election in 1807, he was credited with much of the
organisation of the opposition's efforts, and in the years that followed
pushed for the creation of a more active and effective opposition. A
formidable debater himself, he was frustrated by the ineffectiveness of

Ponsonby, and despaired at the lack of organisation of the opposition's efforts. At times he considered giving up politics altogether but stuck with it, despite struggling to find a seat to fight, which happened a number of times during these years. Tierney was active in opposition from 1815, deputising for Ponsonby during his absences and perceived as much more effective in debate. He was particularly effective on financial matters, with one biographer describing him as having been 'shadow Chancellor'.[5] This was somewhat ironic, given that his own finances were in a parlous state. In 1815 he urgently required £10,000 (over £700,000 in 2023 prices) to avoid bankruptcy and was quietly bailed out by a consortium of his wealthier colleagues.

When Ponsonby died in 1817, Tierney didn't press his own claim to be leader, perhaps partly due to his health, which had not been good for most of that year. He was also depressed at the state of the party and may not have had the appetite to take on the challenge at that time. However, he remained active in opposition, and the following year mounted a sustained attack on the government's continuation of the Bank Restriction Act, making, according to one colleague, 'as clever and amusing a speech as I suppose ever was made on a subject so dry and intricate'.[6]

At the 1818 general election, the Duke of Devonshire arranged for Tierney to be returned as MP for Knaresborough, a secure seat which he represented for the rest of his life, ending his rather fraught electoral situation up to that point. This new security of tenure perhaps contributed to his decision to accept the leadership when he received the letter from his colleagues the following month requesting him to do so.

Once in the leadership, he set about organising a more disciplined opposition for the 1819 session, working hard to ensure a high attendance by his own backbenchers and pitching his speeches to maximise support from independent members. He renewed his attack on the continuation of bank restriction and delivered a number of impressive speeches which delighted his Whig supporters. It was a good start, but Tierney continued to be dissatisfied with the question of the party's overall leadership. He believed it was important for the opposition to be seen as a credible alternative government, and that meant having a recognised and active overall leader and potential Prime Minister. Feeling strongly that Grey was not doing this, he pressed Grey to tackle the matter and privately complained that he felt like 'a captain without an admiral', but Grey refused to address the point.[7]

For much of this first session Tierney was active but careful, subjecting the government to detailed scrutiny and winning occasional victories in the division lobbies whilst keeping the party united by not being excessively confrontational. Then on 18 May he made an error of judgement, abandoning his usual caution, and moved for an inquiry into the state of the nation, ending with a call for the government to be thrown out. This full-frontal attack backfired – his speech was uncharacteristically muddled, leading to the motion being more heavily defeated than expected. This was followed a few days later by the embarrassment of being openly attacked in debate by one of his own members on the floor of the House, and another heavy defeat on a finance resolution.

Later that year, he pressed for the Whigs to organise national protests in the wake of the Peterloo massacre in order to prevent the radicals exploiting the issue. In November he moved for an inquiry in Parliament and argued that the disaffection of the protesters had arisen from genuine grievances that needed to be addressed. Tierney was active on other issues during the following weeks, skilfully tempering his attacks on the government to maximise support in the House, and as the end of the year approached could look back on a successful first full year as leader. Then, on 22 December, he was taken ill and some feared he might be about to expire as Ponsonby had. He recovered, but soon told Grey that he would have to limit his activity as leader. He continued contributing to debates over the next year, but in March of 1821 formally resigned the leadership. He remained an MP, and in 1827 took office again as Master of the Mint in the Tory George Canning's government, retaining his post under Viscount Goderich. However, he was dismissed when the Duke of Wellington took office the following year.

On 25 January 1830 he was at his house in Savile Row, where he breakfasted with his family. He then went to his study, where he worked for the next few hours, writing notes and discussing household accounts with his butler, who found him 'as well as I had seen him'.[8] In the early afternoon a Colonel Phipps called to see him, and the butler entered the study to announce the visitor. Tierney was sitting in his chair, apparently asleep, and failed to respond twice when the guest was announced. They approached and found him quite dead from what was later concluded to be sudden heart failure. The news was at first revealed via a fourteen-word notice in the deaths column of *The Times*, a modest entry which was brought to the attention of the newspaper's reporters. In their fuller report they considered what might have been had his career taken him to higher office:

The death of the Right Hon. George Tierney, M. P., was announced last night through the ordinary channel of an advertisement. Had this distinguished statesman's career been as successful as his principles were fixed and unaccommodating, couriers might have been waiting to announce the fatal event, and the precise moment of its occurrence, to the Sovereign in his Palace, and reporters stationed to collect the details of his last illness. We can now do little more than announce the fact that Mr Tierney is no more.

We know not with certainty what was his age; but he must be the last of nearly ten of that galaxy of talent which illuminated the House of Commons by its brilliancy, from the close of the American war and during the tempestuous season of the French Revolution. Fox, Burke, Sheridan, Windham, Pitt, are all gone before him. Inferior in brilliance, but almost equal in argument, to Fox, less burdened with the trappings of learning, and less perplexed with the refinements of metaphysics, than Burke or Windham, second in wit, but more abounding in wisdom, than Sheridan, less sonorous and imposing than Pitt – Mr Tierney was generally heard with attention equal to any of these illustrious persons, in the debate ... Mr Tierney's speeches were more like colloquial good sense spoken in the parlour, than lofty or studied eloquence uttered in the senate: and he was therefore spared the pain of many a broken metaphor and redundant clause, given merely to round a sentence. He was sagacious to an eminent degree. His enemies have given the quality a less engaging epithet; but whether it were sagacity or cunning, in him it was a pure and useful quality; for it is but too obvious that it was never exerted to promote his own personal interests.[9]

Tierney's time as Leader of the Opposition may have been short, particularly if we consider it to have ended in all but name at the end of 1819, but he was not an insignificant figure. His recognition of the need for an organised and active opposition, and particularly one which would be seen as a responsible and credible alternative government, was important. It certainly shows a more sophisticated understanding of the role of the opposition than his oft-quoted maxim that it is merely about opposing everything and proposing nothing. In truth, he had a pragmatic and nuanced understanding of what it took to oppose effectively, and in this he was perhaps ahead of his time.

4

Henry Petty-Fitzmaurice,
3rd Marquess of Lansdowne

Whig, Leader of the Opposition in the House of Lords
1824–27, 1828–30, 1842–46, 1852

As Archibald S. Foord notes, after George Tierney stood back from the leadership at the end of 1819 'the Whigs had no head in the Commons' for over ten years.[1] To continue our list of contenders, we must therefore look to the upper House. As Tierney had discovered, the division of party leadership between the two Houses at this time was a potential cause of confusion about who was ultimately in charge, not to mention a source of frustration when the overall leader neglected their duties, as he felt Earl Grey did.

Grey stood increasingly aloof from politics during the mid-1820s, and in 1824 he instructed the Whigs' whip in the Lords to deal instead with the Marquess of Lansdowne 'as the person whom his friends were to look upon as their leader'.[2] We can therefore justify the addition of Lansdowne to our list as the de facto leader of the Whig opposition whilst the leadership position in the Commons remained unclear.

Henry Petty-Fitzmaurice was born at Lansdowne House in Mayfair in 1780 to (unsurprisingly) an aristocratic political family. But, like the last few leaders we have considered, he had an Irish connection. His father was born in Dublin and had been elected to both the Irish and British House of Commons, though he never took up his seats. Before he could do so, he had succeeded to the titles of Earl of Shelburne in the peerage of Ireland and Baron Wycombe in the peerage of Great Britain. These entitled him to sit instead in the House of Lords of both countries.

When Henry was two years old his father became Prime Minister (as the Earl of Shelburne), but that government lasted less than a year, brought down by the resignation of our old friend Charles James Fox in 1783. After that, Shelburne was created Marquess of Lansdowne, and his son therefore acquired the courtesy title of Lord Henry Petty, which is how he was known in his early political career.

Henry was educated at Westminster School, then at the University of Edinburgh and Trinity College, Cambridge. Despite the aristocratic background, he did not expect to inherit his father's titles as he had an elder half-brother, John Petty, who was fifteen years his senior. John had already entered Parliament and become an ally of Fox in opposition to William Pitt. It was he who inherited the title of Marquess of Lansdowne when their father died in 1805.

By then, Henry had followed his brother into the House of Commons and was a rising star. He became Chancellor of the Exchequer in the Ministry of All the Talents in 1806 but was in office for just over a year before he lost his seat at the election in 1807. Then in 1809 his half-brother died childless, and Henry succeeded him as 3rd Marquess of Lansdowne, propelling him into the House of Lords. There he supported the Whig leaders Lord Grenville and Earl Grey during the long years of opposition to the Tories, whilst George Ponsonby and Tierney were leading the opposition in the Commons. From this time and throughout his career he was a supporter of progressive social reform – arguing for the abolition of the slave trade and an end to discrimination against religious minorities including Catholics and Jews.

Once he established himself as a leading figure in the Whig Party, he then enjoyed a long and distinguished career as one of the leading statesmen of the next few decades. He had not just one but several stints as Leader of the Opposition in the Lords over that period, beginning with that first de facto tenure after Grey stood back in 1824. But he was also in government for long periods too. In May 1827 he split the Whig Party by going into office with George Canning, whilst Grey and his followers remained in opposition. Entering the government as Minister without Portfolio, he was promoted to Home Secretary two months later – in which role it fell to him to break the news of the Prime Minister's untimely death to the king in August.

This was the first occasion when he might have become Prime Minister himself, but the king instead chose another Tory, Viscount Goderich, under whom Lansdowne served unhappily until the government collapsed in early 1828. He remained a leading figure in opposition to the Duke of Wellington's government for the next two years, and his pre-eminence was recognised by Grey, who offered to stand aside to allow him to become Prime Minister when the Whigs returned to office in 1830. Lansdowne turned this down, leaving Grey to take the top job whilst he settled for being Lord President of the Council. He held that office for nearly eleven years, with just one brief interruption (the four-month government of Peel, 1834–35).

Given the focus of this book is opposition leaders who might have been Prime Minister, Lansdowne stands out as particularly noteworthy on this criterion. Not only had he been in contention for the top job in 1824 and 1830, but on several other occasions during the rest of his career he was consulted by the sovereign about the formation of governments, and often encouraged to become Prime Minister himself, but always turned it down or resisted pressing his claim. At the end of the Whig government in 1841, the outgoing Prime Minister Viscount Melbourne continued to lead the party in the Lords, but after he suffered a stroke the following year Lansdowne became its effective leader in the upper House.

By this time, Lord John Russell had become Leader of the Opposition in the Commons, facing the Prime Minister Robert Peel. Here we can see another feature of opposition politics at the time – greater prominence was given to whichever House contained the Prime Minister of the day. It was therefore Russell who was in the forefront of the political dramas over the repeal of the Corn Laws, which split Peel's Tory government. Lansdowne and Russell had earlier come out for repeal, and it was with their Whig votes that Peel eventually passed the measure in 1846, to the fury of protectionist Tories. When Peel's government was brought down shortly afterwards, Russell was called upon to become Prime Minister of the new Whig government, in which Lansdowne again became Lord President of the Council and played a leading role for the next six years.

When the Liberals (as the party had now become) returned to opposition in 1852, he expressed his wish to retire. However, the party was divided, and when the Tory government of Lord Derby fell after a short while, Lansdowne was again suggested as a possible Prime Minister. He discussed the matter with the Earl of Aberdeen, who eventually became Prime Minister, and joined his Cabinet as Minister without Portfolio. When that government fell, Queen Victoria again pressed Lansdowne to take over as Prime Minister, but he protested that his age and health would not allow it. Instead, Lord Palmerston formed a government in which Lansdowne continued to serve until 1858. At the end of this government he finally retired from the frontline of politics, having declined the offer of a dukedom the previous year.

Five years later, in January 1863, having become increasingly frail, he fell and hit his head on the terrace of his country house, Bowood, and died soon afterwards at the age of eighty-two. His obituary in *The Times* spanned across two pages of dense text, reflecting a long and distinguished career. 'His life is the history of the Whigs during the present century,' it read. 'In youth he was the hope of the party, and in declining years he was the sage on whose counsel they relied.'[3]

We talk a lot these days about 'senior party figures' or 'grandees' in politics – but Lansdowne was the genuine article. It is quite extraordinary that someone of his seniority and popularity declined on several occasions the chance to become Prime Minister. As his obituary puts it, he was:

> A statesman utterly unselfish, a nobleman perfectly genial, a man of large sympathies and thoroughly well-balanced mind – such was Lord Lansdowne to the last. The head of a great party, he was not a party man – for there was no conceit in him. He never put himself forward. Almost all the incidents of his political life are instances of self-denial … He was not without ambition, but his ambition was completely under the control of his judgment.[4]

Such modesty was remarkable, and his attitude towards power was not one which many of his successors in opposition would hold. Where modern politicians are so often ruthless in elbowing their way to the front of the queue for every promotion, looking back at the restraint of figures such as Lansdowne is somewhat refreshing by contrast.

5

John Spencer, Viscount Althorp

Whig, Leader of the Opposition in the House of Commons
March–November 1830

Having been without an agreed single leader in the Commons since 1821, the Whigs were by 1830 more united and determined than they had been for many years, as they faced the Tory government of the Duke of Wellington. At midday on 3 March that year, a deputation of Whig MPs travelled to the Albany on Piccadilly, the home of their colleague John Spencer, Viscount Althorp. There they pressed him to take the leadership of the party in the lower House. With the blessing of Earl Grey, and after a further meeting of over sixty MPs a few days later, Althorp agreed to do so. The post that had been vacant since George Tierney's resignation nine years earlier was finally occupied, and once again there was a recognised Leader of the Opposition in the Commons.

At forty-eight years old, the new leader was not a particularly young man. John Charles Spencer had been born in 1782 at Spencer House in London, the eldest child of prominent Whig politician George Spencer and his wife Lavinia Birmingham. Just a year later his father succeeded to the title of 2nd Earl Spencer, and John took on the courtesy title of Viscount Althorp, by which he was known during his political career in the Commons. His mother, Lavinia, has been described as a 'formidable but controlling' woman who reportedly subjected her children to a brutal regime of verbal abuse, which Althorp's biographer suggests harmed his self-confidence well into adulthood.[1]

He was sent away to be educated at Harrow, where he was a contemporary of four future Prime Ministers: Viscount Goderich, Robert Peel, Lord Aberdeen and Lord Palmerston. He then went to Trinity College, Cambridge, before embarking on a grand tour of Europe in 1802, where his political views were shaped by the experience of seeing countries ruled by absolutist regimes. As he wrote to his father, 'They have no more idea of a limited monarchy on the Continent, than a horse has of the Scriptures.'[2]

On his return, Althorp made his first steps towards following his father into politics, being elected to the House of Commons for the pocket borough of Okehampton in 1804. He resigned this seat two years later at his father's insistence, in order to contest Cambridge University, the seat vacated by William Pitt's death. He lost heavily but was elected later in the year for a county seat in Northamptonshire, which he held for the rest of his time in the Commons.

It cannot be claimed that he was a particularly active parliamentarian, however. He did not make his maiden speech until 1809, five years after his first election. He was more interested in fox hunting than politics, becoming master of the local hunt near the Spencer family seat in Northamptonshire. In 1814 he married his wife Esther, the daughter of a rich country gentleman from Nottinghamshire. They were deeply in love, and it was an immense personal tragedy when she died in childbirth four years later at the age of twenty-nine. Althorp was devastated, withdrawing into a deep depression, and wore mourning clothes for the rest of his life. He also gave up fox hunting as a penance and turned his attention instead to agriculture on his estate.

He became more politically engaged in the aftermath of the Peterloo massacre of 1819, which sparked mass protests and uprisings
across the country. Lord Liverpool's Tory government imposed severe
restrictions aimed at quelling insurrection by gagging radical newspapers and preventing large gatherings. Althorp vigorously opposed
the measures, and allied himself with protesters seeking parliamentary
reform, even appearing at a protest rally in Covent Garden alongside
notorious radical leaders.

The cause of parliamentary reform became a theme of Althorp's
political life, and he pursued it in opposition throughout the 1820s.
He became convinced that the Whigs needed to present a strong
and cohesive alternative to the government, which could eventually
take office. Unlike Lord Lansdowne, he refused to take office in the
Canning government in 1827, which improved his standing amongst
his Whig colleagues. It was this strengthened support that resulted
in increasing calls for him to take on the leadership in the Commons.
However, he resisted such suggestions, protesting in the most self-
effacing terms in a letter to a colleague in late 1828:

> I agree with you that a great many of our party fancy that I should
> make a good leader ... but I know I should not. I should not have
> been two months before I should have fallen into the greatest possi-
> ble contempt. At present I am overrated, then I should be underrat-
> ed ... I assert that I am not equal to the post of the leader of a party.[3]

Over the next year and a half, the Tory government of the Duke of
Wellington came under increasing pressure, with Grey having returned
to more active politics in the upper House and the Whigs beginning
to co-ordinate with other supporters to start looking like a viable alternative government. It was in this context that Althorp eventually

agreed to take on the formal leadership of the party in the House of Commons. When King George IV died shortly afterwards in June 1830, it triggered a general election, at which parliamentary reform was a major political issue. Wellington was vehemently opposed to it, whilst the Whigs under Grey, Lansdowne and Althorp increasingly saw it as their main objective. The Tories lost a significant number of seats, and when the new parliament sat, the Whigs began to ramp up their opposition to the government.

Despite being a reluctant leader, Althorp had a sound grasp of the job, holding meetings of his MPs to discuss tactics on how to proceed in the new parliament. There had been some talk after the election that Wellington might have sought to strengthen the government by bringing in prominent Whigs, but this had not happened. Althorp was concerned that his increasingly vehement opposition should not be seen as sour grapes at being denied office, but as a principled response to the government's failure. At a party meeting in November, he announced that he had previously sought to avoid bringing down the ministry, but the 'inefficiency' of Wellington's government now meant he was prepared to do so. His own account of the meeting stated:

> We agreed for war against the ministry, but ... to be conducted in a reasonable manner. I am therefore to say today that I have no confidence in the government, but that if they propose good measures they may depend upon our support.[4]

The idea of 'war ... in a reasonable manner' is a rather splendid description of what we would today describe as 'responsible opposition' and deserves its place in the hall of fame of opposition quotations. The extract above was followed by confirmation that he would not shy away from supporting a motion in the House that would bring about the fall of the government, should the opportunity arise. Within a few weeks this is what happened, with the Whigs joined by rebel Ultra Tories to inflict a defeat on Wellington over the Civil List. Grey was called to form a Whig government, and briefly pressed Althorp to take the premiership as First Lord of the Treasury. But once again, modesty got the better of Althorp, and he conceded only to take office as Leader of the House of Commons and Chancellor of the Exchequer. He nevertheless became a key figure in the new Whig government, navigating the passage of the Great Reform Act of 1832, the historic legislation enacted to widen the electoral franchise and abolish the most egregious abuses of the election process. He steered it through with great skill, winning round sceptical MPs, which earned him the nickname of 'honest Jack'. As if playing a key role in this landmark legislation was not enough, he also pushed through the Act abolishing slavery in the British Empire and enacted legislation to improve conditions in factories, which was nicknamed 'Althorp's Act'.

In 1834 his father died, and he was forced to resign as Chancellor on being removed to the House of Lords as the 3rd Earl Spencer. Grey had by then resigned as Prime Minister and been replaced by Viscount Melbourne, but divisions amongst the Whigs over the issue of Ireland had weakened the government. Althorp's removal helped bring it down, with King William IV dismissing his ministers in November of that year, the last time a monarch would exercise that direct prerogative.

Out of office, the new Earl Spencer happily returned to life as a country aristocrat and resisted appeals to return to politics. He made rare appearances in the House of Lords and devoted most of the rest of his life to rescuing the finances of the Spencer estates, selling off property and living frugally in his late wife's house in Nottingham. In 1845 he fell ill and died there of kidney failure.

Not an impressive speaker or a dynamic leader, he owed his

reputation to his honesty and common sense, and his solid reliability, being described by Melbourne as 'the tortoise upon whom the world rests'.[5] He saw service in government as a duty and a burden, as can be seen from his reluctance to take on the leadership of his party in opposition and in government. After his death, *The Times* commented on his status as the acknowledged leader of the Whig opposition prior to 1830, but said of his time in government:

> In that position he was placed with as slender personal qualifications for the post as ever fell to the lot of mortal man, although no one will be disposed to deny that he was a person of great private worth; that he possessed some intellectual vigour, and was distinguished by many amiable qualities; but his attempt to be a leading Minister in a popular assembly partook so largely of the ridiculous that it reached the burlesque ... for, though he possessed many qualities highly deserving of respect, and justly entitling him to the confidence of his party, that man could never have found himself at home in the Treasury Chambers at Whitehall, whose tastes and knowledge almost exclusively qualified him for rural pursuits; whose eye was better filled by the image of a plethoric ox than a full exchequer, and who will be best remembered in the history of his race as the 'Bucolic Earl Spencer.'[6]

Rather a harsh assessment, but from what we know of his own correspondence, probably one with which Spencer himself would have agreed when reflecting on what the newspaper had described as 'the strange career which led to these absurd results'. Once again, we have a rare example of an opposition leader who had a chance of being Prime Minister but turned it down after concluding he was not really up to the job.

6

Lord George Bentinck

Protectionist, Leader of the Opposition
in the House of Commons 1846–47

Many politicians today are described as having had a 'meteoric' rise to fame. The metaphor is usually rather misplaced, given that the definition of a meteor is actually a falling object, which burns up as it enters the atmosphere. However, in the case of Lord George Bentinck's political career it is perhaps more fitting. He appeared suddenly in the parliamentary firmament at a time of great drama and blazed brightly across the sky, before burning up and disappearing equally quickly.

He was born in 1802 at the family seat of Welbeck Abbey, the third son of the 4th Duke of Portland. His grandfather was the 3rd Duke, who had been Prime Minister in 1783 and was to be again for two years from 1807. The young boy was actually given the first name William, but in an eccentric quirk typical of the British aristocracy, so were most of the other men in his family. In order to avoid confusion he was known throughout his life by his second name, George.

As a younger son of a peer, he was educated privately at home and not sent to university, spending most of his childhood honing his sporting skills and becoming accomplished at horse riding, shooting, rowing and cricket. At the age of sixteen he was sent off to join the army but frequently got into trouble for insubordination and disrespectful behaviour towards his superiors. In a notable incident, he faced an inquiry after allegedly calling his commanding officer Captain John Ker a 'poltroon', and whilst he was cleared, he nearly fought a duel after Ker refused to let the matter rest.

He changed regiments, and a plan was made for him to be sent out to India as aide-de-camp to his uncle, George Canning, who was expected to become governor general there. Instead, Canning was appointed Foreign Secretary in Lord Liverpool's government, and Bentinck became his private secretary for two years before returning to the army and then to his first love, horse racing.

Bentinck was a distinctive figure – over six feet tall, attractive and strikingly well dressed, with a reputation for rudeness. He was elected to Parliament as MP for King's Lynn in 1828 and declared himself independent of party politics, but was generally considered a follower of his uncle, Canning, whose death the previous year had cut short his premiership. In the 1830s he joined the grouping around his friend Lord Stanley (later the 14th Earl of Derby) known as the 'Derby Dilly', which broke from the Whigs and drifted across to support Sir Robert Peel's modernised Conservative Party. Bentinck acted as unofficial whip for the group as they became increasingly aligned with the Conservative opposition. He turned down office when Peel formed a government in 1841, much preferring to remain focused on his love of horse racing.

Despite his flirtation with politics, it was racing that was his major preoccupation. He later claimed to have sat in the Commons through eight Parliaments without once having 'ventured to trespass upon its time on any subject of great debate'.[1] His short temper and obsession with matters of the turf nearly led to him being killed in 1835 when he fought a duel against a man called Osbaldeston in a dispute over a bet. They met at Wormwood Scrubs at 6 a.m. on 14 April 1835, marched twelve paces and turned. Bentinck fired into the air, but his opponent, a skilled marksman, fired at him, putting a bullet through his hat.

This colourful character might have remained an amusing footnote in history, remembered exclusively for his prowess in the field of horse racing, were it not for the political crisis sparked by debates over the repeal of the Corn Laws that propelled him into parliamentary history and into the pages of this book. As he himself said, he had not previously taken part in any major debate in the House until the issue arose, and he then found himself playing a leading role in the drama.

Having been a loyal supporter of Robert Peel, he was outraged when the Prime Minister sought to abandon protectionism and embrace free trade by abolishing the Corn Laws. The split within the Conservative ranks over the issue has sometimes been described as the Brexit of its day, and whilst the comparison can be overdone, the ferocity with which the two sides fought the battle and the damage it did to the party's unity were certainly similar.

Bentinck was outraged not just at the measure itself, but at the way he considered Peel had broken his election pledges to maintain the Corn Laws. Writing to his fellow protectionist Lord Stanley, he said that if politicians went in for 'political lying and pledge-breaking' it would seriously damage trust in the political classes.[2] Breaking his long silence in the Commons, he made a major speech on 27 February 1846 in opposition to the measure, emphasising the point about honour:

Sir, I wish to God I thought that this change could be carried by this House of Commons with honour, without loss of character, loss of influence, and loss of station with the country … It is but candid to [Whig] Gentlemen opposite to say that their honour is not arraigned; for they have been the consistent advocates of free-trade principles … But when we are told by hon. Gentlemen, and more especially by the hon. Gentleman the Secretary of the Treasury, that this is not a protection Parliament, I am at a loss to understand upon what principles they and he ground their assertion ... I must repeat that in my opinion no Member of the old majority of this House can give his consent to this measure, as proposed by Her Majesty's Ministers for the repeal of the Corn Laws, without dishonour.[3]

He then went on to give a detailed speech over two hours, illustrated with specific analysis of agricultural prices, on the substance of the proposal. But he returned at the end to his earlier point, making another appeal to honour as he closed his speech: 'If we are a proud aristocracy, we are proud of our honour, inasmuch as we never have been guilty, and never can be guilty, of double-dealing with the farmers of England – of swindling our opponents, deceiving our friends, or betraying our constituents.'[4]

It was an impressive performance, which, along with similar performances during subsequent debates, raised his profile amongst Conservative protectionists. Whilst his friend Lord Stanley took on the overall leadership of the protectionists from the House of Lords, Bentinck came under pressure to lead in the Commons. Reluctantly, he agreed in April 1846 to take on the responsibility and, alongside Benjamin Disraeli, co-ordinated the opposition to repeal of the Corn Laws, bringing two thirds of Conservative MPs over to their cause. As a result of such dissent in his ranks, Peel was only able to pass the measure with the votes of the Whigs in the Commons. On the same night that it passed the House of Lords, the protectionist Tories allied with the opposition Whigs to defeat the government on the Irish Coercion Bill, resulting in Peel's resignation and the formation of a Whig government under Lord John Russell.

With the Conservatives now out of office and split between the Peelites and the protectionists, Bentinck was the leader of the larger faction and thus became Leader of the Opposition in the Commons. He was to remain in this position for just eighteen months, operating in close co-operation with Disraeli, who was the better strategist. It was an effective partnership and developed into a close friendship, with Bentinck and his family providing a loan of £25,000 to Disraeli to buy his country house, Hughenden Manor – the most notable example of the patronage that was to be a major factor in bringing the future Prime Minister to greater prominence.

Together, the pair committed the Conservatives to protectionist measures to increase income to farmers and fought the 1847 election on that platform. They also promoted a number of significant measures to provide assistance to Ireland, which had been badly hit by famine. Bentinck's personal loyalty to Disraeli, who was of Jewish ancestry, also played a part in his downfall as leader. He had made it a condition of accepting the leadership that he would remain free to vote with his conscience on matters of religious freedom, and became increasingly estranged from his party on these questions. In late 1847, the Jewish Disabilities Bill was proposed by Russell's government to remove the ban on Jewish members taking their seats in Parliament, and Bentinck was firmly committed to supporting the measure. In the face of opposition from his own ranks, he gave an emotional speech in favour on 17 December 1847, saying that it was with the 'deepest regret' that he found himself 'compelled to act in opposition' to so many of his own party.[5] In a letter to John Wilson Croker nine days later, he explained the consequences of his actions:

I have ceased to be the leader of the House of Commons 'Opposition!' My vote and speech on the Jew Bill gave dire offence to the party, and on the Monday morning I got a long letter from Beresford, who, as you know, is the whipper-in of the party, the long and short of which was an intimation that for daring to make that speech I must be prepared to receive my dismissal. I need not tell you that a hint that any considerable portion of the party were dissatisfied with and wearied of me, was quite enough for me to proffer a resignation with good grace, without waiting to be 'cashiered.' Appointed on account of my uncompromising spirit, I am dismissed for the same reason; that which was my principal virtue in 1846 is my damning vice in 1847.[6]

He went on to condemn the fact that the 'great Protectionist Party' had 'degenerated into a "No Popery" "No Jew" Party', and that this being the case, he was not the right person to lead it. The leading figures in pushing religious intolerance had, he said, 'raised all this artificial zeal in the cause of religion, and fanned the flickering embers of bigotry, till they have raised a flame, of which, as a matter of course, I am necessarily the first victim'.[7]

It was a dramatic and principled resignation, bringing an end to his eventful leadership. This political demise was followed nine months later by a final tragedy. On Saturday 23 September 1848, *The Times* carried the contemporary equivalent of a breaking news alert 'forwarded by electric telegraph from our correspondent at Nottingham'. The message, sent at 9.45 a.m. on Friday, read:

A messenger from Welbeck Abbey has just arrived, announcing the death of Lord George Bentinck. His Lordship left the Abbey, on foot and unattended, at 3 o'clock yesterday afternoon, for Thoresby-park, the seat of the Earl Manvers, where he had an engagement to dine. Not arriving, inquiries were made, and at 9 o'clock last night he was found on the footpath quite dead, having evidently expired of apoplexy.[8]

His sudden death at the age of forty-six, seemingly of a heart attack, was a shock to his colleagues, and particularly to Disraeli, who wrote a glowing biography as a tribute to his late friend in which he observed mournfully: 'At the very moment ... when the nation, which had long watched him with interest, began to congratulate itself on the devotion of such a man to the business of the country, he was in an instant taken from us.'[9] In its obituary, *The Times* also considered the unfulfilled potential of his never having served in government. Its observations on his contributions as an opposition leader are insightful:

> Though he effected many amendments in measures proposed by his political opponents, yet the greater part of his Parliamentary career was devoted to the exciting but barren toils of opposition ... it may without hesitation be asserted that he was one of the most formidable members of Her Majesty's Opposition who at any time occupied a place at the Speaker's left hand ... come what might, Lord George Bentinck almost always succeeded in giving a heavy blow to his opponents ... What he might have been in power no man can tell – what he has been in Opposition is best seen in the fact that scarcely any series of Parliamentary labours ever obtained for a member of either House so much influence in so short a time.[10]

Looked at from a greater historical distance, the impact made by Bentinck during his brief time in active politics remains as striking as that contemporary assessment claims. He had played a leading role in bringing down a formidable Prime Minister, splitting apart the Conservative Party and changing the political landscape of the nineteenth century, whilst launching the career of one of the most celebrated Prime Ministers of the age. All this within less than two years after making his first major speech in the Commons. Combined with his principled resignation and the tragedy of his early death, he would be a hard act to follow.

7

Charles Manners,
Marquess of Granby

Protectionist, Leader of the Opposition in the House of
Commons February–March 1848, Joint Leader 1849–51

It is inevitable in a book like this that some leaders will merit more attention than others. Whilst every life and political career contains something of interest, there are some whose efforts have left less of an impression in the histories of their time and have proved challenging to biographers seeking to justify their subject's significance.

Charles Manners, later the 6th Duke of Rutland, is sadly such a man. Known during his political career by his courtesy title of the Marquess of Granby, he does not even have the distinction of having given his name to the many British pubs that bear that title. These are instead named after his more distinguished great-grandfather, a military hero.

Born in 1815, Charles was the son and heir of the 5th Duke of Rutland. He had a typical aristocratic education at Eton and Trinity College, Cambridge. Unlike some of the leaders we have looked at so far, he was a Conservative from the beginning of his political career, and was elected as MP for Stamford in 1837, the same year Queen Victoria came to the throne. He was appointed a Lord of the Bedchamber to her consort, Prince Albert, between 1843 and 1846, under Robert Peel's government, but received no higher political office.

He was instinctively and firmly committed to the cause of protectionism, representing as he did the traditional landed interest of the aristocracy. He therefore joined the protectionists under Lord Stanley in opposing the repeal of the Corn Laws and followed the leadership of Lord George Bentinck in the Commons. When Bentinck resigned in December 1847, Stanley wrote to Granby suggesting that he take over as leader. At a meeting at the end of January, hosted by Granby's father, the Duke of Rutland, at Belvoir Castle, the unwilling nominee accepted the 'unenviable office' suggested for him.[1] On 9 February, Stanley held a large party meeting to announce the succession, and this was confirmed without dissent by a meeting of Conservative MPs the following day.

It was not an auspicious choice. His own brother, the rather more talented Lord John Manners, predicted he would make a 'miserable leader', whilst Bentinck was furious that Benjamin Disraeli had not been chosen and refused to speak to Stanley for several months.[2] The new leader spoke a number of times in the Commons in response to finance motions proposed by the Chancellor of the Exchequer, but after less than a month he resigned on 4 March, 'conscious of his own inadequacy', as the historian Robert Blake memorably put it.[3]

The party continued without a leader in the Commons for the rest of the parliamentary session, with the whips following instructions from Stanley. The impasse was largely the result of Stanley's continued refusal to give the leadership in the Commons to Disraeli, whom he did not trust. Discussions continued into the following year, when it was eventually agreed to try a peculiar form of joint leadership – Disraeli would share the duties of leadership with Granby and the elderly John Herries. This arrangement was sold to Disraeli as a means by which he could emerge as the main leader of the party in the Commons, overcoming what Stanley believed was widely shared nervousness about him at the time.

Disraeli was not happy with the plan, but it turned out just as Stanley had predicted: Disraeli shone as the natural leader, and the other two gradually faded from prominence. In September 1851, Granby resigned from the joint leadership in protest at what he believed was a lack of commitment to protectionism by his colleagues.

Early the following year, Stanley, having now succeeded to the title of Earl of Derby, formed his first government, with Disraeli as Chancellor of the Exchequer. Granby was not appointed to ministerial office and remained critical of the new government's growing acceptance of free trade. Instead, he was made Lord-Lieutenant of Lincolnshire, in the hope this might keep him quiet, if not happy.

From this point on, Granby's political significance (such as it was) was at an end. He succeeded his father as Duke of Rutland in 1857, and spoke infrequently in the Lords, mostly to repeat his continued belief in the need to restore protectionism. He lived for another thirty years, and at his death, the obituary in *The Times* was padded out with a lengthy history of his aristocratic forebears before turning its attention to his own life. It concluded by remarking:

> While the deceased Duke could lay no claim to eloquence or to original capacity for statesmanship, he was respected by men of all parties for the frankness and courage with which he expressed his political opinions. It was his pride that he never changed his views upon fiscal and commercial questions, and to the last he predicted

that a change would yet come over the convictions of Englishmen in the direction of Protection. In private life, among his tenantry and neighbours, he was much esteemed.[4]

There is perhaps little else to say about this minor entry in our catalogue of opposition leaders. He followed a colourful and consequential predecessor – any leader would have had difficulty living up to Bentinck's effectiveness, and Granby succeeded only in meeting the low expectations of his performance. His main contribution to the political history of the times was the way his failed leadership helped pave the way for Disraeli to emerge as the true successor to his old friend Bentinck.

8

John Charles Herries

Conservative, Joint Leader of the Opposition
in the House of Commons 1849–51

The previous chapter has already outlined the peculiar arrangements put in place for the Conservative opposition leadership
in the House of Commons between 1849 and 1851, which amounted
to a job-share between three individuals. The one who achieved pre-
eminence, Benjamin Disraeli, is excluded from this book by virtue of
his later success, and we have already covered the meagre contribution
of the Marquess of Granby. The third member of this troika was over
seventy years old when he took on the role and was the only one of the
three to have served in high office.

Born John Charles Herries in November 1778, he was known
throughout his career by his initials, as J. C. Herries. Unlike his colleague Granby, he was no aristocrat, being the son of a London merchant, Charles Herries, and his wife, Mary. He was educated first at
Cheam, before going abroad to Leipzig University, where, amongst
other things, he learnt French and German.

After his education, he returned to London to find that his father
had gone bankrupt. At the age of twenty, Herries took a job as a junior

clerk in the Treasury, where he showed a talent for business and economics and was swiftly promoted to a position in the revenue department on three times his initial salary. In 1801 he had an early encounter with the opposition, after being assigned to help the Prime Minister William Pitt draw up counter-resolutions against George Tierney's financial proposals.

He then became private secretary to Nicholas Vansittart, who was Secretary to the Treasury under Pitt and Henry Addington, later serving in the same role during Lord Grenville's Ministry of All the Talents. Herries served him until 1807 but lost that job when the government fell. At this point his father's connections assisted him in finding alternative employment, and he was taken on as private secretary to the new Chancellor of the Exchequer, Spencer Perceval. He flourished under the patronage of his new boss, helping him write the 1810 Budget. Herries was then appointed as Commissary-in-Chief, the Treasury official in charge of the army's finances. He held this powerful and lucrative post until it was abolished in 1816, forming an alliance with the banker Nathan Mayer Rothschild to pay Wellington's troops during the Napoleonic Wars. He then took on other Treasury appointments, writing the report that merged the Irish and British revenue services.

His positive reputation as an effective administrator set him up to take office himself, and after being elected to Parliament for Harwich in 1823, he was appointed Financial Secretary to the Treasury by Lord Liverpool, continuing the role when George Canning formed his government in 1827. By this time, his interests in the City of London were the cause of some suspicion, and when Canning died and Viscount Goderich asked him to become Chancellor of the Exchequer, the proposed appointment was considered controversial. *The Times* recorded the controversy, highlighting the perception in Tory circles that

Herries was being pushed by the king and was at odds with William Huskisson, another possible Chancellor:

> Let us, then, assume on Tory authority, that a 'King's candidate' for the place of Chancellor of the Exchequer has actually been discovered in the person of Mr Herries. Mr Herries has been brought up in the Treasury, and is said to know something of finance. He is said to have a certain bias on public questions – a bias adverse to the liberal principles of Mr Canning on questions of high state policy – diametrically adverse to the practical wisdom of Mr Canning's friend and colleague, Mr Huskisson, on what concerns our manufactures, maritime interests and commerce. Other things have likewise been asserted of Mr Herries, to which it gives us no pleasure to allude – but let them pass.[1]

The newspaper then criticised the notion that a candidate for office should be unconstitutionally forced on the government by the king and suggested that other ministers should resign rather than accept it. Herries himself initially declined the post, but was prevailed upon to accept and was appointed on 3 September 1827. The fragile coalition of moderate Tories and Whigs under Goderich made it an unhappy period in office, beset with tensions and suspicions. A row over the appointment of the chair of the finance committee in Parliament led both Huskisson and Herries to threaten resignation. With the government disintegrating, Goderich resigned as Prime Minister and was replaced by the Duke of Wellington, who formed a Tory government.

Under Wellington, Herries was moved from the Exchequer to become Master of the Mint. He had a seat in the Cabinet, and in this less demanding office he was able to continue giving the government the benefit of his economic advice. He was additionally appointed as

President of the Board of Trade in February 1830, and he served in that office until the fall of the government in November 1830.

Out of office, his talents as an administrator might have been wasted. But instead, he devoted himself to the new challenge and played a significant role in organising the Tories in opposition, alongside Robert Peel. He managed relations with the press, and, along with a number of parliamentary colleagues, established a new headquarters for the party in Charles Street, a development which led directly to the foundation of the Carlton Club as an explicitly political base for the Conservatives. He also took a leading role in drafting motions criticising the Whig government and directing the opposition's parliamentary activity.

His role in improving the party's organisation impressed Robert Peel, who made Herries Secretary at War in his brief government from 1834–5. Returning to opposition, he became an influential figure in attacking Viscount Melbourne's government over subsequent years, but missed the opportunity to return to office when he lost his seat in Parliament in 1841, at the election that brought the Conservatives under Peel back to power. He was therefore absent from the drama of the Conservative split over the Corn Laws during the next few years, though he was a supporter of the protectionists.

He returned to Parliament in 1847 and was therefore available in the House of Commons when the question of the leadership of the protectionist Conservative opposition arose, following the resignation of Bentinck and the disastrous experiment with Granby. As discussed in the previous chapter, Lord Stanley resisted endorsing Disraeli's claim and instead considered a number of possible alternatives to him. In December 1848, Stanley offered Herries the Commons leadership, telling him the party would not have Disraeli as leader. However, the idea failed to get off the ground, with Herries turning down the proposal and Disraeli refusing to serve under him.

In the new year, Herries and other protectionists suggested the formation of a 'shadow Cabinet' made up of five or six members as a means of settling the leadership question.[2] It was this idea which Stanley developed into the eventual proposal of the leadership troika of Herries, Granby and Disraeli. Whilst Disraeli emerged as the pre-eminent leader, Herries remained an influential figure, and he was lined up to return as Chancellor of the Exchequer had a Conservative government been formed in 1851. However, when the Earl of Derby did eventually take office the following year, he made Disraeli his Chancellor instead. Herries, denied the office for which he felt he was most qualified, declined to take another senior role, accepting instead the less demanding post of President of the Board of Control. Derby's first government lasted less than a year, and after leaving office for the last time, Herries retired from Parliament in 1853 and died in 1855.

Looking at the life of Herries from a 21st-century perspective, it is impossible not to see a number of strikingly modern features to his career. He earned his place in politics not through privilege of birth, but through recognition of his talents in his field of expertise, namely government finance. The story of the son of a bankrupt merchant joining the Treasury as a clerk and ending up as Chancellor of the Exchequer has a pleasantly meritocratic flavour to it when compared with the continued dominance of aristocratic figures of questionable ability at this time. That he was to end up sharing the leadership with the epitome of the upper-class politician, Granby, is a rich irony.

The other modern resonance is the way in which Herries effectively learnt his political skills as an adviser to senior politicians, before following them into Parliament and ministerial office. He was a close aide to multiple Chancellors of the Exchequer and Prime Ministers and was rewarded with their patronage to set him on course for his own political career. He then took an active role in modernising the political operation of the Conservative Party in opposition, setting up a new headquarters and taking responsibility for media relations. Though he ended his career as a venerable elder statesman, his route to the top took him via the now-familiar roles of special adviser, spin doctor and campaign co-ordinator. In doing so he can be said to have made a notable contribution to the development of modern professional politics.

9

Granville Leveson-Gower, 2nd Earl Granville

Liberal, Leader of the Opposition in the House of Lords
1858–59, 1868, 1874–80, 1885–86, 1886–91

As we discovered with the Marquess of Granby, the first thing to spring to mind when many of us hear the title of certain British peers is the name of a pub. In a slight variation on this theme, I cannot resist beginning this chapter by recording that its subject conjures up memories for me of childhood road trips to France with my parents, embarking at Portsmouth for crossings to Cherbourg on a Sealink car ferry that also gloried in the name 'Earl Granville'. I have been unable to confirm which earl it was named after despite there being a lengthy history of the vessel available on the internet, in which I see that it ended its days sailing around the Greek islands as the 'Express Olympia' before being sent to the breaker's yard in 2005.

If any politician deserved to be commemorated by lending their name to a ship, however, it would be one with a career as long and distinguished as this particular Earl Granville. His time in active politics spanned more than half a century: he was Foreign Secretary three times, leader of the Liberal Party in the Lords for a total of twenty-eight years and very nearly became Prime Minister on several occasions. That he did not eventually do so owes a lot to the fact his later career was overshadowed by the rise of his close ally William Gladstone, who came to dominate politics during that period. Having considered in recent chapters those leaders whose careers were over-shadowed by the rise of Disraeli, it is fitting that we should now turn our attention to a colleague of his great rival.

Granville George Leveson-Gower was born in London on 11 May 1815, into a family well versed in public life. His grandfather had served in the Cabinet of Pitt the Younger, and his father, Lord Granville Leveson-Gower, had been a Whig MP and a diplomat, including a spell as Ambassador to Russia. This posting, during which he rejected appeals for help from a certain John Bellingham, could have cost the elder Granville his life and prevented his son from ever being born. Bellingham nurtured his grievance against the government and in 1812 plotted to shoot Lord Leveson-Gower, lying in wait for him in the lobby of the House of Commons. It was simply a twist of fate that the Prime Minister, Spencer Perceval, entered the lobby instead and became the victim of the infamous assassination.

With his father spared and raised to the peerage as the 1st Earl Granville, the young Lord Leveson (as he was then known) was edu-cated at Eton and then Christ Church, Oxford. He also spent much time in Paris, where his father was by now serving as Ambassador to France, became fluent in French and briefly became an attaché at the embassy himself. On his return to the UK, he was 'elected' to the House of Commons in 1837 for the pocket borough of Morpeth, whose MP wished to take a temporary break. Leveson made a well-received maiden speech on foreign policy, assisted by having spoken to and stolen all the best arguments of his colleague Henry Bulwer, an expe-rienced diplomat who had also been attempting to speak in the debate.

This first spell in the Commons was brief, ending in early 1840 when his predecessor wanted the seat back. Leveson was then invited to become Undersecretary at the Foreign Office under Viscount Palmerston, a demanding and abrasive boss. He held this position until the Conservatives took office the following year, and soon after that he returned to the Commons in a by-election for the safe Whig seat of Lichfield. In January 1846 his father died, and Leveson was elevated to the House of Lords as the 2nd Earl Granville.

Granville therefore entered the Lords just as the drama of the Conservative split over the Corn Laws was reaching its climax. A committed free trader, he gave his first speech in the upper House in favour of repeal, and after Peel's government fell he was appointed to office by the new Whig Prime Minister, Lord John Russell. At first he was given only minor posts but was gradually promoted, becoming Paymaster General in 1847 and joining the Cabinet in 1851, where he took a leading role in promoting the Great Exhibition of that summer.

Then, in late 1851, he made a surprising jump into high office when he was appointed Foreign Secretary following the resignation of Lord Palmerston. However, he was in office for just two months before the government fell in February 1852, to be replaced by a short-lived Conservative minority government under the Earl of Derby. When the Earl of Aberdeen formed a coalition of Peelites and Whigs later that year, Granville returned to Cabinet as Lord President of the Council, before being demoted in 1854 to Chancellor of the Duchy of Lancaster, a ministerial position outside of the Cabinet.

In 1855, Aberdeen resigned over the conduct of the Crimean War and was replaced by Palmerston, who reappointed Granville to the Cabinet as Lord President. Granville also became the leader of the Whigs in the House of Lords for the first time. (Viscount Palmerston's title was in the Irish peerage, so he sat in the Commons.) This meant that when the government fell from office in 1858, Palmerston led the opposition overall from the Commons whilst Granville became Leader of the Opposition in the upper House for the first time, against Derby's Conservative government. Somewhat unusually, he seemed to relish the experience, writing to a friend in July 1858, 'You will be glad for me in these circumstances that I am getting to like opposition. Although I have not made one good speech this year, I am accepted as Leader and I never knew our side of the House so cordial and united.'[1]

The conduct of opposition at that time was rather more informal, but there is an interesting reference in one of Granville's letters at this time to the holding of what he calls a 'quasi Cabinet' meeting at Palmerston's house – an interesting term which prefigured the later use of the term 'shadow Cabinet'.[2]

Governments during this period, you will have noticed, tended to be short-lived, and Derby's government fell only the following year. There was a lack of consensus on the Liberal side (as the coalition of Whigs and former Peelites had now become) as to whether Russell or Palmerston (both former Prime Ministers) should form the new government. In an attempt to resolve the impasse, Queen Victoria sent for Granville as a compromise candidate. After conducting delicate negotiations with the two big beasts of the party, Granville discovered that whilst both would tolerate being second to the other in government, neither wanted to be third. As Granville wrote later, this left him with no way forward as Prime Minister:

As soon as I found … that I was an obstacle instead of a facility towards the formation of a strong Government, I went to the Queen to ask her to excuse me from the task which she had so unexpectedly and so graciously imposed upon me. In answer to a question, I stated to her Majesty that it was disagreeable to me to advise as to which of you and Palmerston she should send for, but that I was ready to do so if it was her wish. The Queen did not press me.[3]

In the end, Palmerston was sent for and formed his second government, in which Granville remained Lord President of the Council. He came close to being Prime Minister again in 1865 when Palmerston died, but Russell, who had by now joined him in the House of Lords, was called on instead. When that government fell after less than a year, Russell continued as Liberal leader but signalled his intention to retire, and Granville again took on more of the duties of leadership in the House of Lords.

By this time, Gladstone had become the overall leader of the Liberal Party, and when the Liberals won the general election of 1868, he formed his first government, with Granville as Secretary of State for the Colonies and Leader of the House of Lords. Eighteen months later, he was promoted to Foreign Secretary again when the incumbent, Lord Clarendon, died suddenly. He later famously told the House of Lords that on his arrival at the Foreign Office following his appointment, the permanent secretary had told him that 'he had never during his long experience known so great a lull in foreign affairs, and that he was not aware of any important question that I should have to deal with'.[4] Just hours later, a telegram arrived informing them that the throne of Spain had been offered to a Prussian prince, an act which led directly to the Franco-Prussian War.

He served as Foreign Secretary for four years, until the government lost office at the next general election. At this point, Gladstone announced he was retiring from the leadership of the party, and Granville took on many of the overall duties of leading the Liberals in opposition, whilst the Marquess of Hartington led them in the Commons. Granville's house at 16 Bruton Street, and later at 18 Carlton House

Terrace, became the political and social centre of the Liberal Party, with distinguished guests attending regular receptions given by him and his wife.

When the party won the election in 1880, there was once again a distinct possibility that Granville would be called upon to become Prime Minister, but he and Hartington instead convinced the queen to send for Gladstone, which she reluctantly did. Granville returned for a third time to the office of Foreign Secretary and served there for another five years, amid numerous crises in different parts of the world. He was not considered to have handled these well, and a withering attack was made on him by the Tory Lord Randolph Churchill, who in a letter to *The Times* in May 1885 accused Granville of misrepresenting him in a speech in the House of Lords about events which had taken place in Afghanistan. In his rebuttal, Churchill wrote that only two conclusions could be drawn:

> Either that Lord Granville is perfectly unscrupulous in his manipulation of papers for the purposes of debate, or that his incompetence for conducting the foreign affairs of this country, which charitable persons were not unwilling to assume to be of recent growth, in reality is to be distinctly traced from the very commencement of his career as Foreign Secretary ... The process of sneaking down to the House of Lords and making there without notice a variety of deliberate misrepresentations, deliberate misquotations, and false assertions is quite in accordance with the little that is known of the public career of the Earl Granville, Knight of the Garter, and, to the misfortune of his country, Her Majesty's Principal Secretary of State for Foreign Affairs.[5]

Privately, some of his colleagues shared this view, with even Lord

Hartington reported to have said of the *Times* letter that every word was true and that Granville 'was probably the worst Foreign Minister England has ever had.'[6]

Granville left the Foreign Office for the last time on the resignation of the government the following month. When Gladstone briefly returned to office in 1886, he demoted Granville to the Colonial Office, appointing the Earl of Rosebery to the Foreign Office instead. By this time, Granville was an old man, increasingly deaf and afflicted by gout. Though he remained leader of the Liberals in the Lords, he was hampered by his party's political problems over Irish Home Rule, despite his efforts to win support for Gladstone's position. As *The Times* later put it:

> He found himself, whether as leader of the Ministerialists or of the Opposition, in command of a scanty and depressed following, for the ablest statesmen identified with Liberal policy had ranged themselves on the Unionist side. His spirit never flagged, his temper rarely showed signs of friction, but his task was a hopeless one.[7]

Granville's health declined through these years, and he was frequently absent from the House due to ill health. He died on 31 March 1891 at his brother's house in South Audley Street, having suffered for some weeks from an abscess on the side of his face, which may have been cancer. The Prince of Wales, later Edward VII, paid a visit of condolence to the house, and a large number of cards of sympathy were delivered.

Whatever the criticism of his stewardship, his long association with the Foreign Office – from being appointed Undersecretary in 1840 to his three spells as Foreign Secretary – spanned nearly fifty years and was an appropriately impressive record for the son of a diplomat. He also ranks high in the list of those opposition leaders who very nearly made it to Prime Minister, having got as far as being asked to form a government once and having been in serious contention twice more. In my book (which of course this is), that achievement certainly justifies the naming of a cross-Channel car ferry.

James Harris, 3rd Earl of Malmesbury

Conservative, Leader of the Opposition in the House of Lords
December 1868–February 1869

I f the last leader on our list, Earl Granville, had spent much of his career in the shadow of William Gladstone, the next leader was even more in the shadow of the equivalent Victorian big beast on the Tory side, Benjamin Disraeli. It might be thought a bit of a stretch to include him in the ranks of opposition leaders at all, given that he was only very briefly and nominally Leader of the Opposition in the Lords, and at a time when Disraeli was unquestionably the overall leader from the Commons. But (spoiler alert) if you think that bending the rules to include such tenuously qualified candidates is unworthy, you might have to skip quite a lot of this book.

James Howard Harris, later the 3rd Earl of Malmesbury, was born on 25 March 1807 in London. His grandfather had been the eminent diplomat Sir James Harris, for whom the earldom had been created, whilst his father, the 2nd Earl of Malmesbury, had only really dabbled in politics, serving as a Tory MP and as Undersecretary at the Foreign Office – an appointment notified to him just hours before his son's birth, as he waited nervously in the next room. The young James would go on to rise to rather higher office in that department.

He was educated at Eton and Oxford and seemed at first destined to follow his father's example as an aristocratic man of leisure, more interested in shooting and the social round than in politics at Westminster. He spent time after university travelling around the Continent as a man of leisure, and during this time he struck up a friendship in Naples with Lord Byron's last mistress, Countess Teresa Guiccioli, five years after the poet's death. Another friend he made during these years was Prince Louis Napoleon of France, the future Emperor Napoleon III, whom he described then as, 'A wild harum-scarum youth ... riding at full gallop down the streets to the peril of the public, fencing, and pistol-shooting, and apparently without serious thoughts of any kind.' Despite this wild nature, he recalled, 'Even then he was possessed with the conviction he would some day rule over France.'[1]

Known as Viscount Fitzharris during this period, he took an interest in foreign affairs (and not just in the personal sense), writing a pamphlet in 1837 critical of the policies of the Foreign Secretary, Viscount Palmerston. He was elected to the House of Commons for the borough of Wilton in Wiltshire in July 1841, in the general election that brought Robert Peel's Conservatives back to office. Of his experience on the campaign trail, he recorded, 'I completed a most tiresome and uninteresting canvass, there being no opposition to me; but it is an extensive borough, entirely agricultural, and necessitated long drives from one point to another.'[2]

His time in elected office was brief, however. His father had been ill during the election and died on 10 September, removing Fitzharris to the House of Lords as the 3rd Earl of Malmesbury just weeks after he had entered the Commons. He remained an interested observer of politics, but he played no significant role until the drama over Peel's repeal of the Corn Laws prompted him to action. He was instinctively a supporter of the protectionists and had been a good friend of their leader, Lord Stanley, for many years. He thus recorded that in 1846:

I for the first time took a strong part in politics – not for any liking of that stormy life, which I had always shunned – but from a sincere conviction that the abolition of the Corn Laws, proposed by Peel, would be the ruin of all who depended directly or indirectly upon land.[3]

Working with Stanley, he helped whip support for the protectionists, and the experience deepened the attachment between the two friends, who now became effective and loyal allies. When Stanley, now the Earl of Derby, formed his first government in 1852, he appointed Malmesbury as Foreign Secretary – a surprise appointment which attracted criticism over Malmesbury's lack of relevant experience. As he noted in his diary:

The only men [in the new Cabinet] who have ever held office before are Lord Derby and Lord Lonsdale; and the country is to a certain degree anxious as to a Government composed of men so inexperienced in public business. The Opposition papers are loud in their abuse of us personally, to an amount of scurrility that does them no honour. With regard to myself, I get a good share of their epigrams and insults, but I thought all this natural enough under the peculiar circumstances, and have cared little for it, until I found out that the most bitter and disparaging articles were written by

Sidney Herbert and Lord Lincoln, both of whom have been for years my most intimate and 'familiar friends', and I confess their anonymous and treacherous warfare gives me great pain; but such are politics, destructive of all the gentler sentiments between man and man.[4]

In fact, Malmesbury recalled, his experience editing for publication the papers of his illustrious diplomat grandfather was an 'accidental education' that had been a significant help in broadening his knowledge of foreign affairs.[5] The Liberal Lord Palmerston, who had previously been Foreign Secretary, was also kind to Malmesbury when he took up office, providing him with a courteous and helpful briefing on world affairs and giving advice on how to handle the business of government. Malmesbury also called on the elderly Duke of Wellington, whose parting advice – 'Mind you keep well with France' – was particularly timely. Malmesbury's old friend Louis Napoleon was now in power there, having been elected President of France in 1848. The French leader had just staged a coup to remain in office with increased powers and was on his way to having himself proclaimed Emperor. The victor of Waterloo added that whilst he did not believe Louis Napoleon intended to go to war with Britain if he could help it, 'He must keep up his popularity, and then God knows what he may do.'[6]

Malmesbury had kept in contact with Louis Napoleon since their friendship in Rome decades before, visiting him in prison after a failed coup in 1840 and spending time with him during his exiles in England prior to his rise to power. This close connection was of significant diplomatic help to the new Foreign Secretary, who received sincere congratulations from the soon-to-be Napoleon III on his appointment. Any fears that the French leader might seek to avenge his uncle's defeat by attacking Britain were quickly quelled, and Malmesbury played an effective role in laying the foundations for a much closer relationship between the two countries.

Despite his own initial reluctance to accept the position, and widespread scepticism about his appointment, he proved to be a competent Foreign Secretary, but his time in office was short. The government lasted less than a year, and Malmesbury soon returned to opposition, where he remained a senior figure in the Tory leadership, alongside Derby and Disraeli. However, his relationship with Disraeli became somewhat strained during this time, with Malmesbury sharing many of Derby's misgivings about their colleague in the Commons. In 1858, Derby formed another minority government, and Malmesbury was again appointed as Foreign Secretary, where he had to navigate the tricky issue of France's war with Austria over Sardinia, in which, despite his friendship with Napoleon III, he ensured Britain remained neutral.

This second tenure lasted a little longer than his first, but the government fell after just sixteen months. When Derby formed his third and final government in 1866, Malmesbury might have returned again to the Foreign Office but instead accepted the post of Lord Privy Seal. He kept this position when Disraeli became Prime Minister following Derby's retirement in early 1868 and was from then also the Conservative leader in the Lords.

This meant that when Disraeli's government lost office in December of that year, Malmesbury was technically Leader of the Opposition in the House of Lords. He had no wish for this position, however, and decided to resign the leadership immediately. Despite an appeal from Lord Derby for him to stay until Easter, he announced his decision at a dinner of Conservative peers on 15 February 1869, proposing as his successor Lord Cairns, who was chosen unanimously. Despite stepping back, Malmesbury returned to office under Disraeli five years later, again as Lord Privy Seal, serving for two years until ill health forced his retirement in 1876.

He lived on until 1889, over twelve years after he was last in government, prompting *The Times* to write in the report of his death in May 1889:

> The death of Lord Malmesbury, which occurred yesterday, will strike many readers with a feeling of surprise, not indeed that he should be dead, but that he should until yesterday have been alive. No one is so speedily forgotten as a statesman who has retired from active politics. No period of political history is so little known to the man in the street as that which coincides with or immediately precedes the childhood of the living generation. Such history is not yet written in books. The memoirs which illustrate and explain it are for the most part still unpublished … Hence it is that Lord Malmesbury has long been practically forgotten.[7]

As the report went on to note, Malmesbury had published a book, *Memoirs of an Ex-Minister*, in 1884, containing indiscreet and revealing extracts from his diaries and letters. It was, *The Times* conceded, 'the literary sensation of an autumn', and served not just as 'an effective vindication of his official career' but also 'a vivid and entertaining picture of social life and manners'.[8] Malmesbury's book has certainly made writing this chapter much more entertaining than it might otherwise have been, though it has also lengthened the process as I kept being drawn into reading the colourful details. I can therefore only end by agreeing with the writer of his *Times* obituary, who reflected, 'The Foreign Secretary of a generation ago is forgotten, and even his death will scarcely revive his memory; but the "Memoirs of an ex-Minister" should certainly rescue the name of the third Earl of Malmesbury from oblivion.'[9]

Amen to that. Malmesbury might not have been the most notable of Foreign Secretaries and did almost nothing as Leader of the Opposition, but at least he demonstrated that publishing a political history book can sometimes earn a modicum of appreciation for its otherwise undistinguished author. For some reason I find this a reassuring thought.

Hugh Cairns, 1st Baron Cairns

Conservative, Leader of the Opposition in the
House of Lords February 1869–February 1870

When the Earl of Malmesbury stepped down from the leadership of the Conservative opposition in the House of Lords in 1869, the successor he proposed was one who would later become an earl but whose background was rather different to his own. Looking at the lists of titled politicians of this age, it is easy for them all to merge into an anonymous blur of ermine and tweed. This can be justified in some cases (as we have seen already), but it also often obscures exceptionally gifted figures who would have made a name for themselves even without the mantle of a peerage.

Hugh Cairns was certainly such a person. A lawyer of great ability, he rose to pre-eminence in his profession and was ranked by one political opponent as the greatest of all Victorian judges. He served twice as Lord Chancellor, at a time when that job was still reserved for distinguished legal figures, instead of being just another Cabinet post for career politicians of variable quality...

Cairns was not from a great aristocratic family. He was born in Northern Ireland on 27 December 1819, the second son of William

Cairns, an army captain in the 47th (Lancashire) foot regiment, and his wife Rosanna. The Cairns family had moved to Northern Ireland from Scotland in the seventeenth century and, though not aristocrats, were from the ranks of the comfortable Ulster gentry of landowners and merchants. They had a townhouse in Belfast as well as their country lodge, Parkmount House in County Antrim.

The young Hugh attended Belfast Academy and was something of a child prodigy, reportedly giving a public lecture on chemistry at the age of eight. He then went on to study classics at Trinity College Dublin and emerged with a first-class degree, before going on to study law. His family were devout Protestants, and his father had intended him (as a second son) to go into the church, having arranged for him to be tutored by the Rev. George Wheeler whilst at Trinity. Instead, Wheeler urged the elder Cairns to allow his son to follow his interest in the law, so after leaving university Hugh went to London in 1841 and enrolled at Lincoln's Inn.

Called to the Bar three years later in Middle Temple, Cairns began to practise as a barrister in the capital, living in some comfort in Eaton Place thanks to the support of a wealthy relative. He was not considered at this time a particularly elegant speaker, but his common sense and directness in his advocacy built him a solid reputation, with appearances in a number of high-profile cases. In 1852, making the most of his hometown connections, he was elected to the House of Commons as the Conservative MP for Belfast and pursued politics alongside his legal career. He became a QC in 1856 and was appointed Solicitor General in the Earl of Derby's brief government in 1858.

It was in this role that he earned a formidable reputation as a parliamentarian, making a notable defence of the government during a debate over the government of India, in which he forensically rebutted the opposition's attacks and was widely praised for his skill and persuasive eloquence. His speech, according to the report of it in *The Times*, had been repeatedly interrupted by noisy acclamation, first by the traditional cries of 'hear, hear', then by 'cheers', then by even more vigorous approval of 'great cheering', 'continued cheering' and, when he sat down, 'loud and continued cheers, which for a few moments prevented the next speaker obtaining a hearing'.[1]

After that government fell, he took a leading role in opposition to the Liberal government over the next eight years, and when Lord Derby formed his next government in 1866, he made Cairns his Attorney General. However, that appointment did not last long, as concerns over his health led Cairns to resign from the government and from the Commons and take a judicial appointment as a lord justice of appeal. He was missed in government, however; and he was induced by his former colleagues to accept a peerage in early 1867, after which he was able to contribute to defending the government in the Lords.

When Benjamin Disraeli took over from Derby as Prime Minister in 1868, he immediately made Cairns his Lord Chancellor, sacking the incumbent Lord Chelmsford, who was greatly upset. Disraeli, however, argued that Chelmsford had only ever been a temporary appointment and that it had always been agreed that Cairns would eventually succeed him. Lord Malmesbury, by now leader in the upper House, wrote that the return of Cairns to government was 'a very efficient addition to our strength in the Lords, where our bench is comparatively weak in debate'.[2]

Disraeli's government lasted less than a year and, as we saw in the last chapter, Lord Malmesbury did not wish to hang around as Leader of the Opposition after the defeat. Cairns himself sounded out the Marquess of Salisbury to see if he would be willing to take on the role, but after he declined it was settled that Cairns would take over, and this he did when Parliament reassembled in February 1869.

For someone of such great ability, who had by now built a formidable reputation as Lord Chancellor and as a parliamentarian, it is somewhat surprising that he turned out to be unsuccessful as leader, lasting little more than a year and seeking to resign several months before that. The cause of his demise was the Irish Church Bill, by which the Liberal government sought to disestablish the Anglican church in Ireland. As a devout Irish Protestant, this was an issue which Cairns felt very personally. He led fellow Conservatives in first opposing the bill, and then in seeking to win greater concessions from the government when the Commons passed it.

The issue led to heated exchanges and nearly escalated into a constitutional crisis after the Lords insisted on amendments that had been rejected by the Commons. To resolve the impasse, Cairns agreed a deal with the Liberal leader in the Lords, Earl Granville, accepting some limited concessions in return for allowing the bill to pass. He did so without consulting his colleagues, many of whom were outraged. Lord Derby was 'so angry that he left the House', according to Malmesbury.[3] In a circular letter to his colleagues, Cairns explained his actions, telling them that the concessions had been offered at short notice and that it had been 'impossible' to consult colleagues or to explain to them the benefits of the deal. Agreeing it, he said, 'secured more for the Church than I believe would ever again have been obtained' as well as enabling them to 'put an end to what was a violent, and was rapidly becoming a dangerous, strain upon the constitutional relations of the two Houses'.[4]

The apologetic tone of the letter, and the retreat from the fight with the government over the bill, greatly damaged Cairns's standing amongst his colleagues, and shortly afterwards he wrote to Disraeli that he wished to give up the leadership, saying that the party should be led in the Lords by someone with more 'traditional and material weight'.[5] His resignation did not take effect immediately, and at the start of the next session in February 1870 he responded to the queen's speech debate for the opposition but had already signalled it would be his last appearance. *The Times* noted its sadness that he would be stepping down (it hoped temporarily), before going on to offer some thoughts on the particular challenges of opposition in the Lords with which he had been contending:

> We were among those who rejoiced to find as the Session grew near that the rumours of his having resigned the leadership of his party were erroneous, and that the House of Lords would have the benefit of his judgment and moderation in directing its decisions. The Conservative party has an abiding and inevitable majority in the Upper House, and its leader must always be a Parliamentary power. Lord Cairns has attained to this position by the force of his own ability, and has borne himself in it after a manner to satisfy friends and foes. The chief duty of the Conservative leader, we presume, is to influence the decisions of the House, so that, while maintaining its dignity, it shall not come into unseemly or dangerous collision with the Commons.
>
> A Peer may easily obtain a noisy popularity with the zealots of his party by persuading his too ready brethren to throw out the Bills of the Commons, or to disfigure them in such a manner as to render them inefficient or even nugatory. This is 'spirited leadership,' and we have had some of the inconveniences of it at various periods in thwarted legislation, in the loss of time and temper, and a discontent with the authority of the Lords which is not the less dangerous because it is silent and smouldering rather than active. Lord Cairns did a service to his party, as well as to his country, by his compromise with Lord Granville on the Irish Church Bill, and, though of course the indignation of extreme partisans waxed hot for a time, the best

men on the Conservative side felt that he showed the ability fitting for a leader.[6]

This was a thoughtful and sympathetic assessment of the episode which had curtailed his time as leader and highlighted a number of issues of principle. What role should the Lords have in opposing and amending measures from the Commons? How far is it legitimate for the opposition to push their disagreement? To what extent can a leader take a stand on an issue when their party is not fully behind them? These questions remain just as relevant today.

Despite the hope of *The Times*, Cairns's retirement from the leadership was confirmed. A meeting of Conservative peers chaired by Cairns at the Carlton Club on Saturday 19 February 1870 passed a resolution that Edward Stanley – now the 15th Earl of Derby, having succeeded his late father just four months before – should take on the leadership of the party in the Lords after Cairns's resignation. The motion was proposed by the Duke of Richmond and seconded by Lord Salisbury. It appears the new Lord Derby turned down the offer of the leadership, as a week later, at a further meeting at the Carlton Club, he seconded a motion proposed by Salisbury that the Duke of Richmond should take on the party leadership in the Lords.

Richmond duly took over as leader but continued to rely on Cairns's advice. Disraeli also came to respect Cairns for his shrewd political instincts, making him Lord Chancellor once more in his next government in 1874. Disraeli never particularly liked him and was known to mock his pious religious faith, but he recognised his talents and value to the government, and an earldom was created for Cairns in 1878, elevating him to the title of 1st Earl Cairns.

When Disraeli died in 1880, some thought Cairns was well placed to succeed him. This was perhaps the closest he came to being back in contention for No. 10, but the post went instead to future Prime Minister Lord Salisbury. Under Salisbury's leadership, Cairns became uncomfortable with the way the Conservatives in opposition sought to use their strength to push back against the elected Liberal government in the Commons. Whilst the new Conservative leader believed in the constitutional right of the Lords to reject measures sent to them by the Commons which lacked a specific electoral mandate, Cairns argued that peers should take a more realistic view of the limitations of their legitimate role. His views led him to join many of his colleagues in refusing to participate in some of the parliamentary showdowns over legislation sought by Salisbury.

Beyond his political inclinations, Cairns was certainly an interesting character – profoundly devout in his Christianity, he read the Bible every morning for an hour and a half and insisted that his house guests attend a Sunday service held at his house during weekend house parties. His religion led him to support a number of charitable causes throughout his life, one of which was the YMCA. This has, I confess, provided me with my shorthand way of remembering him, as I picture the pious earl in full Lord Chancellor's robes dancing the disco routine later associated with that organisation. It is a bizarre mental image that I have found hard to shift, and by mentioning it I realise the same might be true for you too. For that, I can only apologise.

He was also a great supporter of Dr Barnardo and was asked to open that charitable pioneer's first children's home in Essex in 1877, which then bore his name as Cairns House. He died on 2 April 1885 at his home in Bournemouth, and the tribute to him in *The Times* commended his skills in government, as well as once again recalling his value as a moderating influence:

His great legal acquirements and acumen, and his sagacious counsels, made him an invaluable leader of his party on all occasions, but more especially in periods of difficultly and of crisis ... The full extent of the loss the Conservatives are called upon to sustain by his death will not be realised until the leaders of the party are once more summoned to undertake the responsibilities of office. The influence of Lord Cairns upon Conservatism was pre-eminently a salutary one – useful in moderating the zeal of the most active members of the party, and invaluable as a constructive force in practical legislation.[7]

His tenure as an opposition leader may have been cut short, but this should not detract from the considerable reputation he built throughout his career. A willingness to compromise and offer pragmatic opposition showed a degree of maturity that has not always been present on either party's front benches. It may have contributed to his downfall, but moderation in politics should not, in my view, be considered a vice. The wider issues regarding 'constructive opposition' are ones with which many future leaders would also have to contend.

12

Charles Gordon-Lennox, 6th Duke of Richmond

Conservative, Leader of the Opposition
in the House of Lords 1870–74

Having noted that Hugh Cairns was something of a break from the ranks of traditional aristocrats who dominated politics at this time, and someone of unusual talent and distinction in his own right, the next leader on our list returns us to the more familiar run of nineteenth-century landed nobles. When Cairns stepped down from the leadership of the Conservatives in the Lords in February 1870, we saw in the last chapter that the role was offered first to the new Earl of Derby, who declined it, leaving the party to turn instead to a traditional safe pair of hands. The new leader was an established hereditary peer – a duke, no less – but one who was memorably dismissed by the historian Robert Blake as 'an amiable but ineffective nonentity'.[1] That might be a little harsh, but it is easy to see why the assessment has proved so enduring.

Charles Henry Gordon-Lennox was born in 1818 at Richmond House, Whitehall – the London residence of the Dukes of Richmond, which sits across the road from Downing Street and is now the site of Richmond Terrace. Like Charles James Fox, he was a direct descendant of the first Duke of Richmond, Charles Lennox, the illegitimate son of King Charles II and the Duchess of Portsmouth. As heir to the dukedom from early childhood, Charles was known as the Earl of March until he succeeded to the title in 1860.

Educated at Westminster School and Christ Church, Oxford, he first joined the army, becoming a captain in the Horse Guards, and was then elected to the Commons as Conservative MP for West Sussex in 1841. He combined this with his military career, serving as aide-de-camp to the elderly Duke of Wellington (who held the post of Commander-in-Chief of the army) from 1842 and later to his successor Lord Hardinge from 1852.

In the Commons, he developed a specialism in agricultural policy, and during the split in the Conservative Party over the Corn Laws, he joined his father as a supporter of the protectionist wing of the Tories. He then held office for a few months as president of the Poor Law Board in Lord Derby's brief second government in 1859. After succeeding his father as Duke of Richmond the following year, he later joined Derby's third government as President of the Board of Trade in 1867, continuing in office for a short while when Disraeli briefly became Prime Minister the following year.

This made Richmond a senior enough Conservative peer to be in contention for the leadership in the Lords when Cairns resigned in 1870, even if he was more of a default option after the Marquess of Salisbury and Derby were ruled out. As *The Times* later put it in his obituary, 'It was thought better to select a man of the highest rank, who had had long experience of the House and of public business, and who had a reputation for sound sense, a fondness for compromise, and not the slightest inclination to epigram.'[2] Given that both the Earl of Malmesbury and Cairns had stepped down in the year prior to Richmond's appointment, he was in some senses the fifth choice for the job, but nevertheless he proved able to provide some stability, remaining in post for the next four years of opposition.

As leader he was later considered to have been 'a prudent and industrious worker in the cause of his party, especially when it was in opposition', with *The Times* further stating that 'if his speeches never rose to oratory, they and the party tactics which they expressed were also correct, and often statesmanlike.'[3] Like Cairns, he faced the delicate strategic dilemma of how far to push his opposition to government measures, given the Conservative majority in the upper House. During one tense exchange in the Chamber over the Ballot Bill, the opposition was accused by the Liberal Earl Granville of seeking to 'exercise a despotism' by using the 'enormous power they wield in this House' to vote against and defeat the government, whilst Richmond himself was accused of seeking to induce his colleagues to vote against their better judgement. Richmond angrily reacted to this turn of phrase by retorting:

> My lords, the noble Earl stated that as we on this side of the House were the majority, I was in the habit of exercising what he is pleased to call a despotism – that is to say, that I have the power and also the inclination to direct the noble lords whom I now see around me to vote on every occasion in the way I prescribe, and that I am the despot who rules noble lords on this side of the House ... The noble Earl the Secretary of State for Foreign Affairs [Granville] has no right to tell me I exercise a despotism ... It is an imputation that I venture to appeal to noble Lords on this side to vote contrary to their views and wishes ... I regret that matter of so personal a character has been introduced by the noble Earl, and, feeling so strongly upon it, and that the noble Earl has not a tittle of foundation for

the language he has used, I have taken the liberty of making these remarks. [Cheers.][4]

As well as being an entertaining, lively spat between an opposition leader and a predecessor whom we have already met, the exchange is fascinating for what it says about Richmond's view of the role of a party leader in the Lords. He takes it as a personal insult that there should be any suggestion he had sought to impose rigid voting discipline on his troops, or tried to whip them into supporting his position. Presumably he took the lofty view that peers should never be swayed by anything except the power of argument in the Chamber, but it is an oddly severe response given the usual nature of parliamentary party politics.

After four non-despotic years in opposition, Richmond remained his party's leader in the Lords when Disraeli formed his next government in 1874, entering the Cabinet as Lord President of the Council. In this role he had nominal responsibility for education but took little interest in the subject and seemed more than keen to get the business of the parliamentary session over with so he could return to his Scottish estates for grouse shooting with his friend and predecessor Cairns.

The one area of government in which he took an interest was agriculture, and he used a tenuous connection to his ministerial portfolio to act as though this was his main responsibility. He oversaw a number of pieces of agricultural legislation, including the drastic Contagious Diseases (Animals) Bill, which sought the compulsory slaughter of foreign cattle at the port of entry to prevent the spread of disease to British cattle. This pleased the domestic agricultural lobby but caused a public outcry over the likely increase in meat prices, and his Cabinet colleagues forced him to make major concessions.

Despite such political missteps, Richmond seemed to believe he remained a contender to be Prime Minister, should Disraeli have to step down through ill health. The idea that this could ever happen had alarmed other party grandees at the outset of the government, with Derby (son of the former Prime Minister) having recorded in December 1874:

> Letter from Salisbury, who has got in his mind the notion that there is in some quarters a project for making the D of Richmond the next premier, when Disraeli's health compels him to resign, an event which Salisbury evidently considers as not far distant. He protests against this, says it must not be allowed, that the Duke is unfit for the post, that his appointment would justify the title of the 'stupid party' as applied to us, and that in the event of a vacancy I must assert my claim to the position ... I answer ... agreeing as to the unfitness of the Duke.[5]

In the event, Disraeli served six years as Prime Minister and, having been elevated to the Lords as the Earl of Beaconsfield in 1876, displaced Richmond as the Conservative leader in the upper House until his death in 1881, a year after losing office. Salisbury then replaced Disraeli as Leader of the Opposition and went on to become Prime Minister. In his brief first government in 1885, he appointed Richmond once again as President of the Board of Trade and in August of that year gave him the added distinction of being the first holder of the new Cabinet post of Secretary for Scotland, albeit for only a few months until the government fell in January 1886.

It was Richmond's last government appointment, and an appropriate one given his family connections and extensive lands in Scotland, which his father had inherited on the death of the last Duke of Gordon. This heritage had been recognised in 1876 when the Dukedom of Gordon was revived and awarded to him by and at the suggestion of Queen Victoria.

After leaving government for the last time, he was free to spend more time on his agricultural interests – an enduring commitment which had led the Prince of Wales (later Edward VII) to refer to him twice in public speeches as 'the farmer's friend'.[6] It was a title the duke was proud to claim and a rather kinder one than some of the other labels we have seen applied. He remained on the council of the Royal Agricultural Society into his old age and is the first of our opposition leaders to have seen the twentieth century, dying at Gordon Castle in Scotland on 27 September 1903 at the age of eighty-five. His obituary in *The Times* devoted considerable space to his achievements as a farmer and landowner, including the prizes won by his Southdown sheep.

Whilst he was clearly not the brightest or most effective of politicians, the 6th Duke of Richmond deserves some recognition for having been a senior player in government and opposition during an age defined by the epic rivalry between the two Victorian titans of Disraeli and Gladstone. Unlike some of the dutiful aristocrats who found themselves leading the opposition, he seems not to have suffered from excessive modesty and was quite prepared to entertain the idea that he might have been called upon to be Prime Minister. Given that this prospect was greeted with derision by his senior colleagues, we can conclude that his ambitions in this direction outstripped his abilities and that he lacked a degree of self-awareness about his own leadership qualities. In this, he is hardly unique amongst politicians then or now.

He could, however, claim to have had an impact on government in the field he cared about most. From 1879 to 1882 he had chaired a Royal Commission on the state of the agricultural interest, which became known as the Richmond Commission. One of its main recommendations was eventually implemented, with the creation in 1889 of the Board of Agriculture, whose president was a government minister. This then evolved into the Ministry of Agriculture, later adding Fisheries and Food to its responsibilities, before being merged into the Department for Environment, Food and Rural Affairs. Having himself acted in government as though he was the Minister for Agriculture before the role even existed, it is fitting that he should then have prompted its creation. For machinery of government nerds, this affords the duke at least some lasting legacy for his otherwise mediocre political career.

13

Spencer Cavendish,
Marquess of Hartington

Liberal, Leader of the Opposition in
the House of Commons 1875–80

Having spent the last few chapters looking at Conservative opposition leaders in the House of Lords, we can now turn our
attention back to the Commons and to the Liberals. This does not,
however, mean we get to take a break from the succession of titled aristocrats. Our next leader could hardly have been grander, given that he
bore the surname Cavendish and was later to become the 8th Duke of
Devonshire. But he did at least make his reputation in the Commons,
where for most of the time we are concerned with him he was known
by the courtesy title of the Marquess of Hartington.

This title lent him to what is perhaps my favourite nickname of any Victorian statesman, with some political gossips referring to him as 'Harty-
Tarty'. He also has another claim to fame for me, in that he gave his
name to the Hartington Hotel on Cavendish Place in Eastbourne, land
owned by the Dukes of Devonshire. This later became the Hartington,
a friendly gay pub where, as a young man, I may or may not have spent
some evenings with friends in the late 1990s being either harty or tarty.

Unlike the clientele of what is now called The Hart, the man himself was resolutely heterosexual. His nickname was in fact partly a reference to his long affair with the society courtesan Catherine Walters, known as 'Skittles'. This led to a glorious practical joke reportedly played on him by his friend the Prince of Wales (later Edward VII), who was another of her alleged clients. Making an official visit to Coventry, Hartington was puzzled to find a visit to a bowling alley had been included on the itinerary. On arriving there, the mayor explained that it had been a suggestion from the Prince of Wales, who had told them of his lordship's great love of skittles... Whilst this has all the hallmarks of being apocryphal, I am afraid it is too good for me not to include here.

Colourful as his private life may have been, my rather flippant opening to this chapter belies the fact that Hartington was a highly consequential political figure of the age, who was actually given the opportunity to become Prime Minister on three occasions but declined each time. He also has the distinction of having led three different political parties during his career, either in the Commons or the Lords. Those achievements make him more qualified than usual for a place in this book.

Born as Spencer Compton Cavendish in 1833, he was educated at home mostly by his father William Cavendish, 2nd Earl of Burlington (later 7th Duke of Devonshire), who was said to have believed in a broader and more demanding education for his children than that on offer in the nation's public schools at the time. Burlington was certainly well qualified to oversee his children's education – a brilliant, prize-winning mathematician when at Cambridge, he became the first Chancellor of the University of London from 1836 and went on to become Chancellor of Cambridge University.

Lord Cavendish (as Hartington was initially known) was not quite so accomplished in his early academic career, but he followed in his father's footsteps to Trinity College, Cambridge, where he achieved a respectable second-class degree in mathematics. On leaving, he spent the next few years as a young man of leisure, discovering a love of horse racing, playing bridge and mixing in high society. Being from a prominent Whig family, he was then prevailed upon to enter politics and was elected to the Commons in 1857 as Liberal MP for North Lancashire. The following year, his father inherited the title of Duke of Devonshire from a cousin, and it is from then that Cavendish became known as the Marquess of Hartington.

He made little impact during his first years in Parliament but was eventually appointed to office by Viscount Palmerston in 1863, first as a junior lord of the Admiralty and then as Undersecretary at the War Office. He lost his seat in 1868 but soon found another at Radnor in Wales, after which he was appointed Postmaster General by new Prime Minister William Gladstone, having first turned down the job of Lord Lieutenant of Ireland. In this role he oversaw the nationalisation of the telegraph system, before being reluctantly moved in 1870 to become Chief Secretary for Ireland for four years.

When the Liberal government was defeated in the 1874 general election, Gladstone proved to be badly suited to opposition. Having relished power, he found the experience of losing it particularly hard, and the hard slog of rallying a defeated and increasingly divided party was one for which he had no appetite. Instead, he took an increasing interest in writing tracts on religious issues, including an attack on papal infallibility. His colleague Sir William Harcourt, who disliked him, vented his frustration at the state of the opposition in a way familiar to today's politicians – by privately briefing the press. He told the editor of the *Daily News*, 'There is no whip, no office, *no nothing*. The thing is ridiculous and disgraceful. You will be safe in saying that nothing is decided, nothing arranged, nothing prepared. The fate of the Liberal party depends on whether G[ladstone] chooses to get out of the sulks.'[1]

It gradually became clear that Gladstone had lost interest in politics and was considering retiring to spend more time with his theological dilemmas. He was out of step with the views of many of his colleagues and didn't have the inclination even to try to bring the party together. In December 1874 he decided to resign the leadership before the new session of parliament and rebuffed efforts from party grandees to get him to stay even as the nominal leader. Another unimpressed colleague, the Duke of Argyll, wrote of the former Prime Minister's abdication of responsibility that he had 'treated the Liberal Party like a young woman whom he has seduced, ruined and then thrown on the streets'.[2]

These were the circumstances in which Hartington became leader of the party in early 1875. His accession was not without controversy, with a number of candidates emerging and jostling for position. Hartington's main competitor was William E. Forster, who had made his name during the recent government as a progressive who had promoted a number of educational reforms. He had, however, alienated some of his natural supporters on the radical wing of the party, and many of them were actively opposed to him taking over.

Hartington, on the other hand, had fewer achievements but also fewer enemies. More of a political amateur, the historian John P. Rossi memorably noted, 'His main interests seemed to be racing, shooting, and his mistress, the Duchess of Manchester, though not necessarily in that order.' Harcourt made the case for a more hands-off leadership as a welcome contrast to the recent dominance of Gladstone, arguing that Hartington would be 'the best constitutional Sovereign in the party after the fall of the despotism'.[3]

SPENCER CAVENDISH, MARQUESS OF HARTINGTON

The man himself showed little interest in the leadership, and the more active candidature of Forster might well have prevailed, particularly after his supporters successfully campaigned for the decision on the new leader to be made by all the party's MPs, rather than by just a handful of grandees. This proposal, confirmed by the calling of a general meeting by the party's Chief Whip William Adam, was something of a constitutional innovation. A week before it took place, an anonymous letter to *The Times* signed 'V' made this very point:

> On no previous occasion has either House of Parliament elected its leader by popular suffrage. I am not at present concerned to prove that the new method is, as I believe it to be, the worst that could be devised; but I think it important that a political revolution should not be accomplished in careless ignorance. The office of Parliamentary Leader has, like many other elements of the Constitution, been gradually established for reasons of practical convenience. Although the Leader of the Opposition in the House of Commons has neither salary nor legal precedence, he is generally next in Parliamentary and political rank to the Prime Minister, and he is often his destined successor. The appointment by universal suffrage among Liberal members of the House of the leader of the Party is practically a usurpation of the prerogative of the Crown, which in modern times is ordinarily exercised by the actual or prospective Cabinet.[4]

For those sad characters like myself who have spent years obsessing about the constitutional position of the official opposition, 'V' makes an interesting argument, which has some contemporary resonance. If it was a novelty then for the choice of leader to be made by the parliamentary party, the modern situation, in which leaders are chosen by party members, presents an even greater concern. We have seen on several occasions in recent decades the effects of opening up lead-ership elections to self-selected political activists, who have gone on to choose such infamous opposition leaders as Iain Duncan Smith and Jeremy Corbyn. Regardless of the merits of those candidates, both of them suffered from a lack of support amongst their parliamentary colleagues, which could have had serious constitutional implications had either won a general election. This is a point on which I could myself be moved to write a pained letter to *The Times*, whether or not its readers are interested.

The Liberal Party meeting took place in the library of the Reform Club on the afternoon of Wednesday 3 February 1875, by which time Hartington had emerged as the sole contender. Forster, much to his supporters' disappointment, had withdrawn his candidature after con-cluding that he would not be able to unite the party. As a result, this innovative 'election' was a formality, with the proceedings reported (of course) in *The Times* the next day. After a resolution was passed noting the deep sense of loss at Gladstone's retirement, Charles Villiers rose to 'loud cheers' to propose the motion 'that the Marquis of Hartington be requested to undertake the leadership of the Liberal Party in the House of Commons'. He was followed by one of Forster's support-ers, who paid tribute to the 'self-denial' of their withdrawn candidate before pledging loyalty to Hartington in the interests of party unity, and the motion was then agreed unanimously.[5]

Hartington himself was not present, having considered it improper to attend the deliberations, but his brother, Lord Frederick Cavendish, spoke on his behalf. In his remarks he stressed that Hartington had not sought the role, and that 'no man in this room would have been more rejoiced than my brother had your unanimous choice fallen upon some other gentleman'. This was more than polite humility, with Cav-endish adding the candid explanation that:

The Marquis of Hartington is not unconscious of the difficulties and of the labour to be encountered in the task of leadership, even in the most favourable circumstances ... Only those who know my brother best can be aware how diffident he feels as to his abilities and qualifications for performing the task.[6]

Despite this reluctant beginning, Hartington proved to be a quiet success as he navigated the next five years in opposition, during a period in which the Liberals remained divided over how to respond to their defeat. Hartington favoured quiet patience, whilst others, including Joseph Chamberlain, believed in a more active approach to stoke popular discontent with the Tory government. Despite his retirement, Gladstone remained an influential figure in the party and caused difficulties for his successor by taking a different view to him, particularly on foreign policy around the Russo-Turkish War.

Nevertheless, by the time of the 1880 election, Hartington had restored a degree of party unity and his attacks on Disraeli's Conservatives were highly effective, resulting in the Liberals winning a large majority in the House of Commons after gaining 110 seats. Queen Victoria invited Hartington to form a government, but it soon became clear that Gladstone, who had come out of retirement to play a prominent role in the election campaign, would not accept a Cabinet position under him. As a result, both Hartington and Granville, the party's leader in the Lords, stood aside and recommended to a reluctant sovereign that Gladstone should be called upon to return as Prime Minister.

Hartington instead joined Gladstone's Cabinet as Secretary of State for India, moving to become Secretary of State for War two years later. His later career was something of a roller coaster, as he split from Gladstone over the issue of Home Rule for Ireland, to which he was opposed, and became the leader of the unionist faction of Liberals in the Commons, allying with the Marquess of Salisbury's Conservatives. At the 1886 election this faction won seventy-eight seats, with the Conservatives taking 316, and Salisbury proposed that Hartington should become Prime Minister of a coalition government, an idea which Queen Victoria supported but Hartington turned down. The following year, Salisbury asked him again after the resignation of Randolph Churchill as leader of the Conservatives in the House of Commons, but Hartington refused the offer once more.

He went on to lead the Liberal Unionists in the House of Lords after he inherited the dukedom in 1891 and later served as Lord President of the Council in the Conservative government of Lord Salisbury for eight years, from 1895. In this role he had responsibility for education policy and passed the 1902 Education Act which established local education authorities for the first time. He was a contender for Prime Minister once more when Salisbury retired in 1902 but instead became leader of the Conservatives in the House of Lords.

As a believer in free trade, the duke resigned from office after Arthur Balfour's government embarked on tariff reform, and he therefore ended his career having fallen out of step with both main parties. He died in 1908 at the Hotel Metropole in Cannes, on his way back from a convalescence trip to Egypt. His *Times* obituary noted he was 'not a man of great intellectual distinction' and had 'in his nature a marked vein of indolence' but had ultimately been 'a signal example of what strong sense, moral worth, and firmness of will can accomplish in public life, even when they are unaccompanied by the more showy qualities by which ordinary politicians rise'.[7]

A reluctant leader, he nonetheless deserves to be remembered as the first leader of a major political party to have been elected by its MPs. This democratic innovation would later be adopted by the Labour Party from its first entry into Parliament and (eventually, many years later) by the Conservatives. Hartington's subsequent time in opposition, during which he held together a fractious party for five years, culminated in him winning a general election with a sizable majority and being asked to form a government. That would usually be a mark of success that would disqualify him from this book, but the fact he turned down such a clear chance to become Prime Minister (and did so again twice more) makes him perhaps the most 'not quite' Prime Minister of all those we will consider. His distinction of having led three different parties in Parliament is also a notable claim to fame. And next time I'm in Eastbourne, I hope to revisit The Hart to raise a glass to old Harty-Tarty.

14

Sir Stafford Northcote

Conservative, Leader of the Opposition
in the House of Commons 1880–85

After William Gladstone emerged from his sulky temporary retirement to become Prime Minister again in 1880, he faced across the House of Commons a Conservative Leader of the Opposition whom he knew particularly well. Their association went back to when the man standing opposite him at the despatch box had been appointed as his young private secretary thirty-seven years before. Since then, the former aide had followed his old boss into politics, though taking a different political path, and had succeeded him as Chancellor of the Exchequer six years earlier.

The name Sir Stafford Northcote is now most famous to students of politics for its attachment to what became known as the Northcote–Trevelyan report, which laid the foundation for the modern civil service in 1853. But few perhaps know that this worthy official became a leading politician of the age, who could very nearly have become Prime Minister and did in fact become First Lord of the Treasury. In a cruel twist of fate, he ended his career at 10 Downing Street but only in the most tragic of circumstances.

Born in 1818 in London, Northcote (pronounced 'Northcut') was from a long-established family of Devon nobility. He was heir to the Northcote baronetcy of Hayne, first held by Sir John Northcote, an MP before the English Civil War. The young Stafford was a precocious child, writing poetry and fiction from an early age. He was educated first in Mitcham and Brighton, before going to Eton and then to Oxford, where he graduated with a first in classics and a third in mathematics.

He aimed to go into the law, entering Inner Temple in 1840, but two years later his career took its decisive turn. Gladstone, who was at the time Vice-President of the Board of Trade in Robert Peel's Conservative government, wrote to Northcote's former housemaster at Eton asking him to recommend a former pupil to be his private secretary. Northcote was chosen and spent the next three years alongside Gladstone in government, handling his correspondence and accompanying him on visits around the country.

The personal nature of the appointment made him more akin to a modern special adviser, so despite Gladstone resigning from government, Northcote remained with him for the next five years and assisted him in his election campaign in 1847. During this time, Northcote was also a legal assistant at the Board of Trade. He was then appointed in 1850 as a secretary to the Great Exhibition, working closely with Prince Albert on the project and winning great praise from him, along with being made a Companion of the Order of the Bath for his efforts.

He remained on close personal terms with Gladstone, who became godfather to his eldest son, whilst Gladstone in return asked Northcote to be an executor of his will. However, their political views had begun to diverge – Northcote had more sympathy with the protectionist cause, whilst Gladstone remained a Peelite free trader and was appointed Chancellor of the Exchequer in the Earl of Aberdeen's government in 1852.

It was at Gladstone's behest that, the following year, Northcote and the Treasury official Sir Charles Trevelyan were invited to write their eponymous report on reform of the civil service, which recommended the creation of a permanent class of impartial civil servants, appointed and promoted on merit. There is a certain irony in this, given Northcote's own career trajectory was the result of personal patronage and that he was by this time becoming increasingly political.

He was elected to Parliament as the MP for Dudley in 1855 as a 'liberal conservative', with the backing of a Peelite, Lord Ward, and with Gladstone's endorsement. He was, however, increasingly out of sympathy with the Peelites, and after voting with the opposition to bring down Viscount Palmerston's government, he decided not to contest Dudley again at the 1857 election and was unsuccessful in his attempt to be elected instead for North Devon.

Out of Parliament, he then received an approach from Benjamin Disraeli, who suggested Northcote stand as a Conservative for Stamford. He wrestled with his loyalty to Gladstone, who he knew would not approve and worried about 'deserting' his old boss. But from the beginning, he and 'Dizzy' (as Northcote called him) hit it off, and for the next twenty-three years Northcote was Disraeli's loyal and trusted colleague, referred to by the future Prime Minister as his 'right hand'. When Disraeli became Chancellor, Northcote served as Financial Secretary to the Treasury, and in Lord Derby's third government in 1866 he entered the Cabinet as President of the Board of Trade. He then became Secretary of State for India, remaining in office when Disraeli briefly succeeded Derby as Prime Minister two years later.

After five years in opposition, during which he took up a position as chairman of the Hudson's Bay Company, he returned to office in 1874 alongside Disraeli, who appointed him Chancellor of the Exchequer, a position he held for the duration of his friend's premiership. When Disraeli went to the House of Lords in 1876, Northcote succeeded him as leader of the Conservatives in the House of Commons and remained in that position after the government lost office in 1880.

When Disraeli died a year later, Northcote took on the joint leadership of the Conservatives alongside the Marquess of Salisbury in the Lords. As Leader of the Opposition in the Commons it was he who now faced Gladstone as Prime Minister. This caused him some difficulties, with his style of opposition attracting criticism from his colleagues for being less than vigorous. He was seen as too deferential to his old boss and mentor, despite the fact their relationship had by now soured, with Gladstone reported to view him with contempt for his 'flabby weakness' as a leader.[1] An organised group of young Conservative backbenchers, including Lord Randolph Churchill, exacerbated Northcote's problems by making similarly withering attacks on him.

Northcote was a dutiful and fair-minded leader for the five years he held the job, but his aversion to partisan political fighting stoked increasing dissatisfaction on his benches. His diminished reputation meant that when Gladstone's government fell in 1885 it was Lord Salisbury, not Northcote, who was called upon to become Prime Minister. He was instead appointed First Lord of the Treasury and given a peerage as the Earl of Iddesleigh, his removal from the Commons having been a condition insisted upon by Lord Randolph Churchill as his price for joining the Cabinet. This government only lasted a year before it was replaced by a short-lived Gladstone government. When Salisbury returned to office in 1886 he made Northcote (or Iddesleigh as he now was) his Foreign Secretary, a position that suited him, but he had little time in which to make an impact.

In December, Lord Randolph Churchill resigned as Chancellor, and as we saw in the previous chapter, Lord Salisbury entered talks with the Liberal Unionists, even offering to stand aside and serve in a government under their leader, the Marquess of Hartington. As these discussions proceeded, Iddesleigh offered Salisbury his own position if required, and in early 1887 the Prime Minister took him up on the offer, appointing himself Foreign Secretary in Iddesleigh's place. Iddesleigh turned down a subsequent offer to become Lord President of the Council and accepted his retirement from government with good grace.

A matter of days later, on 12 January, Iddesleigh came to London to visit his old office, and before going on to speak at an event in the City later that day, asked to call in briefly on the Prime Minister. *The Times* provided a vivid account of what happened next:

Lord Iddesleigh walked across from the Foreign Office, where he had lunched, to No. 10 Downing-street at 2.45, and was received there and conducted upstairs to Lord Salisbury's offices, which are on the first floor, by Mr Maddams and Mr Foote, official messengers. Mr Maddams noticed that Lord Iddesleigh was not well directly after he entered the house. He seemed to be oppressed, his breathing was laboured, and evidently he had considerable difficulty in ascending the flight of stairs. Directly he reached the ante-room he sank at once into the nearest chair by the door, while Mr Foote, who was walking in front of him, went to announce his arrival to Lord Salisbury. When the messenger returned in a few moments to usher Lord Iddesleigh in, his lordship was still sitting on the chair, and instead of rising and following the messenger he said, feebly, 'I will be with Lord Salisbury in a minute,' and began to groan … Lord Salisbury was then told, and was speedily in the room, together with the other secretaries. Lord Iddesleigh, who had sunk to the floor, was lifted to a sofa in the room. His neckerchief and collar were loosened, and restoratives were applied, but all attempts to revive him proved fruitless.[2]

He was pronounced dead twenty minutes after arriving at No. 10, at the age of sixty-eight. It was a dramatic end to a fascinating life, during which he held the unique distinction of having been a close colleague and trusted friend to two of the age's great Prime Ministers and rivals, Gladstone and Disraeli. He rose to occupy two of the great offices of state and to lead his party, but his lack of partisan political drive prevented him from reaching the highest office.

The fact that he died at No. 10 is an irresistibly poetic tragedy, particularly given that he is one of the few people to have been First Lord of the Treasury without being Prime Minister, and so was technically entitled to have lived there during the time he held that office, though he chose not to. His sad death secures for him a place in the history of that building, as well as in the wider histories of the period. But it is perhaps still the Northcote–Trevelyan report for which he will be best remembered. There is not space here for a lengthy treatise on its enduring significance in the UK's constitutional arrangements, but the great Peter Hennessy provided an effective summary when he described it as being:

The greatest single governing gift of the nineteenth to the twentieth century: a politically disinterested and permanent Civil Service with core values of integrity, propriety, objectivity and appointment on merit, able to transfer its loyalty and expertise from one elected government to the next.[3]

In the twenty-first century, those core values remain the bedrock of the British civil service, even if they are perhaps coming under greater strain. It is certainly fitting that one of the main architects of that model demonstrated throughout his own career the ability to transfer loyalty to politicians of different parties, even if his tendency to appear objective and 'politically disinterested' made him unsuited to being a forceful opposition leader.

15

Sir Michael Hicks Beach

Conservative, Leader of the Opposition in
the House of Commons February–July 1886

In the space of little more than a year, from June 1885, the UK saw
no fewer than four different governments. After the fall of William Gladstone's administration in June, the Marquess of Salisbury's
Conservatives took office for seven months, followed by the return
of Gladstone's Liberals for just five, after which the Conservatives
returned in July 1886. Amid this rapid alternation of power, it would
be easy to lose track of who was leading the opposition at any given
month (and believe me, I had to draw a diagram to work it out).

The removal of Sir Stafford Northcote from the Commons at the
start of the brief Salisbury government in June 1885 ended his time as
leader of the Conservatives in that House. Instead, Salisbury appointed
a different baronet as Chancellor of the Exchequer and Leader of the
House of Commons – Sir Michael Hicks Beach. Unlike Northcote,
Hicks Beach had enjoyed a rise in his reputation during the preceding
years of opposition to Gladstone, as he was seen as an effective critic of
the government. When the Conservatives left office in the new year, it

was therefore Hicks Beach who took up the leadership of the opposition in the Commons, albeit only briefly.

Born in 1837, he had been educated at Eton and Oxford and had
striking looks, tall and thin with a mop of curly brown hair. He inherited his baronetcy from his father, who had briefly been a Conservative
MP in 1854 before dying later that same year. Having spent some time
touring the Middle East after university, Hicks Beach settled down
into the life of a country gentleman in Gloucestershire for a number of
years, declining invitations to stand for Parliament himself. It was only
in 1864 that he was persuaded to stand in a by-election and was elected
for East Gloucestershire at the age of twenty-seven.

He seemed to have little political ambition and was shaping up
to be a traditional Tory squire and backbench rebel but was offered
a junior post in Benjamin Disraeli's government in 1868 and earned a
reputation as a good minister, with the ability to master his brief. As a
result, when Disraeli returned to office in 1874, he made Hicks Beach
Chief Secretary for Ireland, though still outside Cabinet. He was then
promoted to the Cabinet two years later, before being appointed as
Colonial Secretary in 1878.

As previously noted, it was after Disraeli's government fell in 1880
that Hicks Beach made his name in opposition, making a number of
acclaimed speeches against Gladstone's government and helping provide the active political attacks which many of his colleagues thought
were lacking in the leadership of Sir Stafford Northcote. One of the
leading critics of Northcote, Lord Randolph Churchill, was a close
friend of Hicks Beach, and this relationship helped the latter build a
following in the party, culminating in his election as chairman of the
National Union of Conservative Associations as a compromise candidate between the different factions.

Hicks Beach also played an unexpectedly decisive role in the fall of Gladstone's government in 1885, when an amendment he proposed to the Customs and Inland Revenue Bill in June 1885, on the subject of property taxation and the relative rates of duty on alcohol, was passed. This defeat on a Budget measure led to the resignation of the government, an unexpected consequence for such a comparatively minor issue. As *The Times* noted the following day, 'The debate on Sir Michael Hick-Beach's [*sic*] amendment, though its conclusion was so momentous, aroused at the outset only a languid interest in the House of Commons.' The paper also suggested that 'the Opposition can hardly be very proud or happy in their success', given the number of problems they would inherit on taking office.[1]

But take office they did, with Hicks Beach taking over the nation's finances as Chancellor, as well as becoming Leader of the House of Commons. This was a significant job considering Salisbury governed as Prime Minister from the House of Lords, but he had little time to make an impact. Having ruled as a minority government for five months, Salisbury called a general election in November, but despite a modest improvement in the Conservative position, the Liberals won the most seats (though not a majority). Salisbury tried to continue, but after Gladstone won the support of Irish nationalists with a pledge in favour of Home Rule, Salisbury's government was defeated in the Commons, and he resigned in January 1886.

Hicks Beach then became Leader of the Opposition in the Commons, facing Gladstone as Prime Minister, who was now attempting to pass Home Rule with his Government of Ireland Bill. This was a hugely controversial issue, and Hicks Beach was in the forefront of the parliamentary campaign against it. After Liberal Unionists split from Gladstone to vote with the opposition, the Bill was defeated, and Gladstone's government resigned.

Another general election followed, and this time the Conservatives, in alliance with the Liberal Unionists, won a large majority. Hicks Beach might have been expected to return to the Treasury as Chancellor, but Salisbury instead appointed Churchill – an ill-fated appointment which did not last long. Hicks Beach, meanwhile, accepted the job of Chief Secretary for Ireland and later President of the Board of Trade, until the Conservatives lost office in 1892.

He remained a leading figure in the Conservative Party, and when Salisbury returned as Prime Minister in 1895 he restored Hicks Beach as Chancellor, a position he retained for the next seven years. He resigned when Salisbury retired as Prime Minister, having by this time fallen out with Salisbury's successor, Arthur Balfour. This was not quite the end of his career in active politics, however. Over the next few years he was heavily involved in the battle in the Conservative Party over tariff reform, leading a large group of free-trade Tory MPs in opposition to protectionist measures. He gave up his seat in the Commons and entered the Lords in 1906 as 1st Viscount St Aldwyn, playing the role of elder statesman for the next decade.

He died on 30 April 1916, having been promoted to Earl St Aldwyn just a year earlier. By a sad set of coincidences, just weeks earlier his son's wife had died, and his son was killed during active duty in the war only a week before Hicks Beach's death. He was summed up in his *Times* obituary as 'a thorough Conservative of the old school' and a 'Parliament man'.[2] This last description was particularly apt, given that before he left the Commons he had spent forty-two years there and had been Father of the House, as its longest-serving member, for the last five.

His time as Leader of the Opposition in the Commons was so brief it is hard to suggest any particular significance of it, but like many other such temporary incumbents, his claim to notoriety comes more from his position as a leading figure in his party during this period.

His association with Randolph Churchill saw him embroiled in the factional infighting that broke out in the Conservative Party following its defeat in 1880, in which different elements wrestled for control of the party organisation. This is a familiar story in opposition up to the present day, and it is generally only when a party manages to put such strife behind it and unite that it is able to present itself as a credible alternative government. That was true in 1885, and Hicks Beach played a central role in agreeing the compromise necessary to make it happen and to lay the foundations for taking power.

16

John Wodehouse,
1st Earl of Kimberley

Liberal, Leader of the Opposition in the
House of Lords 1891–92 and 1897–1902

After our excursion to the House of Commons, we return to the
Lords for our next subject, a Liberal peer who has the distinction
of being the first in this book to have served as leader into the twentieth century. However, like many of those on our list, his periods in
government contribute much more to his place in history than his time
as Leader of the Opposition. In his case, these periods in government
include the accolade of having been a minister in every Liberal administration from 1852 to 1895, culminating in a year as Foreign Secretary.

At the time of his birth in 1826, John Wodehouse was third in line
to the peerage of his elderly great-grandfather, the 1st Baron Wodehouse. But in 1834 his father died, followed exactly a month later
by Lord Wodehouse. This family tragedy made the young John heir
to his grandfather, who had succeeded to the title as the 2nd Baron
Wodehouse.

Now a widow, his mother Anne Wodehouse took particular care
over her son's education. He was sent away to Rutland before the age

of ten to be taught by a theologian called the Reverend Thomas Kerch-ever Arnold. This regime was strict, but Wodehouse later said Arnold was a good influence and removed from him 'a vile habit of falsehood', teaching him always to be truthful and accurate. We can only speculate about whether that might have helped or hindered him in his later career in politics.

After this distinctive early education, he followed the more well-trodden path of Eton and then Oxford, where he studied classics at Christ Church. He was gifted academically, being repeatedly commended for good work, and supplemented his formal education with several months on the Continent, as well as extra tuition before his final exams. Whilst still at university, in 1846, he succeeded his grandfather and became 3rd Baron Wodehouse, also inheriting the family estates of around 10,000 acres in Norfolk and further land in Cornwall. He set about putting the estates in better financial order, succeeding over the years in paying off accumulated debts.

He was reported to be disappointed that his peerage deprived him of his chance to join the House of Commons, but as a young, political-ly interested member of the House of Lords he had the opportunity to make his way, and he became Undersecretary at the Foreign Office in the Earl of Aberdeen's government in 1852. He was good at the job and was later appointed to a sensitive diplomatic post in Russia just after the Crimean War.

Wodehouse returned to the Foreign Office as Undersecretary when Viscount Palmerston formed his government in 1859 but resigned two years later when Foreign Secretary Lord John Russell was sent to the House of Lords, apparently not wishing to serve under a minister in the same House. After refusing offers from Palmerston of senior co-lonial posts in India and Canada, he returned to government in 1864 as Undersecretary at the India Office and was then promoted later that year to Lord Lieutenant of Ireland. In this role, as the head of the Irish government, he oversaw reform of the universities and the disestablishment of the Irish Church but was a staunch opponent of Home Rule.

The growing nationalist movement and militant action by Irish republicans was becoming a serious problem, and in September 1865 Wodehouse acted on suspicions of a planned uprising by ordering a crackdown, which began with a raid on an address in Dublin. *The Times* report stated, 'A large force of police was despatched from Dublin Castle to Parliament Street, where they divided into two bodies and blockaded both ends of the street. Admission was then demanded at the office of the *Irish People*, the organ of the Fenian Brotherhood.'[1] After breaking down the door, police took a dozen people into custody, and other arrests followed during the course of the night. In total, twenty-one people were initially charged with offences relating to conspiracy to commit treason, and the government under Wodehouse was widely praised in London for its actions. As a reward, in May the following year he was awarded an upgrade to his peerage, with *The Times* announcing that 'Lord Wodehouse is to be raised to the dignity of an earl by the title of Earl of Kimberley, the name of his lordship's seat in Norfolk'.[2]

The new Earl of Kimberley left Dublin later that year on the fall of the Liberal government but returned to office when William Gladstone became Prime Minister and appointed him as Lord Privy Seal in 1868, before moving to the Colonial Office in 1870, where he served for four years. A lasting legacy of his tenure is the name of the capital city of the Northern Cape of South Africa, site of a huge diamond mining operation, which was renamed Kimberley after him. Less flatteringly, the Kimberley diamond mine, once claimed to be the largest hand-dug excavation on Earth, is more commonly known as the Big Hole.

When that government lost office, Kimberley became active along-side Earl Granville in opposition to Disraeli, particularly after Disraeli had entered the Lords in 1876. He returned to the Colonial Office when Gladstone became Prime Minister again in 1880 and was then appointed as Secretary of State for India, having previously turned down the offer to be Viceroy there. He remained in this post for nearly five years, and on the fall of that government he was once again active in opposition, acting as Granville's de facto deputy. In March 1891, the long-serving Granville died, and after a meeting of senior Liberal peers, a statement was issued that:

> It is not intended to appoint at present a successor to Lord Granville as leader of his political friends in the House of Lords. On the occasions of Lord Granville's absence from his place, Lord Kimberley has habitually conducted any communications with the Government which were required by the course of business, and he will continue to discharge this duty with a view to the general convenience.[3]

The decision not to make a formal appointment was attributed to the imminent general election, though this did not in fact take place for over a year. Kimberley meanwhile remained active, combining the role of acting leader of the Liberals in the Lords with touring the country in support of Liberal candidates. After the 1892 election, Gladstone was able to form a minority government with support from the Irish nationalists. Kimberley returned to office as Secretary of State for India but was now also Leader of the House of Lords and Lord President of the Council.

When Gladstone retired in 1894, he was replaced by the Earl of Rosebery, who appointed Kimberley to succeed him as Foreign Secretary. Whilst the two were largely in agreement on foreign policy, the new Prime Minister's continuing interest in his old brief left Kimberley little room to develop a distinctive record in the year that remained until the government lost office.

Returning to opposition, Kimberley was now an elder statesman, known as 'Uncle Kim' to his younger party colleagues – an affectionate nickname, despite it today sounding rather like a North Korean dictator. Rosebery remained as leader for just over a year but retired at the end of 1896. At a meeting of opposition peers at Spencer House on 18 January 1897, ahead of the new session of Parliament, 'the Earl of Kimberley was unanimously invited to resume his former position as leader of the Liberal peers in the House of Lords'.[4] He remained leader until his death five years later. His obituary noted his reputation for common sense, modesty and moderation, before paying him this rather weak tribute:

> In the course of his long official career he acquired an experience which made him most valuable as a departmental chief. As the leader of an insignificant minority in the House of Lords he did as well as could have been expected. If he made no great successes, he knew how to avoid great failures, and he leaves behind him a memory associated with the sincere respect and liking of both colleagues and opponents.[5]

As we know by now, the crafting of a backhanded compliment has been raised to a high art by the writers of obituaries, but I think the writers of this one underestimated the significance of being able to say that a politician managed to 'avoid great failures' during their time in office. Often, that can be counted a major victory. And as for the patronising assessment that 'he did as well as could have been expected' – I wonder if that is not perhaps a fitting epitaph for any politician, particularly in relation to the job of opposition.

17

Sir William Harcourt

Liberal, Leader of the Opposition in
the House of Commons 1895–98

Shortly after 3 p.m. on Monday 24 June 1895, the House of Commons was filled with an 'unusually large attendance' of MPs, whilst
the side galleries were crowded with peers and other spectators.[1] Those
on the government benches cheered as Sir William Harcourt, Chancellor of the Exchequer and Leader of the Liberal Party in the Commons, rose to announce that the Earl of Rosebery's government had
decided to resign, following their defeat on a motion of censure the
previous Friday. In an emotional speech, he declared that it had always
been his aim 'to maintain the ancient dignity and the great traditions
of this famous assembly' and ended by saying:

> For every man who has spent his life in the noble arena of Parliamen-
> tary conflict, the chiefest ambition must always, whether in the maj-
> ority or in the minority, be to stand well with the House of Commons.[2]

He was received with cheers and kind words from both sides, and many
took it to be a final farewell to public life after an illustrious political

career. But whilst he never served in government again, he was not in fact saying goodbye to the Commons. Instead, he was simply about to embark on his final challenge in the House, as Leader of the Opposition. Like many of those in this book, his tenure in that job is vastly overshadowed by his career highlights in government. Harcourt was one of the most prominent statesmen of the age, serving in two of the great offices of state, and had a real chance to become Prime Minister. Had he been a little nicer to his colleagues, he might well have been.

He was born as William Venables Vernon in 1827, the son of a clergyman and the grandson of the then Archbishop of York, Edward Venables Vernon. The archbishop was a younger son of the 1st Baron Vernon and adopted the name Harcourt on inheriting the estate of his cousin, the last Earl Harcourt, in 1830. That estate centred around the family seat at Nuneham Park in Oxfordshire – a very fine mansion, set in acres of parkland and originally designed by Capability Brown. King George III had visited in 1786 and called it 'the most enjoyable place I know', a view later endorsed by Queen Victoria, who stayed there in 1841 and wrote that 'this is a most lovely place'.

Now also known by the surname Harcourt, the young William was educated at home and then at a small private school by a clergyman, before going to Cambridge to study mathematics and classics. His father wanted him to pursue a political career or become an academic, but he initially chose the law and journalism and began practising as a barrister at Lincoln's Inn. Whilst doing so, he also wrote for a number of Liberal-leaning publications on international affairs and began drifting towards greater political involvement, though taking a different direction to his family's traditionally Tory instincts.

He first stood for Parliament unsuccessfully in 1859 but remained committed to his legal career, becoming a QC in 1866. He did however build a reputation as a political commentator during this time, writing a series of letters to *The Times* (of course) on international affairs, which he signed 'Historicus'. Despite this increasing profile, it was not until 1868 that he was first elected at the age of forty as the Liberal MP for Oxford. During his first years in Parliament, he was something of an independent-minded radical, frequently criticising his party's government on a number of issues with forceful speeches. Nevertheless, he earned the respect of William Gladstone, who in 1873 offered him the post of Solicitor General, which he accepted, along with a knighthood.

However, he was only briefly in this office as the government fell the following year, and for the next six years he played a leading role in opposition to the government of Benjamin Disraeli. When the Liberals entered government again in 1880 he was appointed Home Secretary by Gladstone, but the law at that time meant that he had to fight a by-election on taking office, which he narrowly lost. This was an unusual setback for such elections, but he was swiftly found an alternative seat in Derby, which he represented for the next fifteen years.

Harcourt's five years as Home Secretary secured his position as a leading figure in the government of Gladstone, to whom he remained close. He faced a number of challenges, not least the growing threat from militant Irish nationalists, which resulted in a bombing campaign in London. But given my penchant for historical oddities and anecdotes, there are two incidents which took place during this period that I have to prioritise for inclusion over such weighty issues.

The first of these was a notorious incident which became known as the 'Harcourt interpolation', involving a certain newspaper not unfamiliar to readers of this book. On 23 January 1882, *The Times* (for it was she) published a transcript of a speech given by Harcourt at Burton-on-Trent, in the middle of which there appeared a very rude phrase. Readers of a delicate disposition should look away now, as the report suggested that Her Majesty's Principal Secretary of State for the Home Department had found time in his speech to tell his audience that he 'felt inclined for a bit of fucking'.

This startling assertion was not, it turned out, an accurate record, and Harcourt had not suddenly given vent to unexpectedly lustful desires whilst discussing the role of tenant farmers in a forthcoming by-election. It later turned out that *The Times*'s compositors, who put together the plates for printing the paper, were at the time in dispute with the newspaper's management, and one compositor who had been sacked had inserted the line into the article without it being detected. Understandably, its discovery after the paper hit the streets caused something of a storm. As Harcourt's son Lewis recorded in his diary:

> In the report of H[ome] S[ecretary]'s speech in today's 'Times' there is a disgraceful interpolation of an obscene line … It was discovered before the second edition was published and so it only appears in the first but so anxious are the proprietors to stop it that they telegraphed to every book stall and news-agent in the United Kingdom to buy back all copies at any price and in this town [Leicester] they have been paying from 7/6 to £2.20 a piece for them.[3]

Before you rush to *The Times*'s digital archive to look for yourself, I regret to inform you that the copy of the paper preserved for that day is the replacement edition without the offending line. You can however find the awkward follow-up, which appeared five days later beneath the Court Circular. The paper assured readers that 'no pains have been spared by the management of this journal to discover the author' of what it called the 'malicious fabrication', which it said was now under legal investigation.[4]

The second incident is rather more gruesome. It arose from a controversy over the closure of a church graveyard in the parish of

Colsterworth and Harcourt's involvement in rejecting proposals from the rector of the parish for its replacement. After the Home Secretary had first received an angry letter, things took a macabre twist: a box containing the dead body of a baby was delivered to the Home Office, addressed to Harcourt. The sender turned out to be the eccentric rector, who admitted later that he had done so as a protest, having obtained the body under false pretences from the parents of a stillborn child.

Such peculiar incidents aside, Harcourt was judged to have been a successful and effective minister, and when Gladstone formed his next brief government in 1886, he made Harcourt Chancellor of the Exchequer. During the years of opposition that followed, Harcourt played a role in trying to bring the Liberal Unionists back to the party, having himself changed his mind and reversed his opposition to Irish Home Rule. He was unsuccessful, perhaps due to his abrasive personality, which is reported to have been a constant problem in relations with his colleagues. One of his private secretaries at the Treasury, Laurence Guillemard, reported being apprehensive of going to work for him, having 'heard disquieting accounts of an overbearing disposition and violent temper' and found that his new boss did indeed have 'the temper of a child, yes and often a naughty child, perverse, unreasonable, petulant, mischievous'. In an otherwise sympathetic portrayal of Harcourt, Guillemard made the following observation:

It was an ungoverned temper. I don't know whether he had ever tried to govern it, but if he had, it beat him. He was ever a fighter, reckless and self-confident, and it was part of his exuberant nature to rejoice in his own personality, failings and all, to let himself go and damn the consequences ... he thought he could do what he liked, and that other people could go hang. Be this as it may, there is no doubt that his temper handicapped him through life, robbed him of the full reward of his abilities, made many enemies, lost him some good friends, and sorely tried many more.[5]

Harcourt returned as Chancellor when the Liberals took office again in 1892, and his 1894 Budget is remembered for significant changes to the regime of inheritance tax, with the introduction of highly controversial death duties. It was quipped that this was a 'second son's revenge', since Harcourt was not in line to inherit his own family's fortune, which had gone to his elder brother's son. That same year, Gladstone retired as Prime Minister, and Harcourt mounted a campaign to succeed him, assisted by his son, Lewis, who served as his private secretary. However, he was not successful, and Queen Victoria instead sent for the Earl of Rosebery, a rival with whom Harcourt had repeatedly clashed in government.

Despite the enmity between them, Rosebery kept Harcourt as Chancellor, also allowing him to become leader of the party in the House of Commons. This is why, when the government resigned the following year, it fell to him to deliver the dramatic speech with which we opened the chapter. On 1 July 1895, ahead of the coming general election, Harcourt and his son went to Parliament and 'took possession of the Leader of the Opposition's room which still had all Arthur Balfour's papers in it'.[6]

The Liberals heavily lost the 1895 general election, and Harcourt himself lost his seat, before quickly being returned for another seat in West Monmouthshire, allowing him to continue as leader in the Commons. Rosebery remained overall leader of the Liberals from the Lords, but he and Harcourt operated entirely separately and refused to meet one another. In 1896, Rosebery stood down as leader in the Lords. Harcourt became overall leader of the Liberals but was unenthusiastic about the job. He was considered to have let the government off the hook over a major foreign policy scandal, and, facing criticism and division within his party, he too resigned as leader in December 1898. It was later drily noted that 'though many polite things were said about him at the meeting of the National Liberal Federation immediately afterwards, no attempt was made to induce him to reconsider his decision'.[7]

He remained a significant elder statesman but turned down the offer of a peerage in the 1902 coronation honours, preferring to stay in the Commons and allow his son, now also an MP, to do so too. In March 1904, shortly after announcing he would be stepping down from Parliament due to failing health, his nephew died childless, and Harcourt inherited the family estates at Nuneham. Ironically, he therefore found himself subject to the harsh death duties he had himself introduced. The impoverished state of the family finances were further compounded when, on 1 October that year, Harcourt himself died suddenly in his sleep at Nuneham, having only just moved into the great house.

His reputation survives as one of the more significant late-Victorian politicians, and one who could have made it to the very top had he been more personable to his colleagues. Harcourt had earned the nickname 'The Great Gladiator' in some quarters, but historians such as Roy Jenkins also remarked on his 'execrable temper and his bullying'.[8] It is perhaps a lesson as valid today as it was then that such behaviour does not always go unpunished in politics.

18

John Spencer, 5th Earl Spencer

Liberal, Leader of the Opposition
in the House of Lords 1902–05

Another milestone now, as we leave the nineteenth century behind and move into the twentieth. Or at least we would, if we were only to focus on our next subject's tenure as Leader of the Opposition, which began in 1902. But as we have come to expect, his time as leader is not the full story, with much of his reputation in fact being formed during earlier parts of his career whilst in government under William Gladstone, navigating the politics of Irish Home Rule.

The other thing to note is that for the first time we have a leader with the same name as a previous entry on our list, John Spencer. This is not exactly surprising, given the two are from the same family and that the earlier leader, the 3rd Earl Spencer, was his uncle. As we search for ways to distinguish one political aristocrat from another, it is particularly helpful that in this case we have a memorable nickname to use: this John Spencer was known as the 'Red Earl' on account of his distinctive long red beard.

He was born in 1835, the eldest son of Frederick Spencer, a former naval officer and Whig MP, who inherited the earldom from his brother when John was ten years old. Educated at Harrow and then Cambridge, the young heir was not very academic, taking more of an interest in cricket and horse riding. After graduating, he followed the by-now-familiar path of election to the House of Commons and was returned as Liberal member for South Northamptonshire in 1857. It was not to be a long career in that House.

Towards the end of that year, he embarked on a three-month tour of North America, arriving back in England in mid-December. On 27 December his father died suddenly, and he became the 5th Earl Spencer at the age of twenty-two. Entering the House of Lords, he took on a number of appointments in the royal household over the next decade, first as groom of the stole to Prince Albert and then to the Prince of Wales, later Edward VII. During this time, he left a tangible legacy to future generations by starting the process of transferring the part of his land that now forms Wimbledon Common to become a public park.

When Gladstone formed his first government in December 1868, he rewarded Spencer, who had become one of his leading supporters. The appointment of the 33-year-old earl as Lord Lieutenant of Ireland came as a surprise to him, as well as to political observers, given he had not previously held any government office or shown any interest in Irish affairs. He crossed to the Irish capital on Wednesday 23 December for a 'flying visit', heading first to the Viceregal Lodge before going in procession to Dublin Castle for his ceremonial swearing-in, accompanied by the firing of gun salutes, before returning to London that evening.[1]

He arrived just two years after his Liberal predecessor, the Earl of Kimberley, had left the job. Like him, Spencer had to spend much of his time in office dealing with outbreaks of violence and issues of law and order, as well as a number of controversial reforms to tenancy rights and the education system proposed by Gladstone's government. The defeat in the Commons of the Irish University Bill in 1873 nearly brought down the government, with Spencer arguing they should resign, but after Benjamin Disraeli refused to form a minority government the Liberals continued for another year, until the general election brought in a Conservative majority.

Released from office, Spencer returned to the traditional aristocratic pursuits of hunting and shooting and took the opportunity to embark on a programme of renovations at his family seat at Althorp House. He was recalled to government when Gladstone next took office in 1880, first as Lord President of the Council and then back in Ireland as Lord Lieutenant from 1882. This second stint as viceroy was more dramatic than the first, with an outbreak of terrorist violence from the very start. On the day of his official return to Dublin Castle in May, his new Chief Secretary Frederick Cavendish (brother of the Marquess of Hartington) and a colleague, T. H. Burke, were brutally assassinated by a group of militant Irish nationalists. Spencer himself had only narrowly escaped.

The murders led to a huge backlash in London and a security crackdown in Ireland. Spencer was given an armed police escort wherever he went, and government buildings were locked down and their military guards increased. It is a striking parallel with the security situation that would prevail in Northern Ireland a century later and the security measures with which British officials would become familiar.

Ireland became the defining political issue of the day as Gladstone made his ill-fated first attempt at implementing Home Rule in 1886. Spencer had become a convert to the policy, unlike many of his colleagues, and stuck with Gladstone in opposition after the brief government fell over the issue. He paid a high social penalty for his position over the following years, being shunned by many of his aristocratic friends and by Queen Victoria, who stopped inviting him to Windsor. During these opposition years he also faced financial difficulties due to falling agricultural prices, and this led to him selling off the extensive Althorp library of rare and valuable books. They were bought by the widow of the Manchester textile millionaire John Rylands and formed the core of the John Rylands Library, which she went on to establish in the city.

On the Liberals' return to government in 1892, Spencer was made First Lord of the Admiralty, a position which eventually led to him precipitating the resignation of Gladstone two years later. Spencer had prepared plans for an increase in naval expenditure, which the Prime Minister strongly opposed. Many in the Cabinet backed the Red Earl, and when he refused to back down Gladstone resigned, retiring from politics for the last time at the age of eighty-four.

This was the first moment Spencer could have succeeded as Prime Minister, and in fact Gladstone favoured Spencer as his replacement, despite their disagreement. Queen Victoria, however, did not ask for his advice and sent for the Earl of Rosebery instead. When the Liberals went into opposition the following year, Rosebery didn't last long before resigning, and the Earl of Kimberley (our friend 'Uncle Kim') became leader of the Liberals in the Lords until his death in 1902.

Spencer then succeeded him as Leader of the Opposition in the Lords, having deputised for Kimberley during his illnesses in the preceding years. In February 1905, *The Times* carried a letter from him setting out a policy manifesto and calling for an early general election. He wrote:

The present Government, although they still have a majority in the House of Commons, ought to recognise that their position in the country is very different, and their endeavour to remain in office without an early appeal to the constituencies strikes me as very much opposed to the best interests of the nation.[2]

In the rest of the letter, he outlined his opposition to the protectionist policies that were being advanced by Joseph Chamberlain and made reference to other issues including Ireland, reiterating his support for 'self-government' there. *The Times* the following day noted that this had provoked interest in Dublin, taking Spencer's letter as an official statement of Liberal policy and 'an indication that in the event of a Liberal victory at the polls Lord Spencer will be offered and accept the Premiership'.[3] By this time it was widely expected that the Conservative government of Arthur Balfour would not last much longer, so it looked highly likely that Spencer would indeed make it to No. 10 this time.

Fate, however, had other plans. Later that year he suffered a debilitating stroke that removed him from active politics just two months before the government fell. It was therefore Sir Henry Campbell-Bannerman, the Liberal leader in the Commons, who was appointed Prime Minister and went on to win a landslide victory at the general election in 1906.

Whilst he made a modest recovery and lived on for another five years, Spencer never fully recovered his health or returned to public office. He suffered a further stroke in July 1910 and died the following month. The personal tragedy for Spencer in being deprived of the premiership in 1905 was well captured by the young Winston Churchill, who wrote to Rosebery, 'It was rather like a ship sinking in sight of land.'[4]

19

George Robinson,
1st Marquess of Ripon

Liberal, Leader of the Opposition in the
House of Lords October–December 1905

The sudden removal of the 5th Earl Spencer from the political scene in October 1905 was a personal tragedy that ended his chances of the premiership, but it was also a significant blow to the Liberal Party, who were on the brink of a return to power. Whilst the overall leadership of the party fell to Sir Henry Campbell-Bannerman, leader in the Commons, there was now a vacancy for the leader in the Lords. This was filled by a peer who, at the age of seventy-seven, was some eight years older than his predecessor.

George Robinson, 1st Marquess of Ripon, was a veteran of Liberal governments, having first served in government under Viscount Palmerston in 1859 and eventually becoming Viceroy of India. Whilst he never became Prime Minister, he did get to live at 10 Downing Street and did so very early in life. He was actually born there, as the son of the serving Prime Minister Viscount Goderich. This fact was all the more remarkable given that Goderich's premiership lasted just 144 days. George was born on 24 October 1827, less than two months after his father took office, and the government fell early in the new year.

His mother and father had suffered the loss of their two previous children, and the period after his birth was therefore one of great anxiety to them. His mother in particular suffered badly from postnatal depression, whilst his father found the stress of the situation added to his political problems and hastened his decision to resign. The outgoing Prime Minister reportedly broke down in tears when he went to see King George IV, who had referred to him previously as 'a damned, snivelling, blubbering blockhead', rather unsympathetically.[1]

The young George was educated entirely at home, and attended neither school nor university, learning to read by copying his father's letters and adopting his mother's evangelical Christian beliefs. When he came of age he spent some time on the Continent at a time of political unrest and revolution, and this reinforced his emerging views as a political radical. He became associated with a group of Christian socialists and joined them in campaigning for increased workers' rights, industrial arbitration and new schemes of education for children and adults. In the 1850s he wrote a pamphlet called *The Duty of the Age*, which attacked the aristocracy and advocated a radical agenda of change.

Elected to the House of Commons in 1852 as MP for Hull, he was then unseated due to an election petition and then re-elected the following year for Huddersfield. For the next six years he led a small group of radical politicians in the Commons, known as the Goderichites. Whilst his views were seen as extreme, he was a conciliatory and balanced debater, which won him friends on all sides, and his faction exerted considerable influence, with him being talked of by some as a potential future Prime Minister.

Then in 1859 his father died, and he succeeded him as the Earl of Ripon and moved to the House of Lords. He also succeeded his uncle the same year as Earl de Grey and became a wealthy landowner. Ripon joined the Liberal government of Palmerston as Undersecretary for War and then entered the Cabinet as Secretary of State for War. He implemented reforms to improve conditions for soldiers, working with and encouraging Florence Nightingale in her campaigns to do so. He then became Secretary of State for India and established a reputation as an effective and reforming administrator.

In 1868, he became a senior member of Gladstone's first government as Lord President of the Council and helped pass some of its most reforming measures on issues such as the secret ballot, education reform and political change in Ireland. He also played a leading role in reaching reconciliation with the United States on a tricky international dispute through the Treaty of Washington, a success which led to him being promoted in the peerage to become the 1st Marquess of Ripon. He resigned from the government in 1873 and converted to Catholicism, which created a significant furore, but by 1880, when Gladstone again came to power, this had faded enough for him to be appointed Viceroy of India. Ripon held this post for four years, during which time he pursued progressive policies including the introduction of self-governing local authorities, improvements to education and working conditions, and attempts at legal reform. There was much opposition to this agenda from Britain, but as he put it:

> Unless we provide these men [in India] with outlets for their political aspirations they will become most naturally our bitter and very dangerous opponents ... it is our duty to raise the people of this country politically and socially ... making the educated natives the friends instead of the enemies of our rule.[2]

In later Liberal governments he served as First Lord of the Admiralty and Secretary of State for the Colonies, before becoming a leading voice in opposition to the Conservative governments of the Marquess of Salisbury and Arthur Balfour. After briefly replacing Spencer as Leader of the Opposition in the Lords in 1905, he returned to government for the final time, as Leader of the House of Lords in Campbell-Bannerman's subsequent Liberal government.

Ripon retired in 1908, declining to continue serving under H. H. Asquith, and died the following year of heart failure. At a lunch given in his honour upon his retirement, he reflected in his speech on the start of his life and his subsequent unfulfilled ambitions, with reference to the Prime Minister, who had spoken before him:

> Mr Asquith has reminded you that I had the fortune, if it be a fortune, to be born at No. 10 Downing-street. I need not explain to you that it was my consistent ambition to die in No. 10 Downing-street (laughter), in occupation, but I am now too feeble to turn him out (renewed laughter), and therefore I had to turn myself out and retire from that honourable dwelling.[3]

Ripon also reflected that having been considered 'a very dangerous young man' at the start of his career, he considered himself still to be a radical, though 'much more respectable'. He explained that in his progressive brand of politics 'I took what I could get and waited to get more', arguing that 'you may easily overshoot your mark, but you can scarcely be wrong if, guided by sound principles, you advance with advancing public opinion'.[4]

20

Henry Petty-Fitzmaurice, 5th Marquess of Lansdowne

Liberal Unionist, Leader of the Opposition
in the House of Lords 1905–16

For those readers who might understandably have been struggling with the succession of titled aristocrats, their associated swapping from one House of Parliament to the other and confusing changes in courtesy titles, I have some good news. We have reached the end of the peer show and the last of our leaders to be drawn from the House of Lords. This also marks the end of the confusing issue of whether the Leader of the Opposition in the House of Commons or the House of Lords should be regarded as the overall leader of their party and aspirant Prime Minister. From here on, the House of Lords was relegated undisputedly to second place to the House of Commons, as a result of a major constitutional upheaval which occurred during the tenure of this chapter's subject.

Henry Petty-Fitzmaurice might strike you as a familiar name from earlier in the book, and the two are of course related. Our latest Henry, who was to become the 5th Marquess of Lansdowne, was the grandson of the 3rd Marquess, who had been leader of the Whigs in the Lords at various points during the nineteenth century. Born on 14 January 1845, this Henry was initially known as Viscount Clanmaurice and was educated at a prep school near Reading before going to Eton, where biographies recall he was 'fag master' to the young Arthur James Balfour, in whose government he would later serve.[*]

He then went to Balliol College, Oxford and was still an undergraduate when, in 1866, his father's sudden death led to his succession to the title of Marquess of Lansdowne at the age of twenty-one. He completed his studies at Oxford under the close supervision of his tutor Benjamin Jowett, a noted theologian who went on to be master of the college and vice chancellor of the university. Lansdowne later credited Jowett with setting him on the course of his career, throughout which the two remained in touch.

As a young Liberal in the Lords, he served as a junior whip in William Gladstone's first government in 1868 and was then promoted to become Undersecretary for War four years later. He wrote to Jowett to tell him of the appointment and received a letter of congratulations in which his old tutor declared himself 'delighted' and advised that once Lansdowne had mastered the details 'I should fancy that you can leave smaller matters to take care of themselves, and fix your attention on the greater ones'.[1]

Lansdowne clearly acquitted himself reasonably well in office, being appointed Undersecretary at the India Office when Gladstone became Prime Minister again in 1880. But he resigned from the post after just two months in protest at the Irish land reforms being proposed by Gladstone, which as an Irish landlord he fundamentally opposed. Alongside the marquessate, one of his other titles was Earl of Kerry,

---

[*] For those of us not familiar with the odd traditions of English public schools, this is apparently the term for a senior pupil in charge of more junior ones, rather than anything more eyebrow-raising in modern slang.

and he now owned extensive lands in Ireland centred around Derreen House, near Kenmare in County Kerry.

Despite Lansdowne's break with the government, Gladstone appointed him three years later as governor general of Canada where he served for five years, falling in love with the remote countryside there and helping negotiate a treaty to resolve a fishing dispute with the United States in 1887. Upon leaving Canada the following year, Lansdowne was swiftly appointed Viceroy of India by the Marquess of Salisbury, the Conservative Prime Minister. His absence from domestic politics in the UK allowed him to keep clear of the divisions over Home Rule for Ireland, but he was increasingly more in sympathy with the Liberal Unionists, who were by this time in alliance with the Conservatives.

When he returned to the UK in 1894, he was therefore naturally aligned with those two parties and served in Lord Salisbury's governments as Secretary of State for War and then Foreign Secretary from 1900, during which time he oversaw the *entente cordiale* with France. After Balfour became Prime Minister, Lansdowne became Leader of the House of Lords and then, when the Conservatives lost office in 1905, Leader of the Opposition in the Lords.

He was to hold this office for the next decade, during a period when the position of the House of Lords, and of the opposition to the Liberal government, took on huge significance. As leader of the Unionist peers (the Conservatives and the Liberal Unionists), Lansdowne had a majority in the upper House, which was at this time equal in its legislative power to the House of Commons. He could, therefore, effectively veto or amend at will the proposals that reached the Lords from down the corridor. He initially used this power carefully, allowing through bills with which he and his colleagues disagreed, in deference to the electoral mandate of the government. But in 1909 this all changed.

When H. H. Asquith became Prime Minister in 1908, he appointed David Lloyd George as Chancellor of the Exchequer, and the following year Lloyd George introduced his 'People's Budget' of tax rises to pay for increased social welfare programmes. In particular, the new land taxes which had been proposed sparked vigorous opposition from the Unionists, many of whom represented landed interests that would be heavily affected by the proposals. Support grew on the opposition benches of both Houses for the Budget to be voted down when it reached the Lords, and neither Lansdowne nor Balfour, leader in the Commons, sought to quell this rising tide of militancy.

On 22 November, Lansdowne rose in the Lords to move the rejection of the Budget. A small crowd had gathered outside Parliament to see peers arrive, but he had avoided them by being driven in by motor car. The following day's *Times* reported on the scene at the 'Historic Debate':

The House of Lords yesterday was crowded to its upmost capacity. The representatives of the Press and the public – men and women – who were so fortunate as to possess tickets were admitted at 25 minutes past 4 o'clock. Just six minutes later Lord Lansdowne was standing by the table, uttering one of the greatest challenges in Parliamentary history. The Leader of the Opposition in the Lords could not possibly have had a larger audience. The benches on the Opposition side were, of course, packed: and the Government benches – where many gaps might naturally have been looked for – seemed almost equally full.[2]

Lansdowne was suffering from a heavy cold, and his voice was so husky that reporters present struggled to hear all he said, as he coughed his way through his speech. But his words were suitably grave: he declared that the Budget should not be passed until it had been given a popular mandate in the country at an election, and he went on to argue that although the step he proposed was 'unusual', the Lords maintained the right to reject a finance bill. They had, he said, 'A constitutional safeguard which they were not justified in dispensing with.'[3]

After six days of debate, the House rejected the Bill and set in chain the constitutional crisis that would lead to the Lords being stripped of its powers of veto. The Liberal government called and (just about) won a general election in early 1910, after which they reintroduced the Budget. The Lords now allowed it to pass unopposed, but by now the issue had become the future of the upper House itself.

Asquith introduced a Parliament Bill to reduce the Lords' power over legislation to only one of delay and to remove entirely their power over financial bills. Balfour and Lansdowne entered discussions with the government to see if they could find a compromise but were unwilling to consider anything which would limit their powers over future taxation. After a second general election in December gave the Liberal government a renewed mandate, the opposition split on the issue between the 'ditchers' committed to resisting the bill and the 'hedgers' who wanted to pass the bill to avoid the government invoking the nuclear option of asking the king to flood the House with new Liberal peers.

Lansdowne himself failed to give a lead at this point, telling a meeting of Unionist peers that he would be abstaining on the bill and taking little part in the final debates on the legislation. He did, however, give tacit encouragement for some of the 'hedgers' to vote with the government, to ensure the bill passed. On 10 August 1911 the crucial vote took place, and when the division was called at 10.40 p.m., 'Lord Lansdowne leading, many members of the Opposition rose and left the House amidst perfect order'.[4] After this walkout by the abstainers, the government prevailed by 131 votes to 114, and the Parliament Act narrowly became law by a majority of just seventeen.

It was not Lansdowne's finest hour, but his actions had helped end the crisis. He was widely expected to stand down when Balfour did so later that year, but instead remained in post alongside the new Commons leader, the inexperienced Andrew Bonar Law, with whom he shared the overall leadership of the party. At the outbreak of the First World War in August 1914, he was strongly supportive of British involvement and sent a note to Asquith offering the 'unhesitating support' of the opposition for military action.[5]

Just two months later his own son was killed in action in France, but he remained committed to the war and joined Asquith's coalition government in May of the following year as Minister without Portfolio, serving until Asquith was replaced by Lloyd George in December 1916. At this point, Lansdowne stepped down from government and handed over the leadership in the Lords of the now-merged Conservative and Unionist Party to Lord Curzon.

Free of office, he began to campaign for a negotiated end to the war, publishing what became known as the 'peace letter' on 29 November 1917, which gained a degree of popular support but led to him being ostracised by former colleagues. After the end of the war, he made fewer appearances in the House of Lords, and his health declined in the succeeding years until his death in Ireland on 3 June 1927.

Lord Lansdowne was one of the last of a fading generation of aristocrats to have governed the British Empire during its heyday in Victoria's reign. Just as that world had begun to change, it is fitting that he also played his own part in the decisive change to the role of the House of Lords in the UK political system. Never again would a party leader in the Lords be considered pre-eminent over their equivalent in the Commons, and never again would there be any prospect of a Prime Minister governing from that House.

21

Joseph Chamberlain

Liberal Unionist, Acting Leader of the Opposition in
the House of Commons 15 February–12 March 1906

In July 1906, crowds flocked to the streets of Birmingham to cheer
a man who had represented the city in Parliament for thirty years
and become one of the most prominent politicians of the age. The
seventieth birthday of Joseph Chamberlain was marked with several
days of official tributes and celebrations, of which the contemporary
coverage in *The Times* gives a flavour:

> There was considerable excitement in the city throughout the day,
> flags were flying, and large numbers of men, women, and children
> wore Chamberlain medals suspended from Unionist-coloured
> ribbon. Some of the motor and other omnibuses were gorgeously
> decorated in honour of the event … As Mr Chamberlain drove from
> Highbury to the city the route along which he passed was lined with
> people who gave him a very hearty greeting.[1]

At the culmination of proceedings, the man at the centre of the fes-
tivities gave a speech in which he mounted a staunch defence of his

political views and declared, 'It is not the amount of the income-tax, not the number of cheques that pass through the Clearing-house that mark the progress of a nation ... It is our advance toward a great laudable aspiration, the greatest happiness of the greatest number'.[2]

It was a fitting speech that exemplified the rise of a self-made man with strong progressive views, at a time when the increasingly democratic age was about to be confirmed by the dramatic restriction on the powers of the House of Lords covered in the previous chapter. But who was the speaker being so publicly lauded? He never became Prime Minister and served only very briefly as Leader of the Opposition, but his impact on politics had been profound.

It is fair to say that the name Chamberlain is today most prominently associated in British politics with someone who did make it to No. 10: Neville Chamberlain, the Conservative Prime Minister from 1937 to 1940. The footage of him waving around his famous piece of paper and declaring 'peace for our time'* and the grave intonation of his broadcast announcing the UK's entry into the Second World War are ingrained upon our national memory. Less well remembered now is his father, who had been the subject of the outpouring of public recognition in Birmingham thirty years before.

Joseph Chamberlain was born in 1836 into a family which for four generations had earned its living as shoemakers (cordwainers) in the City of London. Having previously lived above their shop, they had moved out to a terraced house in Camberwell just before his birth, and he was educated first at a small local school before being sent to University College School where he proved to be an able student, winning a number of academic prizes.

Upon leaving school at the age of sixteen, he became an apprentice

---

* Yes, that is what he said, despite the pervasive misquotation.

in the family firm, first making shoes before moving over to book-keeping. He then moved to Birmingham to work in his uncle's factory making metal screws, where he became a partner and helped significantly grow the business into an international success. He became involved in Liberal politics, making his name campaigning for increased provision of education for working-class children, and was elected Mayor of Birmingham in 1873, where he oversaw a huge programme of public works and became a national political figure.

Chamberlain was elected to the House of Commons a few years later in 1876 as member for Birmingham and became a leading figure in the group of radical Liberals. Unlike many MPs of the time, he maintained a strong link to his constituency and made his main residence there, building himself a new home in the south of the city which he named Highbury. There he had eighteen acres of grounds in which he indulged his passion for gardening, particularly for breeding orchids. Whilst this sounds like the basis for a blissful domestic life, he had by this point been afflicted by a series of personal tragedies. His first wife Harriet had died in childbirth in 1863, just two years into their marriage, and his second wife Florence, a cousin of Harriet's, had then suffered the same fate in 1875. His grief drove him to devote even more time to work, firstly in business and then later to politics.

When William Gladstone was returned to office in 1880 he made Chamberlain President of the Board of Trade, a job Chamberlain found frustrating for its lack of scope to make significant change. At the general election in 1885 he stood on a progressive unofficial manifesto called the 'Radical Programme', advocating free public education, increased direct taxes, universal male suffrage and protection for trade unions. He was hailed by his supporters as 'your coming Prime Minister', and his campaign attracted large crowds and much interest from other progressives, including the young Ramsay MacDonald and David Lloyd George.

His stance prompted friction with Gladstone and other mainstream Liberals, but he took office again as President of the Local Government Board, before resigning just a few months after Gladstone revealed his plan for Irish Home Rule. Chamberlain was passionately opposed to the proposal and formed a breakaway group of Liberal Unionists to fight it. This faction, led by Chamberlain and the Marquess of Hartington, united with the Conservative opposition to defeat the Home Rule Bill at its second reading in the Commons, bringing Gladstone's government to an end. They then agreed an electoral pact with the Conservatives in the 1886 general election, winning a large majority for the Unionist alliance.

The split was rancorous, and when Chamberlain entered the Commons Chamber his former Liberal colleagues greeted him with shouts of 'Judas!' and 'Traitor!' He didn't take office with the Conservatives but continued to work closely with them, motivated partly by his fear of the rise of socialism, which he opposed. He did however still hold out hopes of reuniting with the Gladstonian Liberals and held a number of meetings with them to try to come to a compromise over Ireland, but this was to no avail.

Gladstone took office again in 1892, at an election which saw the Liberal Unionists fall back in their number of seats and Chamberlain's position weakened. After Lord Hartington went to the House of Lords as the Duke of Devonshire, Chamberlain replaced him as leader of the Liberal Unionists in the Commons and developed a strong working relationship with Arthur Balfour, the Conservative leader there. When the Conservatives took office under the Marquess of Salisbury in 1895, he declined an offer to be Chancellor and instead asked for, and was given, the post of Secretary of State for the Colonies, in which he served for eight years.

It was during this period that he made his reputation in government, using his responsibility for most of the British Empire to pursue grand schemes to increase trade and improve education and research into tropical diseases, raising money to found the London School of Hygiene and Tropical Medicine. Previously seen as a second-rank ministerial job, he raised the Colonial Office to greater significance in government, becoming known as the 'First Minister of the Empire' and being seen as the second-most senior figure in Salisbury's government. At the 1900 'khaki election' he took the leading role in the Unionists' victorious campaign, shamelessly using the Boer War as a patriotic rallying cry and relishing the cult of personality that grew up around him in what was called by some 'Joe's election'. When Salisbury resigned two years later, Chamberlain could have become Chancellor but did not press his claim – a fateful decision which set the scene for the coming turmoil over economic policy.

He was by now committed to proposing a policy of 'Imperial Preference' to impose tariffs on foreign imports and favour instead those from the British Empire. This broke the free-trade consensus that had endured since the scrapping of the Corn Laws and was resisted by the Chancellor and much of the Cabinet. Instead of accepting defeat, he began a concerted effort to campaign for the policy publicly, making a landmark speech in Birmingham in May 1903 criticising government policy on the issue and repeating his views in the House of Commons. In the autumn of that year, Balfour's Cabinet again refused to endorse the policy and Chamberlain resigned.

He did not go quietly, and stepped up his campaign for Imperial Preference, speaking at public meetings across the country supported by the Tariff Reform League, a grassroots organisation that attracted considerable support and funding from Conservative activists. Despite efforts by Balfour to broker compromise in the Conservative ranks, the party became increasingly divided, and the Prime Minister resigned in

November 1905, bringing the Liberals back to office ahead of a general election.

The issue had fatally split the Unionist alliance, who suffered a landslide defeat at the 1906 election, being reduced to just 157 seats. Balfour himself lost his seat, and Chamberlain became acting Leader of the Opposition for a couple of weeks as the accepted leader of the Conservatives and Liberal Unionists until Balfour returned in a by-election. He used his position to pressure Balfour to make concessions in favour of tariff reform, and he was to continue playing a leading role in the opposition and in reshaping the Conservative Party, which was moving closer to a formal merger with the Liberal Unionists.

The celebrations of his seventieth birthday, which took place shortly after the election, were thus a fitting testimonial to his political career so far, confirming his huge public profile and influence in national politics. But they turned out to be a final curtain call. Less than a week later, he suddenly collapsed after suffering a debilitating stroke. This ended his active career, and though he was returned unopposed as MP for Birmingham in the 1910 general election, he never recovered his health and died on 2 July 1914. The report of his death, accompanied by a specially drawn portrait depicting him wearing his trademark monocle, recorded a flood of tributes. These were led by King George V, who sent a message to Chamberlain's widow with his 'heartfelt sympathies' on 'the loss of one of whom I had the greatest admiration and respect'. The dowager queen Alexandra mourned 'one of the greatest men this Empire has ever known', whilst David Lloyd George paid tribute to the 'dazzling career' of a 'great municipal reformer'.[3]

Chamberlain's impact on British politics was unquestionably significant. By taking a prominent role in the campaigns against Irish Home Rule and in favour of tariff reform, he helped split both major parties of government and reshaped their politics. But it was his commitment to progressive social improvements, forged in Birmingham even before his election to Parliament, which perhaps provides his greatest legacy. Though never a Conservative himself, the alliance and then merger of his Liberal Unionists with the Conservative Party gave the Conservatives a renewed appeal to the working classes, just as the age of mass democracy was beginning.

More than a century after his death, Chamberlain's reputation received renewed scrutiny when Nick Timothy, a Birmingham-born admirer of 'Our Joe', became chief of staff to the Prime Minister, Theresa May. He had earlier written a biography of Chamberlain and called him the Conservative Party's 'forgotten hero'. Political commentators pored over Timothy's writings and speculated about the influence of Chamberlain to the agenda pursued by May. Such influence was curtailed by the result of the 2017 general election, in which the Conservatives lost their majority and Timothy lost his job. But it is testament to Chamberlain's impact that his ideas should be seen to have continued relevance to electoral politics in the twenty-first century.

22

Sir Edward Carson

Irish Unionist, Leader of the Opposition
October 1915–December 1916

If you visit Northern Ireland and approach Parliament Buildings at
Stormont, your eyes will inevitably be drawn to the imposing statue
which stands in front of the classical edifice of the building. The figure
of a man, his right arm raised dramatically in mid-speech, is set on a
tall plinth staring down the long tree-lined drive towards the gates of
the estate. Engraved on the base is the single name 'Carson'.

As is the case for much in Northern Ireland, the symbolism is powerful and controversial. Edward Carson, later elevated to the peerage as
Lord Carson, was the leader of both the Ulster Unionist Party and the
Irish Unionist parliamentary party for eleven years before the partition
of Ireland in 1921. He could have become the first Prime Minister of
the new Parliament of Northern Ireland but turned down the opportunity, having fought throughout his political career for Ireland to
remain within the United Kingdom.

His tenure as Leader of the Opposition at Westminster took place
in unusual circumstances, given he was not the leader of one of the
major political parties in the House. In May 1915, during the First

World War, H. H. Asquith formed a coalition government which contained Liberal, Conservative and Labour members. In this government, Carson was initially appointed as Attorney General but resigned in October 1915 over the conduct of the war. Given that all the main parties, including the nationalist Irish Parliamentary Party, were either in or supporting the government, this left Carson as the leader of those unionists who stood outside the government and de facto Leader of the Opposition.

Born in Dublin in February 1854, Carson was from a Protestant family that had moved to Ireland from Scotland forty years earlier. They were affluent, and he was educated at boarding school before going to Trinity College Dublin, where he read classics. He was a contemporary of Oscar Wilde, whom he had known since they were both children, and this connection was to take an ironic twist later in their respective careers.

After university he studied for a career in the law and was called to the Irish Bar in 1877, to the English Bar sixteen years later and was made an Irish QC in 1889. He served briefly as Solicitor General for Ireland in 1892 and was elected as Irish Unionist MP for Dublin University in the same year. Carson built a successful legal practice, and in 1895 he took on his most celebrated case when he was engaged by the Marquess of Queensbury to defend him in the libel trial brought against Queensbury by Oscar Wilde. When Wilde heard who was to be opposing him in the case he remarked with trademark wit, 'No doubt he will pursue his case with all the added bitterness of an old friend.'[1] So it proved, with Carson conducting a devastating cross-examination in which he described a love letter from Wilde to Lord Alfred Douglas as 'an abominable piece of disgusting immorality'.[2] The following day, he continued his opening statement, declaring his intention of calling a number of young men to testify against Wilde as to his behaviour. Before he was able to do so, Wilde's lawyer rose to announce that his client would not contest the case, and the jury was directed to find Lord Queensbury not guilty.

The collapse of the case led immediately to Wilde's arrest on charges of gross indecency, on the basis of the evidence that had been acquired by Carson for Queensbury's defence. Despite Carson privately asking the Solicitor General if they might not 'let up on the fellow now', the criminal case proceeded.[3] Wilde was found guilty and sentenced to two years' hard labour, after which he fled to France and died in poverty.

Carson meanwhile was thriving, and by 1900 he was said to be earning £20,000 per year in fees, the equivalent of £2 million at 2023 prices. That same year he was appointed Solicitor General for England and Wales in the Marquess of Salisbury's government and given the customary knighthood. He remained as Solicitor General until the Conservatives left office in 1905. As a unionist, he was now firmly aligned with the Conservatives, despite his natural political affiliations being more on the Liberal side of the political spectrum. In his alliance with the Conservatives, he remained committed primarily to the unionist cause and motivated in his alignment by his opposition to the new Liberal government's renewed plans for Irish Home Rule.

Following the passing of the Parliament Act in 1911, which removed the ability of the Lords to veto a Home Rule bill, the Liberal government sought to return to the issue at the insistence of the Irish Parliamentary Party, whose support gave the Liberals their majority in the Commons. Carson had by now become leader of the Irish Unionists and led the campaign against the proposed Government of Ireland Bill. From 1912 to 1914 he was at the forefront of the Home Rule crisis, which threatened to bring civil war to Ireland. With the prospect of an Irish nationalist government being established in Dublin, the unionists of Northern Ireland declared their intention to resist the proposals by force if necessary. In September 1912, Carson became the first of nearly half a million people to sign the Ulster Covenant, committing them to 'using all means which may be found necessary to defeat the present conspiracy to set up a Home Rule Parliament in Ireland' and to refuse to recognise any such Parliament's authority.[4]

This was no empty threat, for at the same time they established the Ulster Volunteer Force, the first armed loyalist paramilitary group in the province, which Carson supported as the means by which a provisional Ulster government could be established in the event of Home Rule being introduced. In July 1912 he attended a march of the volunteers and told them he had come to 'make the personal acquaintance of every man who is my follower and prepared to go with me into the coming struggle'.[5]

Carson himself was not in favour of the partition of Ireland, hoping instead that the fierce resistance of the Ulster Unionists would lead to the whole idea of Home Rule being dropped. This proved a vain hope, and instead he and other unionists reluctantly turned their attention to trying to amend the bill to exclude Ulster from its provisions. With the threat of civil war growing, the government duly introduced an amending bill to exclude Ulster temporarily from Home Rule, but the details were still not finalised. It was only the outbreak of the First World War that ended the crisis, with the government passing an Act to suspend the operation of Home Rule for the duration of the conflict.

As we have seen, Carson was subsequently appointed Attorney General in the coalition government that was formed the following year, and it was his resignation from office that made him effectively Leader of the Opposition from October 1915. This was, however, more of a technical distinction, as to all practical purposes there was no organised opposition in place during this period. As *The Times* noted in its report on his resignation statement in the Commons:

The fact that the statement was made from what used to be known as the front Opposition bench is not to be taken as a sign that Sir Edward means to range himself as a definite opponent of the Government. Probably he has very little in common with the miscellaneous body which now occupies the old seats of the Unionist leaders, and still less with the sharp-shooters who have lately played the part of an Opposition.[6]

In any case, he was not himself to 'play the part' for very long. After helping to bring down Asquith as Prime Minister in favour of David Lloyd George in December 1916, he returned to government as First Lord of the Admiralty, before moving to become Minister without Portfolio in the war Cabinet until January 1918, when he resigned to concentrate on the resolution of the Irish question.

In 1918 he accepted Lloyd George's pledge that Ulster would not be included in new Home Rule proposals, and at the general election in December he swapped his Dublin constituency for a seat in the Duncairn division of Belfast. When the government proposed partition of Ireland, with parliaments in north and south, a meeting of the Ulster Unionist Council with Carson in the chair accepted it, but he remained personally unhappy with the outcome and resigned the leadership of the Ulster Unionists in February 1921, accepting a peerage shortly afterwards and becoming a judge as a Lord of Appeal.

Carson settled in Kent and only visited Ulster three times more during his life – receiving an honorary degree from Queen's University Belfast in 1926, attending the opening of Parliament Buildings at Stormont by the Prince of Wales in 1932 and then attending the unveiling of his own statue there in July 1933. On that occasion he delivered a reflective speech, in which he remarked:

I remember well many a night lying awake and wondering what it was that had happened to the great English nation and the great English people, for what we were demanding was nothing but that our birthright as loyal citizens of the United Kingdom under a King that we loved should be preserved. We never made any other demand but that, and, looking back on it, does it not seem a strange thing that all these years of strain and sometimes obloquy should have happened merely because we were loyal subjects of the King in the United Kingdom and were determined to retain the position?[7]

He died two years later at home in Kent and was given a state funeral before his burial at St Anne's Cathedral in Belfast. A warship had brought his body to the city, and soil from each of the six provinces of Northern Ireland were scattered over his coffin.

Whilst only Leader of the Opposition for a brief time, his life had been defined by opposition in the most profound sense, to both Home Rule and partition. He failed in that objective, but it is sobering to think that he had been willing to encourage and support armed resistance by the Ulster Volunteer Force in order to help his cause – an entirely different spin on the usual notion of 'loyal opposition'.

23

William Adamson

Labour, Leader of the Opposition (contested) 1918–21

W e now reach another milestone, with our first Labour leader. His claim to be his party's first official Leader of the Opposition has been somewhat overlooked in accounts of the period, for reasons that are not wholly clear. It certainly deserves to be given greater prominence, and I shall do my best to serve that cause. But let us first consider the man himself.

Described by a colleague as a 'canny Scot', William (Willie) Adamson was about as much of an antidote to the preceding litany of aristocratic leaders as it is possible to devise.[1] Born in Halbeath, near Dunfermline, in 1863, he was the son of a coal miner and attended a small local school before going down the mines himself at the age of eleven. He remained a miner for twenty-seven years, becoming active in the Fife and Kinross Miners' Association as a branch delegate and rising eventually to become its vice president and then general secretary.

He was a devout Baptist and teetotaller, and his politics were initially those of a Liberal. But he gravitated in the direction of the organised Labour movement and was elected to Dunfermline town council in 1905 as a Labour member. This led to his first attempt at winning a parliamentary seat, fighting West Fife for Labour in the general election of January 1910 against the sitting Liberal MP. He was unsuccessful that time, but in the second election of that year he triumphed, making headline news for having 'wrested a seat from the Liberals', the only Labour candidate to have done so.[2]

During his first few years in Parliament Adamson made little impact, asking occasional questions and speaking briefly on technical matters relating to mine safety and workers' rights. He did however speak on behalf of the Labour Party's forty-two MPs to give their support to the second reading of the Temperance (Scotland) Bill, which allowed communities north of the border to hold local referendums on whether to ban or allow the sale of alcohol. He was no pacifist and was recorded to have been firmly in support of Britain's involvement in the First World War, despite his elder son being killed in the conflict.

In October 1917 he succeeded Arthur Henderson as Chairman of the Labour Party, a role he would hold until 1921. He was described on his appointment as 'popular and fearless' by *The Times* and was greeted by shouts of 'hear, hear' when he made his first appearance in the House in his new position.[3] At the start of the following year's session, he made a well-received speech following speculation about a possible change of government, telling the House, 'Before we make another change I want to be convinced that we are going to put a better Government in the place of this one.'[4] Later that year he was made a privy counsellor in the king's birthday honours.

The election of December 1918 then saw the alliance between the Conservatives and the coalition Liberals under David Lloyd George win a landslide of 506 seats. H. H. Asquith's non-coalition Liberals collapsed, falling to just thirty-six seats, and Asquith himself lost his seat. The split in the Liberal Party made politics particularly confusing at this time (though having grappled with the complex factions of the eighteenth- and early nineteenth-century Parliaments, we should be well prepared). Essentially, the Liberals had split between supporters of Lloyd George ('coalition Liberals' or 'national Liberals'), who remained as Prime Minister heading the coalition government, and those who backed their ousted leader Asquith ('non-coalition Liberals' or 'independent Liberals'). The 1918 election is now known as the 'coupon election', as Conservative and Liberal candidates who supported the coalition were given a letter of endorsement from Lloyd George and the Conservative leader Andrew Bonar Law, which became known as the 'coalition coupon'. Over 150 Liberals were issued with the 'coupon', and 136 of them were elected.

Against this backdrop of Liberal infighting, the Labour Party increased its support significantly, winning 2 million votes – more than either of the Liberal factions – and increasing its number of MPs from forty-two to fifty-seven. Whilst this appears only a modest increase, its effects were significant. On paper, the largest opposition party was now the Irish nationalists Sinn Féin, with seventy-three MPs, but they refused to take their seats in the Commons. As the largest opposition bloc actually sitting in the House, the Labour Party now had a claim to be considered the official opposition in the House of Commons. And, contrary to what has sometimes been asserted in histories of the period, they did indeed press that claim.

At a joint meeting of the National Executive and the parliamentary party at Westminster's Central Hall, Labour resolved, with just one vote against, 'That it be an instruction from this conference that the Labour Party in the House of Commons make the necessary arrangements to become the official Opposition.'[5] In a subsequent meeting of its MPs, Adamson was unanimously re-elected as chairman of the party in Parliament. The significance of the development was not understated by *The Times*, which declared:

> The decision of the Labour Party to accept the responsible position of the official Opposition is a landmark in our Parliamentary history … It is a great opportunity for a party which was only born in the opening years of the present century. It is also a great test of its capacity. The Opposition is a very different thing from a small group below the gangway, which has been the status of Labour in the last three Parliaments.[6]

The paper went on to declare that the party's privy counsellors and ex-ministers would now take up their place on the opposition front bench as the alternative ministry, prepared to take up the reins of government should the need arise, a prospect it described as 'little less than a revolution in the history of the British Parliament'. It also noted that the re-election of Adamson as chairman meant 'a new Leader of the Opposition has stepped upon the parliamentary scene', and commented, 'In training and outlook he is the antithesis of his predecessor, Mr Asquith. Mr Adamson has little scholarship, and no dialectic, but he is as shrewd as he is sincere.'[7]

Despite these emphatic words, matters became somewhat more confused when Parliament met the following month, in February 1919. Under a headline noting 'Two Opposition Parties', *The Times* reported that 'for once a great deal more attention was given to the Front Opposition Bench than to the Treasury Bench' and recorded a jostling for position between Labour and the remaining non-coalition Liberals under Sir Donald Maclean.[8] The latter 'drew first blood', with Maclean occupying the seat of the Leader of the Opposition, alongside a number of his colleagues, and Adamson and his colleagues sitting on the front bench to their left (though whether this meant below the gangway is not clear). Adding to the confusion, two senior supporters of the coalition Liberals and two Unionists also exercised their rights as ex-ministers to sit there, on what sounds to have been a rather crowded bench.

The slightly farcical scenes continued as MPs were summoned to the House of Lords to hear the Royal Commission. The Leader of the House of Commons, Bonar Law, led the procession of MPs out of the Chamber, with Maclean and Adamson both assuming the Leader of the Opposition's prerogative of walking alongside him, neither 'giving away any point in the game'.[9] When it came to offering congratulations to the Speaker on his re-election, Maclean again prevailed by speaking first after Bonar Law, though he acknowledged that this was only due to his length of service. The issue did not rest there, and the following week it was Adamson who succeeded in being called first after the mover and seconder of the Humble Address to give the opposition's response to the King's Speech. Before sitting down, he made a pointed reference to the position of his party:

> I want, in conclusion, simply to say that the party with which I am associated, the Labour party, have been ambitious enough to intimate to the country, and to others concerned, that they intend to fill the role of the principal Opposition to His Majesty's Government. That claim may be contested, but I can assure you that it is a claim that is made by the members of the Labour party in all seriousness, and in the course of the proceedings of this House they will endeavour to justify the claim which they have put forward.[10]

He went on to describe how Labour's opposition would be different to that of the past, with the party not simply opposing for its own sake and instead supporting those measures it felt able to support. For the next three years, Adamson did his best to live up to these lofty sentiments, and as a later assessment put it, 'His handling of the thankless task ... was competent, if not inspiring.'[11] Others were more scathing, with Beatrice Webb saying, 'He had neither wit, fervour nor intellect; he is most decidedly not a leader', and Emmanuel Shinwell calling him 'a dour and phlegmatic Scottish miners' leader very much out of his depth in the Commons'.[12] Troubled by ill health, he stepped down at the start of the new session of Parliament in February 1921, with J. R. Clynes being elected to replace him.

Adamson had secured for himself a significant place in history. Whatever Maclean's protestations, it was clear Labour was now the official opposition and on its way to becoming a serious party of government. Five years later it duly took power, and Adamson was appointed Scottish Secretary, a role he returned to in the next Labour government in 1929. He did not shine in the role, recording few achievements and being considered a poor performer in the House.

He joined the vast majority of Labour members in resigning office when Ramsay MacDonald formed the National Government in 1931, and in the subsequent general election he lost his seat along with many of his Labour colleagues. He sought to win it back in 1935 but was again unsuccessful, with West Fife instead returning Scotland's first communist MP, Willie Gallacher. Just a few months later, Adamson died at the age of seventy-two. His obituary noted, 'He lacked the temperament of the popular leader, but his colleagues respected his judgement and stability of character.' Alongside the other details of his career, it also found space to state categorically that he was 'the first leader of the Opposition in the history of the Labour Party'.[13] As an epitaph, I think that should certainly count for something.

24

Sir Donald Maclean

Liberal, Leader of the Opposition (contested) 1918–20

S hortly before 5 p.m. on 15 June 1932, members of the Cabinet received news of the sudden death of one of their colleagues. The President of the Board of Education, Sir Donald Maclean, had succumbed to a heart attack at home at the age of sixty-eight. The news caused 'a profound sensation' amongst his friends at Westminster, and sincere condolences were paid to his family.[1] One of his sons, also named Donald, was midway through his degree at Cambridge, and his father's death certainly had a profound effect upon him and upon world events. Freed from his moralistic upbringing, he felt more able to embrace the growing communist sympathies which he and his close contemporaries at Trinity Hall had developed. Just a few years later they were recruited as Soviet agents and have become immortalised in history as the Cambridge spy ring. Maclean Jr, beginning a career in the Foreign Office, was given the codename *Sirota*: Russian for 'orphan'.[2]

Much has been written about the life of the spy Maclean, with biographers seeking clues to the development of his political views and explanations for what drove him and his colleagues to betray their country. Understandably, this has included consideration of his childhood and the influence of his family. What emerges is in many ways a classic tale of teenage rebellion against the views of the political establishment represented by his Cabinet minister father. But it has also been noted that his sense of self-righteous conviction and near-religious devotion to his cause owed much to the paternal example he had been set. In this way, our next leader (who is also the last Liberal to appear) had an impact neither he nor anyone else would have predicted.

Sir Donald Maclean had been born in Farnworth in Lancashire in 1864. He was the son of John Maclean, a Scottish cordwainer (shoemaker) who had travelled to England to pursue his business. The family then moved to Wales, where Donald was educated at Queen Elizabeth Grammar School in Carmarthen before training as a solicitor and beginning to practise law in Cardiff. Raised as a Presbyterian, he was a teetotaller and active campaigner for the temperance movement, as well as for other social causes.

His politics were firmly Liberal, with a resolute commitment to free trade, as befitted the son of a businessman. Maclean stood unsuccessfully for Bath at the 1900 general election but was later elected for the constituency at the election in 1906, having played a leading role in organising the Liberal campaign in the surrounding area. He took up residence in London, married his wife Gwendolen and became a partner in a law firm there alongside his parliamentary duties. He became close to H. H. Asquith during this time, and whilst he was not appointed to ministerial office, he was given a number of responsibilities within the party, including overseeing the running of the *Westminster Gazette*, a Liberal newspaper.

His career in the Commons was briefly interrupted when he was defeated in the January 1910 election, but he rediscovered his Scottish roots and returned to the House as MP for Peebles in the December 1910 election. After this, his standing in Parliament increased as he was made Deputy Chairman of Ways and Means (a deputy Speaker) in 1911. Maclean chaired a number of committees, including ones on enemy debts and local government. He was made a privy counsellor in 1916 and knighted in 1917.

He remained loyal to his friend and former Prime Minister Asquith after David Lloyd George formed his coalition government, and after Asquith lost his seat at the 1918 election, Maclean, as one of the only remaining non-coalition Liberals, stepped in as Chairman of the Parliamentary Liberal Party, known disparagingly as the 'Wee Frees'. He later recalled how, after the electoral disaster, a group of twenty of them had gathered in Committee Room 9 in the Commons on the evening before the new session 'sore and disheartened – blaming everybody and everything' and complaining of the 'moral iniquity' of the election. After discussion, they decided to form themselves into a party and face a House of Commons which was 'hostile and, indeed, derisive'.[3]

He remained their chairman and de facto parliamentary leader until Asquith returned to the Commons in a by-election in February 1920. As we saw in the previous chapter, this brought Maclean into competition with Labour's William Adamson to be recognised as Leader of the Opposition in the Commons. Labour had agreed with the Speaker that they should occupy the opposition front bench, but as noted by *The Times*:

This decision, of course, does not dispose of the claim of other Privy Councillors like Sir Donald Maclean and one or two Liberal ex-Ministers to sit on the Front Bench. The Asquith Liberals are making a point of the fact that, although Labour has passed them in the House of Commons, they still form the Opposition in the

Lords. It is, indeed, one of the ironies of the Parliamentary situation that the Asquith Liberals will be far stronger, both in numbers and in debating power, in the hereditary Chamber than in the popularly-elected House.[4]

The tussle with Labour for pre-eminence in opposition continued, with questions over who should occupy the opposition whips' room and Maclean's colleagues briefing that 'in the unprecedented Parliamentary situation, the mere counting of heads should not be allowed to determine the question.' As they put it, the role of the official opposition should be considered 'in commission' until one or other party established a clearer claim.[5] The running battle for speaking privileges and seating arrangements in the Chamber continued after the House met, and for the next few years Maclean vied to remain relevant, whilst playing a leading role alongside Asquith in attempts to revive the party's fortunes in the country, making use of their continued control of the Liberal Party machinery.

He was judged to have been an effective leader in difficult circumstances, and some of his colleagues reportedly wished he could have continued after Asquith returned at a by-election in February 1920. At this point, the vexed question of who could claim the title of Leader of the Opposition resurfaced, with the former Prime Minister considered by many to have the best claim, despite Labour's continued greater numbers. *The Times* reported on the day Asquith took his seat:

Sir Donald Maclean will at once resign the position of Sessional Chairman of the group, which will forthwith disappear from the category of Westminster titles. He will naturally fall into the position of Mr Asquith's second in command. It will be interesting to see how the Labour Party takes the return of Mr Asquith. At the opening of this Parliament the Labour Party staked out a claim to be regarded as 'the Opposition.' Mr Adamson, the Sessional Chairman of the party was put forward for recognition as 'the Leader of the Opposition.' The Speaker, however, wisely reserved his decision until the political situation should have further developed, and impartially called on Mr Adamson and Sir Donald Maclean in turn to discharge the functions of Leader of the Opposition. As the Labour Party based its claim a year ago on the number of its members, it may not accept without a protest Mr Asquith's resumption of his former position. The wiser course clearly would be to accept the inevitable with good grace.[6]

Whilst Asquith was back in charge, Maclean was set to remain a significant figure in Liberal politics during the 1920s, which were set for further upheaval after the Conservatives voted to withdraw from the Lloyd George coalition and cast the coalition Liberals into opposition. At the ensuing general election in 1922, the non-coalition Liberals duly increased their numbers, but Maclean lost his own seat. Nevertheless, he became president of the National Liberal Federation and oversaw the reluctant reunion of the Liberal Party, which involved him cooperating in an uneasy truce with Lloyd George. He returned to the Commons as MP for North Cornwall in 1929, and as a senior figure in the party helped negotiate its participation in the National Government of Ramsay MacDonald in 1931, in which he was appointed a minister for the first time as President of the Board of Education. He was then promoted to the Cabinet and served in that office until his sudden death in June 1932.

Maclean's time as an opposition leader (if not 'The' opposition leader) came at a particularly difficult time for his party. His contribution in that role was recognised by his colleagues after Asquith's return in 1920, when a dinner was held in his honour. At this event, Asquith paid tribute to him:

> It was in one of the darkest hours of our political fortunes that he was called on to undertake what was certainly a thankless, and what to many observers appeared to be an impossible, task … I remember quoting what was said of an Irish politician in the 18th century, that he was a man who was ready to go out in all weathers, and that is what Sir Donald Maclean is … He has brought to the work of leadership the most priceless of all assets – the asset of character.[7]

The speech – and Maclean's reply – were greeted with cheers, and he was presented with a silver inkstand inscribed to him 'as a token of personal affection and a tribute to his leadership, 1919–20'. It was clearly a heartfelt gesture of appreciation and demonstrates why Maclean deserves his place in the history of his party and of the opposition. If the notoriety surrounding his son's later treachery has any positive effect, it should be to prompt the rediscovery of this Not Quite Leader of the Opposition.

25

Arthur Henderson

Labour, Leader of the Opposition 28 August–27 October 1931

For some of the leaders we have considered, their tenure in opposition has been significantly overshadowed by other achievements in their career, such as serving in one or more of the great offices of state. To this category we can certainly add our latest contender, who, as well as having served three times as leader of the Labour Party, was also Home Secretary and Foreign Secretary. If that were not enough, he was also awarded the Nobel Peace Prize. I think it's fair to say that raises the bar somewhat.

Having made the case in an earlier chapter for William Adamson to be acknowledged as the first Labour Leader of the Opposition, we now reach a name more familiar to historians. Arthur Henderson, despite only being officially Leader of the Opposition for a couple of months in 1931, is a hugely significant figure in Labour history. When he first served as the party's leader in 1908 he took over from Keir Hardie. He was also the first ever Labour Cabinet minister.

His origins, like many early Labour figures, were in Scotland. He was born in 1863 in Glasgow to working-class parents – his mother was a domestic servant, whilst his father was a textile worker who died when Arthur was ten years old. The family moved to Newcastle, and he became an apprentice at an iron foundry from the age of twelve, working in the industry for the next twenty years. He had a strong commitment to Christianity and was a regular attendee at the Wesleyan Methodist Mission chapel in Elswick Road.

He entered politics through the trade union movement, becoming a district representative and achieving prominence for his role during a major industrial dispute in the north-east in 1894. Like many in the labour movement of the time, he began as a Liberal and had been elected as a local councillor in Newcastle in 1892, representing Westgate North ward. He was election agent to the Liberal MP for Barnard Castle before being elected in 1898 as both a county and district councillor for Darlington, where he would go on to serve as mayor.

As a representative of the Friendly Society of Iron Founders, Henderson was a delegate at the conference which founded the Labour Representation Committee in 1900. As a result of his prominence in the union, he was invited to contest Barnard Castle with their sponsorship as the Labour candidate when the incumbent MP died in 1903, and the contest attracted a fair amount of interest, with almost daily reports in the national press. The campaign was characterised by an increasingly bitter dispute with the Liberal candidate about whether the Liberal should stand down to avoid splitting the progressive vote against the Conservative candidate. On the day of the count, *The Times* reported the Conservatives were expected to prevail, with the Liberals in second place. This was entirely wrong, as Henderson triumphed by the narrow margin of forty-seven votes over the Conservative Colonel Vane, with the Liberal candidate trailing in third. In his speech, Henderson claimed it had been 'a workers' fight, and to them was due the credit of a glorious victory'.[1]

The victory, coming soon after that of Will Crooks in a by-election in Woolwich, was a significant one. Henderson became only the fifth Labour MP and the first to have been elected against both Liberal and Conservative opposition. *The Times* devoted several columns to reporting on its significance but observed rather sniffily, 'We still believe that Mr Henderson and his friends take themselves and their movement much more seriously than do most of those who have voted for Labour candidates.'[2]

Despite such scepticism, the party continued to advance, with Henderson joined by considerably more colleagues after the 1906 general election, when twenty-six Labour MPs were elected. He served as the party's Chief Whip at the start of the new parliament, and when Keir Hardie stood down as Chairman of the Parliamentary Labour Party in 1908, Henderson was elected to replace him. As de facto leader for two years, he gave support to the Liberal 'People's Budget' and aligned Labour with the government in the fight against the House of Lords during the crisis that followed. At the January 1910 election, Labour's numbers increased further to forty MPs, and in the wake of this further advance Henderson stood down as chairman, to be succeeded first by George Barnes, who only served a year, and then by Ramsay MacDonald.

At the outbreak of the First World War, MacDonald was heavily opposed to Britain's entry, and finding himself at odds with the party's more supportive position, resigned as chairman. Henderson therefore returned to the role, and when H. H. Asquith formed his coalition government in May 1915, he was appointed to the Cabinet as President of the Board of Education, before moving to be Paymaster General the following year. After David Lloyd George took over as Prime Minister, Henderson joined the war Cabinet as Minister without Portfolio but resigned acrimoniously in 1917 after a row about a proposed international socialist conference, which he had committed to attend after visiting Moscow for talks with the Russian provisional government.

Out of government, Henderson also stood down again as chairman of the parliamentary party and instead focused on strengthening Labour's political organisation and policy platform in his role as the party's national secretary, which he had also held since 1912. He took a leading role in the fundamental redrafting of the party constitution, which committed it to socialist objectives and was approved at the June 1918 party conference.

Having done a successful job of strengthening the party's overall electoral machinery, Henderson then encountered a series of electoral setbacks himself. He unwisely abandoned his seat in the north-east at the 1918 general election, standing instead in East Ham South, which he lost. Returning in a by-election for Widnes the following year, he again became Labour's Chief Whip, but lost the Widnes seat in 1922, returned in another by-election for Newcastle East and then lost this seat in the 1923 general election. Two months later he was back in the Commons as MP for Burnley and was appointed Home Secretary in the first Labour government under MacDonald. When the party returned to office in 1929 he was made Foreign Secretary, giving him a key role during the crisis which led to the party's split two years later.

When MacDonald proposed cuts to unemployment benefits, Henderson joined the majority of the Cabinet in opposing him. At this point Henderson could have become Prime Minister, as the most senior figure in the government when MacDonald resigned. But instead, King George V persuaded MacDonald to stay on and form a National Government with the Conservatives, whilst Henderson led his Labour colleagues in going into opposition. He was elected leader

of the party for the third time on 28 August 1931, after initially suggesting that the job should go to J. R. Clynes, another former leader. When
the Commons resumed in September, Henderson was Leader of the
Opposition and led his colleagues in a concerted attack on MacDonald's government, a fortnight after having served in his Cabinet. It was
an extraordinary spectacle in the House, where 'the Opposition were
numerous enough to make their benches crowded and restless enough
to make them noisy'.[3]

After this dramatic split, Henderson would not have long in office
as Labour leader. He led the party into the general election called just
two months later, at which the party suffered a disastrous result, reduced from 287 MPs to just fifty-two. Henderson was not amongst the
remaining MPs, having himself lost his seat. For someone who had
played such a pivotal role in building the Labour Party from its very
foundations to be a party of government, it was a bitter blow. Under-
scoring the scale of the disaster, *The Times* published a full page head-
lined 'Labour Leaders Beaten' featuring photographs of some of the
prominent Labour losses, led by Henderson. The Conservative leader
Stanley Baldwin, meanwhile, was pictured at his party's headquarters
smiling in satisfaction as he read the tickertape machine churning out
the results.

A total of thirty-four former Labour ministers were defeated, including thirteen ex-Cabinet ministers. Speaking to the press at Burnley, Henderson attempted to strike a defiant note, saying that although
'a shattering blow has been dealt at Labour in Parliament' the party
was 'not broken' and 'its spirit is not crushed'. But he went on to warn
of the effect of the result:

The new House of Commons will be a mockery of democratic Parliamentary representation, and from the standpoint of general national

interest this is a danger and a disaster. Experience has shown that the absence of an adequate and effective official Opposition undermines faith in Parliamentary institutions.[4]

In an attack that has echoes of later complaints from defeated Labour leaders, he blamed the 'propaganda directed against us' by 'unscrupulous' methods, saying, 'The electors, panic-stricken and deceived, were stampeded to an extent unparalleled in British politics.' But he vowed that the Labour movement would 'rise again stronger and more vigorous than ever'.[5]

Despite being out of Parliament, he was unanimously re-elected as leader of the party at a meeting at Transport House the following week, with a resolution passed expressing continued confidence in him. George Lansbury, one of the few surviving former ministers, was chosen as chairman of the parliamentary party, to 'act as the Leader of the Opposition until such time as Mr Henderson finds his way back to the House of Commons'.[6] In the event, however, Henderson formally stood down from the leadership the following year.

He also had another duty to perform, having previously been nominated when in government to chair the world disarmament conference in Geneva, at which sixty-one states were represented. He duly went and presided at the opening session on 2 February 1932, continuing to oversee its lengthy proceedings for the next two and a half years. His efforts led to him being awarded the Nobel Peace Prize in 1934, but the conference was ultimately a failure, with the new German leader Adolf Hitler pulling Germany out, leading to understandable unwillingness by France and other nations to disarm. By this time Henderson had been re-elected to Parliament in a by-election in September 1933, but his health was failing, and he died in October 1935.

His political career was marked by an unstinting commitment to the trade union movement and to the Labour Party, serving in various official capacities in the party's organisation from its foundation in 1900 until 1934, when he reluctantly stood down as national secretary after twenty-two years in the job. He was at other times its treasurer, Chief Whip, chairman and of course three-time leader in Parliament. It is an extraordinary record, and he was no mere placeholder. Henderson played an active role in developing its constitution, policy programme and electoral machinery, whilst also holding office as its first Cabinet minister and serving in high office in its first two governments. It is a tantalising prospect to think what might have been had Ramsay Mac-Donald refused to form the National Government in 1931 and instead allowed Henderson to succeed him as Labour Prime Minister. The devastating split of that year would have been avoided, and history would have taken a very different course during the 1930s.

26

George Lansbury

Labour, Leader of the Opposition 1931–35

'George Lansbury looks a go-er.' So said the actor Peter O'Toole, playing the title role in the play *Jeffrey Bernard Is Unwell*. The subject of his comment was a cat, named after the former Labour leader and mimed by the actor playing an eccentric gentleman by the name of Caspar, who had invented the sport of 'cat racing' with his two pets (the other one named Keir Hardie). If this sounds like a surreal fever dream, I can only apologise and suggest you look up the relevant video clip online to make (some) sense of it. I was taken to see the play at the Old Vic in 1999 by my brilliant and much-missed friend Peter Taylor, a lifelong Labour supporter with an encyclopaedic knowledge of the party's history and a wicked sense of humour. He died far too young in 2019, but amongst the many happy memories I cherish of him is the association in my mind between the subject of this chapter and the participant in a feline flat race.

It was another Taylor, the historian A. J. P. Taylor, who once described Lansbury as 'the most lovable figure in modern politics', which is not a bad accolade for anyone to receive.[1] If that were not enough, he was also the grandfather of the actress Angela Lansbury and of the animator and puppeteer Oliver Postgate. So as well as a significant contribution to twentieth-century political history, his legacy could also be said to include *Murder, She Wrote*, *Bagpuss* and *The Clangers*.[*]

After Labour suffered its crushing defeat in 1931, Arthur Henderson remained as overall party leader for a year, but as we have seen, the roles of chairman of the parliamentary party and Leader of the Opposition would fall to George Lansbury. Compared to some of the more moderate early Labour figures he was an unambiguous left-winger, seen by many as a natural protester rather than a responsible figure of government. He had, however, served in Cabinet before the Labour split and was one of the few senior figures in the party to have survived the 1931 election.

Lansbury was born in Suffolk in 1859, the son of a railway worker (also named George) and his progressive-minded wife Anne, who had a great influence on the young George's thinking and politics. They moved to London's East End when George junior was nine, and he left school at fourteen to take up manual work, which included a spell unloading coal wagons. He entered politics as secretary of the Bow and Bromley Liberal and Radical Association, before becoming a socialist in 1892 and a leading member of the Social Democratic Federation (SDF). This organisation, unlike its later near-namesake, was not a moderate political force. It was explicitly Marxist and indeed included amongst its members Karl Marx's daughter Eleanor.

Under the SDF banner, Lansbury was the parliamentary candidate for Walworth in a by-election and then the general election of 1895. He was heavily defeated, but in 1900 achieved a more respectable share of

---

[*] For the sake of completeness (and after asking for opinions on Twitter), I should include also the other iconic roles associated with Dame Angela: Miss Price in *Bedknobs and Broomsticks*, Mrs Eleanor Iselin in *The Manchurian Candidate* and, of course, the voice of Mrs Potts in Disney's *Beauty and the Beast*. As for Oliver Postgate, I was much more a fan of *Ivor the Engine* than the frankly creepy Bagpuss.

the vote when he stood in Bow and Bromley, despite still losing to the Conservative incumbent. He had, however, already been elected as a Poor Law guardian in Poplar in 1893, and ten years later he became a Poplar borough councillor, having resigned from the SDF to join the Independent Labour Party.

In 1905 he was appointed as a member of the Royal Commission on the Poor Laws, alongside Beatrice Webb, and argued for the introduction of a system of old-age pensions and a minimum wage, ideas which the pair included in a minority report. Lansbury then stood in the 1906 general election as an independent socialist candidate, on a platform which highlighted his support for women's voting rights, a cause he had been advocating since his days in the Liberal Party. He was again unsuccessful, as he was when he stood in Bow and Bromley in January 1910, but after fighting the Bow and Bromley seat again in the December 1910 election he finally won, defeating the Conservative candidate and future Cabinet minister Leo Amery.

In Parliament he made the issue of women's suffrage his main political campaign, denouncing the treatment of imprisoned women suffragettes and being suspended from the Commons for disorderly conduct after angrily challenging the Prime Minister and refusing to obey the Speaker's instruction to leave the Chamber. The parliamentary column of *The Times* described the scene:

There were loud cries of 'Order!' while the hon. member advanced to the end of the Treasury bench and in an excited tone continued … You are beneath contempt (waving his arm towards the Treasury Bench). You call yourself gentlemen! You forcible feeders of women! You ought to be thrown out of public life.

The Speaker said: I ask the hon. member for Bow and Bromley to leave the House.

Mr Lansbury (amid cries of 'Order!') – I am not going out when this contemptible thing is being done, this torturing of women, murdering or driving them mad. You ought to be ashamed of yourselves, you who talk about principle ... The women are showing you what principle is, and you ought to honour them, not laugh at their sufferings. You should honour them for their womanhood.[2]

His militant stance was not shared by some of his colleagues on the Labour benches, and frustrated by their failure to be more assertive, he resigned his seat in order to fight a by-election on the single issue of votes for women. This drew much attention, but after a lively campaign, he was defeated. The following year, Lansbury was sent to prison for three months for incitement to commit crime after making a series of speeches in which he said, in relation to the suffragettes' campaign:

I am still a believer in militancy. I think myself that women who are outlaws ought to break the law on every possible occasion, short of taking human life, in any way which suggests itself to them ... Every single agitation that has been carried out in this country has really been successful that has had a militant movement ... I would like to see London severely tackled, and every big town tackled systematically.[3]

During the First World War he was editor of the socialist *Daily Herald* and used this position to campaign against the war, which he blamed on capitalism. He also welcomed the Russian Revolution in 1917, writing in an editorial that 'a new star of hope has risen over Europe'.[4] In 1920 he visited Russia and met Lenin, writing an account of his visit on his return.

Lansbury had remained a councillor in the London Borough of

Poplar, one of the poorest boroughs in London, and in 1919 had become its first Labour mayor. In 1921 he and his Labour colleagues set an illegal budget, refusing to levy precepts to fund the London County Council and Metropolitan Police, in protest at the unfairness of the rates system, which penalised poor boroughs like Poplar by making them bear the burden of paying poor relief. The Poplar Rates Rebellion, as it became known, caused a huge controversy, and the councillors were taken to court, marching there led by the council's macebearer and accompanied by a brass band and a banner reading 'Poplar Borough Council marching to the High Court and possibly to prison'. Ordered to levy the precepts, they refused and were imprisoned for contempt of court.

After six weeks they were released, and the government backed down, passing legislation to equalise the burden of poor relief across London boroughs. As a result, the rates in Poplar fell by a third, and the council received significant extra funding. It was a huge personal victory for Lansbury. On the back of this triumph, he was returned to Parliament in 1922 as MP for Poplar, Bow and Bromley and held the seat until his death.

Just ahead of the formation of the first Labour government, he caused offence in royal circles by issuing a public warning to the king not to stand in the way of the party taking office. Speaking at a meeting at Shoreditch Town Hall, he said:

A few centuries ago one King who stood up against the common people of that day lost his head – lost it really. (Laughter and cheers.) Later, one of his descendants was told to get out as quickly as he could. Since that day Kings and Queens had been what they ought to be. They never interfered with politics, and George V would be well advised to keep his finger out of the pie now.[5]

Unsurprisingly, Lansbury was not offered a position in the Cabinet when Labour took office later that month and declined a more junior post. In the second Labour Government in 1929, however, he was appointed First Commissioner of Works, with a seat in the Cabinet. In this role he was in frequent contact with the king and, somewhat surprisingly, was reported to have developed a cordial relationship with him. He was an active minister and achieved a positive public profile with a programme of improving public recreation facilities. These included a public lido in Hyde Park on the Serpentine that became known as 'Lansbury's Lido'. This particular achievement is commemorated today on the side of the lido cafe with a metal plaque which bears his name and image and records that he 'made this bathing shore for our enjoyment'.

Then came Labour's acrimonious split in 1931, and Lansbury's assumption of the leadership of the party in the Commons after the disastrous election. As we have seen, he had a long reputation as a self-declared militant socialist, and he did little to moderate his views in the leadership, continuing to speak out based on his personal platform of pacifism, unilateral disarmament and dismantling of the British Empire. He was an unlikely leader, as he himself acknowledged in a speech to the party conference in 1934, in which he said:

> I never dreamed in my wildest imagining that I would ever be called upon to act as the spokesman. I have never considered myself leader – but as spokesman of my colleagues in the House of Commons I am proud to have been one of that little band ... It was an accident that put me there – the accident of the last General Election – and I am only there as long as my colleagues think it wise for me to be there. When they think change is needed, then I shall go.[6]

As well as being the spokesman for the little band at Westminster, he also appeared to be the authentic voice of much of the party's wider membership at the time. Pacifism was an issue which had always tended to split the party, but for the time being it seemed to be in the ascendent. The 1933 Labour Party conference had passed a notably pacifist resolution, and Lansbury felt at liberty to give full vent to his own views. He was reported to have sent a message during a by-election contest in East Fulham that year saying, 'I would close every recruiting station, disband the Army and disarm the Air Force. I would abolish the whole dreadful equipment of war and say to the world: "Do your worst".'[7]

This extreme commitment to pacifism was causing growing unease in the party amongst his more moderate colleagues. In 1935, the fascist government of Italy was preparing to invade Abyssinia (Ethiopia), and the Labour National Executive tabled a resolution at that year's party conference calling for sanctions against the aggressor. Lansbury was opposed to this as a form of economic warfare and spoke against it vehemently in a speech from the platform, extolling his belief in Christian pacifism.

Whilst this was well received by many delegates, his position was then fiercely attacked by Ernest Bevin, the leader of the Transport and General Workers' Union, who condemned Lansbury for failing to abide by the party's agreed policy to oppose fascist aggression. Bevin's speech won round crucial union votes, and the resolution in support of sanctions was passed by a large majority. Realising his position was untenable, Lansbury resigned a few days later. He was succeeded on a temporary basis by his deputy, ahead of the general election the following month. At that election, Labour significantly recovered its parliamentary strength, and that temporary leader, Clement Attlee, remained in post for the next twenty years, going on to become the party's most revered Prime Minister.

Lansbury continued to occupy himself with politics, serving an-other term as Mayor of Poplar 1936–7 and campaigning for pacifism through the Peace Pledge Union, of which he became president in 1937. In this cause he travelled widely, meeting President Roosevelt in the United States and European leaders including Adolf Hitler and Benito Mussolini, encounters he recorded in his book *My Quest for Peace*, published in 1938. At the outbreak of the Second World War he spoke in the House of Commons of his hope 'that out of this terrible calamity there will arise a real spirit, a spirit that will compel people to give up reliance on force, and that perhaps this time humanity will learn the lesson and refuse in the future to put its trust in poison gas, in the massacre of little children and universal slaughter'.[8]

He did not live to see the restoration of the peace he craved, dying of cancer less than a year later on 7 May 1940. His whole career had been marked by commitment to pursuing his core socialist beliefs, wheth-er or not they accorded with his party's official line and even when doing so involved endorsing militant activism. He was uncomfortable in the leadership and was never reconciled to the strictures required of an establishment politician. In this, there are perhaps more than a few comparisons to be made between him and a more recent Labour leader from the far left. Like Jeremy Corbyn, Lansbury is perhaps best regarded as a man of firm principles who refused to compromise on them throughout his career. Whilst such consistency can be viewed as admirable to those who already share those convictions, it presents problems when a party seeks to broaden its electoral appeal. Lansbury was unsuited to doing so, but his lifelong commitment to the Labour cause and his willingness to fight his campaigns inside and outside Parliament have earned him a prominent place in the pantheon of left-wing Labour heroes.

27

James Maxton

Independent Labour, Leader of the Opposition
(contested) 1940–45

One of my favourite pub quiz questions when speaking to my
students is to ask them, 'Who was the Leader of the Opposition
during the Second World War?' Clement Attlee was leader from 1939
until he entered government in May 1940, so he can be said to qualify
for the early stages of the war. But then who was it? One answer could
be James 'Jimmy' Maxton, a Scottish left-wing rebel and leader of the
Independent Labour Party, but his claim is rather contested.

Like many at Westminster, I first encountered his name at some
point in the late 1990s in connection with the then Chancellor, Gordon
Brown. One of the biographical points which stuck in the mind about
Brown was his precocious academic prowess when at the University of
Edinburgh, during which time he wrote his PhD thesis on the Labour
Party in Scotland from 1918–29, with a particular focus on his hero,
the Clydeside socialist James 'Jimmy' Maxton, of whom he published
a biography in the 1980s. The ascent of Brown to the top of politics
therefore prompted something of a spike in interest in Maxton (and

second-hand book sales), as commentators sought to discover more about the object of Brown's political fascination.

The future Prime Minister was not the only writer to have focused on Maxton, with a number of other biographies having been published about the 'beloved rebel', as one of them called him. I can therefore direct readers to those for a fuller appreciation of his life and confine myself to a rather more brief sketch.

Maxton was born in a suburb of Glasgow in 1885, the son of two schoolteachers. He attended grammar school and went to the University of Glasgow before becoming a teacher himself. At that time he described himself as a Conservative, but he underwent a conversion to socialism after seeing the poverty of the children he taught and joined the Independent Labour Party (ILP) in 1904. The ILP was then a separate party but affiliated to the mainstream Labour Party.

His profile rose during the First World War, which he opposed, and his pacifism was a major theme of his life, as it was for other Labour figures such as George Lansbury. He was a conscientious objector during the conflict and was imprisoned for a year for sedition after a speech in defence of Clydeside shop stewards who were facing deportation. Having been Chairman of the Scottish ILP from 1913 to 1919, he was elected to Parliament in 1922 as the MP for Bridgeton in Glasgow, one of ten Labour MPs returned for constituencies in the city. He became a fiery speaker and cut a distinctive figure, being tall and thin with a long mane of black hair. In 1923 he was suspended from the House for calling Conservative MPs 'murderers' for cutting funds to health authorities.

He and his colleagues sought to influence the mainstream Labour Party in a more left-wing direction, and his relationship with its leader Ramsay MacDonald was an uneasy one. He became National Chairman of the ILP in 1926 and oversaw the publication of its policy programme of that year, entitled *Socialism in our Time*. Two years later, he and the miners' leader A. J. Cook published what became known as the 'Cook–Maxton manifesto', advocating class warfare, which provoked tensions within the party's ranks after he was accused of not consulting his senior colleagues about it.

During the second Labour government from 1929 to 1931 he became a staunch critic of its lack of radicalism, and the relationship between the ILP and the Labour Party became ever more strained. After the fall of the Labour government and the Labour Party split, the ILP formally disaffiliated and arguably lost their remaining influence. From this time on, Maxton was more of a fringe figure and during the 1930s turned his attention to international affairs, pursuing a strongly pacifist line (except in regard to the Spanish Civil War, where he said he would be willing to fight for the Republicans). When the Second World War began, he opposed British participation and was predictably critical of the decision by the Labour Party under Clement Attlee to join the wartime coalition under Winston Churchill.

It is at this point that the question of his inclusion in a list of Leaders of the Opposition requires consideration. With the Labour Party ceasing to be a party of opposition, the same issue arose as had done during the coalition in the last war. Who were the official opposition? Whilst the issue had been fudged in 1915, there was now another factor to take into account, which should have been decisive.

In 1937, Parliament had passed the Ministers of the Crown Act, which gave a salary to the Leader of the Opposition for the first time. For the purposes of that payment, the Act defined the position as being the leader of the largest party outside the government. Clement Attlee had been the first leader to qualify and had received the salary. Now he and his Labour colleagues were in office, along with the Liberals and the National Labour members. The law was therefore quite straightforward: the next largest party in the Commons was Maxton's ILP, with four members.

This fact did not escape Maxton's notice. On 21 May, a Labour back-bencher raised the issue of the salary during questions to the Prime Minister. Churchill responded that in view of the coalition govern-ment being formed, 'His Majesty's Government is of opinion that the provision of the Ministers of the Crown Act, 1937, relating to the payment of a salary to the Leader of the Opposition, is in abeyance for the time being.' This prompted Maxton to intervene, saying, 'The answer seems to indicate that not only is the salary of the Leader of the Opposition being put into abeyance but that there is an attempt being made to put opposition into abeyance.' At this, Labour members shouted, 'No,' and 'Leave that to us'.[1]

The debate continued during the business statement, when Maxton addressed the precedent of the last war, arguing that at that time there had been no 'distinct and separately organised Opposition to the Gov-ernment' but that 'on this occasion there is such an Opposition'. At this, a number of MPs shouted 'Where?', prompting Maxton to reply 'Here'. The Speaker then made a statement about the occupation of the opposition front bench, ruling, 'The present circumstances are, as far as I know, unprecedented. It cannot be said that there is now an Opposition in Parliament in the hitherto accepted meaning of the words; namely, a party in Opposition to the Government from which an alternative Government could be formed.' On that basis, he said, the opposition front bench could be occupied by ex-ministers of any party. This prompted another rejoinder from Maxton, who replied:

It may be that, in the minds of hon. Members who are endeavour-ing to be in the Government and out of it at the same time, this is a waste of time. To me, it appears that we are now making vital decisions. If as you say, Mr. Speaker, the Opposition is to be abolished, then we are on the Reichstag level at once. The Opposition are those who are in opposition to the major policies of the Government ... I am not to be bound by a Ruling of this description, which gives the strategic position of Opposition to anybody at all who may have been in a Government 50 years ago, and who may be 100 per cent in agreement with the present Government's policy.[2]

It is a fascinating issue (though, to quote my husband, 'I'll be the judge of that'), which goes beyond the narrow issue of parliamentary seating arrangements and salaries into a wider debate over the need for opposition during times of national crisis. With the Speaker and the Prime Minister united on their interpretation, however, the question was considered closed, and Maxton's legitimate claim to be considered Leader of the Opposition was denied.

He remained a marginal figure but a regular presence in the Chamber, speaking often to provide a critical voice against the government during the wartime consensus. In 1942, he was the only one of 465 MPs to vote against a motion of confidence in Churchill's government. He died in 1946, and the tributes paid to him recalled his great skills of oratory, along with his personal warmth, which seems to have won him friends across the House. Many descriptions of him involve the word 'rebel', and as he himself once said, 'My function as an agitator is to fan the flames of discontent.'[3] It was certainly a role he appeared to relish, even without being paid the salary for doing so in the House.

28

Hastings Lees-Smith

Labour, Acting Leader of the Opposition
May 1940–December 1941

On 13 May 1940, Winston Churchill delivered his first speech to the House of Commons since taking the reins of power as Prime Minister. In words that have echoed down the decades, he declared that he had 'nothing to offer but blood, toil, tears and sweat', and defiantly outlined the government's aim as 'victory at all costs'.[1]

Less well remembered is who spoke next. Rising in the Leader of the Opposition's place on the front bench opposite was the 62-year-old Labour MP for Keighley, who had previously served as Postmaster General and President of the Board of Education in the second Labour government nine years before. To cheers from across the House, Hastings Lees-Smith declared his support for Labour's inclusion in the new National Government and drew a contrast with Nazi Germany, saying, 'We have had unity by discussion, persuasion, good will and good sense, instead of unity by the concentration camp, the rubber truncheon and the executioner's block.' The experience of forming the government, he said 'convinces me that our form of Parliamentary government is the most civilised in peace and is the most formidable weapon in control in war'.[2]

Despite that political unity, the parliamentary system he was so keen to celebrate remained built around the idea of a House divided between government and opposition. In order to make the normal procedures work, someone had to face the government benches and respond to ministers. As a result, the Labour leader Clement Attlee, now the Lord Privy Seal, had nominated Lees-Smith, as the most senior of his colleagues not in government, to perform the duties of the Leader of the Opposition: 'Asking questions as to the business of the House and so on.'[3]

On that first occasion, Lees-Smith said he had been 'asked by my colleagues on this occasion' to speak after the Prime Minister, but at a meeting of the Parliamentary Labour Party ten days later, he was unanimously elected as acting chairman, whilst Attlee remained leader of the party.[4] As *The Times* noted, 'This means that Mr Lees-Smith will be the spokesman of the Labour Party from the Opposition front bench in the Commons.'[5] As we saw in the previous chapter, however, he would not officially be Leader of the Opposition, or receive the new salary for that post. This, as the Prime Minister and the Speaker had declared when challenged by James Maxton, was 'in abeyance' for the duration of the National Government.

The arrangement remained somewhat contentious, with Maxton remaining unhappy that a Labour member was assuming the duties of opposition whilst supporting his colleagues in government. After the evacuation of Dunkirk at the end of the month, Churchill made another famous speech to the Commons, declaring, 'We shall fight on the beaches ... we shall never surrender.' When he sat down, Lees-Smith again rose to respond, but this time he was interrupted by Maxton, who raised a point of order to the Speaker about the propriety of any response being made to such a statement. After a number of other interventions, the Speaker suggested Lees-Smith not proceed. Similar squabbles followed the first few times he attempted to ask the business question, but after a few weeks the system appeared to settle down.

Hastings Bertrand Lees-Smith had been born in 1878 in India, the son of a major in the Royal Artillery and his wife, Jesse Reid. After his father died two years later, the young 'Bertie' was brought back to England to be raised by his grandfather. He was educated privately, attended a military academy in Hertfordshire and was set to follow his late father into the army, but this proved not to be right for him. Instead he pursued a more academic path, going to Queen's College, Oxford, to study history.

At university, Lees-Smith was a Liberal but showed signs of his future trajectory by also joining the Fabian Society. After graduation he served as a lecturer at Ruskin Hall, known then as the 'Workman's University', which provided education to working-class men on trade union scholarships. He was then appointed as a lecturer in public administration at the London School of Economics, where he taught on and off for the rest of his life.

He was first elected as Liberal MP for Northampton in the January 1910 election and proved something of a radical, supporting nationalisation of industry, land reform and a minimum wage. During the First World War he joined the army, serving in the ranks and reaching the rank of corporal, despite having been highly critical of the conflict as a founding member of the anti-war Union of Democratic Control, alongside MPs including Ramsay MacDonald. This connection, and his increasing disaffection with the Liberal Party after its split in 1916, led Lees-Smith to abandon his constituency and stand in the 1918 general election for Don Valley as an independent radical. He lost, but joined the Labour Party the following year and was elected MP for Keighley in 1922. He lost the seat in 1923 but won it back again in 1924.

He gained some prominence amongst his new colleagues in the

Commons by being elected to the executive committee of the Parliamentary Labour Party in 1924 and re-elected in the succeeding years. When Ramsay MacDonald formed the second Labour government in 1929, Lees-Smith was made Postmaster General before being promoted to the Cabinet in early 1931 as President of the Board of Education. He was only in this role for a few months before the drama of the Cabinet split over unemployment benefit, during which he appears to have initially backed MacDonald over the proposed cuts. However, after the party split occurred he went with his Labour colleagues into opposition and was elected again to the party's executive committee, before losing his seat at the 1931 general election.

After his defeat he returned to full-time teaching at the LSE but remained active in politics and returned to Parliament in 1935 after narrowly regaining his seat in Keighley. He became an active frontbench opposition spokesperson under Attlee's leadership, speaking frequently on various pieces of business, particularly those of a procedural or constitutional nature. One of these was the Ministers of the Crown Bill, which rationalised various ministerial salaries and introduced the new salary for the Leader of the Opposition. In view of the role he would take on three years later, it is interesting to see the part of his speech supporting that proposal, which started from the basic principle that 'if a man gives the whole of his time to the public service, he ought to be paid for it' but then added some thoughts on the broader issue:

In our view, the proposed payment is the logical outcome of the whole conception of Government which we present as an alternative to the totalitarian States. In a totalitarian State, no opposition is allowed. Our whole conception is that an Opposition is necessary in order to represent the views of the minority which is inevitable in any nation of free men who are able to call their souls their own.

If that be the case, the worth of the Opposition in Parliament, not in defeating Government legislation, for it cannot do that, but in modifying Government legislation so as to adapt and adjust it to the reasonable views of the minority, is just as much a part of the function of good government as that which is carried on by the Government itself.[6]

It is something of an irony that having made that case, he was then required to take on the duties of the leader at the outset of the wartime coalition without such payment. In doing so, Lees-Smith won respect for his diligence in carrying out those responsibilities, but they perhaps took their toll. After a year and a half in the role he fell ill with a bout of influenza, complicated by asthma, and died suddenly on 18 December 1941 at the age of sixty-three. His loss was keenly felt by his colleagues, with Attlee paying him this tribute:

In Mr. Lees-Smith we have lost a colleague whom we could ill spare in these difficult and dangerous times ... For 40 years, first at Ruskin College, Oxford, and then at the London School of Economics, he taught generations of students the principles of democratic government. For the greater part of 30 years he practised those principles in Parliament. He was a great lover of this House and was deeply versed in its history and procedure. Few men better understood, not merely the forms, but the living tradition and spirit of the greatest democratic Assembly in the world.[7]

29

Frederick Pethick-Lawrence

Labour, Acting Leader of the Opposition
December 1941–March 1942

Returning to the pub quiz question of who was the Leader of the Opposition during the Second World War, we now reach one of the trickier answers, with a contender who only served in the role for a few weeks. As we have seen, Hastings Lees-Smith had acted in the role for procedural purposes from May 1940, despite James Maxton fitting the statutory definition rather better. When Lees-Smith died suddenly in December 1941, there was a vacancy for the procedural role, and *The Times* reported:

> By the sudden death of Mr Lees-Smith the Parliamentary Labour Party has lost the acting chairman of its administrative committee and its official spokesman in the House. Mr F. W. Pethick-Lawrence is to fill this office temporarily, and it is thought probable that the Labour Party will later elect him to succeed Mr Lees-Smith.[1]

Indeed, the seventy-year-old Frederick Pethick-Lawrence had already been deputising for Lees-Smith in asking the business question on various occasions since November and continued to do so in the new year. On 21 January 1942 he was formally elected as acting chairman of the administrative committee of the Parliamentary Labour Party, after other potential candidates withdrew from contention. He therefore succeeded as 'the party's official spokesman in the House while Mr Attlee is serving in the Government'.[2]

Born in 1871 in London as Frederick Lawrence, his father was the owner of a building firm and died when Frederick was three years old. After attending a prep school in Wokingham, he went to Eton and then Cambridge, where he studied mathematics and became president of the union. He was elected a fellow of Trinity College but decided against an academic career, and after going on an extended world tour he settled in Canning Town, becoming treasurer of the Mansfield House university settlement, an initiative to bring social and educational opportunities to the deprived local community. At the same time he studied for the Bar and became a barrister at Inner Temple. The death of his brother in 1900 brought him a degree of wealth, which allowed him scope to pursue his political and social causes.

Meanwhile, he had met and fallen in love with Emmeline Pethick, who was to be a huge influence on his life and political views. She was a progressive radical, and her views reinforced his own move to the left. Despite the disapproval of his family, they married in 1901, and as a marker of their equal partnership, combined their surnames to become the Pethick-Lawrences.

Together, they became active supporters of the Women's Social and Political Union (WSPU), with Fred using his legal practice to defend suffragettes in court, publishing supportive articles in the press and paying bail money for them. In 1912 they were both sentenced to nine months in prison alongside Emmeline Pankhurst for conspiracy to incite violence and went on hunger strike, with both of them being force-fed. They were released after five weeks, and after disagreements with the Pankhursts over the increasing use of violence as a tactic, both were expelled from the WSPU but continued to support the cause.

During the First World War, Pethick-Lawrence advocated a peaceful settlement and refused to serve in the armed forces, assigned instead to work on the land as a conscientious objector. He became treasurer of the anti-war Union of Democratic Control, where he worked alongside Ramsay MacDonald, Arthur Henderson and Lees-Smith, and stood as the 'Peace by Negotiation' candidate in a by-election in South Aberdeen in 1917 but was heavily defeated. Having now joined the Labour Party, he stood unsuccessfully for South Islington in the 1922 general election, then in 1923 was elected as MP for West Leicester after sensationally defeating Winston Churchill to win the seat. He had by this time developed a reputation for economic policy, publishing a number of books on the subject, and Churchill himself described his victorious opponent as 'the prospective Chancellor of the Exchequer of a Labour Government'.[3]

This was a rather premature prediction, and Pethick-Lawrence was not included in the first Labour government the following year. He did, however, become a prolific speaker in the House, concentrating mostly on financial matters and making the case for a capital levy. When the second Labour government was formed in 1929 he became financial secretary to the Treasury, a role that he seemed to enjoy and which played to his strengths. It did mean, however, that he was at the centre of the financial crisis that engulfed the government in 1931, although not in the Cabinet.

When Ramsay MacDonald formed the National Government, Pethick-Lawrence declined to join, and having gone with his Labour colleagues into opposition, circulated a letter to the Parliamentary Labour Party in which he gave his view of the economic crisis, writing, 'The action taken by the Prime Minister has been fundamentally wrong ... It was wrong to disrupt the Labour Party by insisting on greater sacrifices by the poorer workers than seemed to a large section of his colleagues a fair proportion.'[4]

He was then elected to the parliamentary executive committee ahead of the 1931 general election, when, like many others, he lost his seat. He returned to Parliament as MP for Edinburgh East in 1935, became the leading finance spokesman for the opposition under Clement Attlee and was awarded membership of the Privy Council in the 1937 coronation honours. In 1938 he was made chairman of the Public Accounts Committee, a role he held until 1941. Despite his carefully prepared speeches, he was not good at engaging his audience and was rather cruelly nicknamed 'Pathetic Lawrence' by journalists in the press gallery. Attlee, in a typically succinct appraisal, later said he was 'very sound, but never really came over in the House of Commons'.[5]

When Labour entered the wartime government and Lees-Smith took on the duties of Leader of the Opposition, Pethick-Lawrence acted as his unofficial deputy and continued to speak on finance matters. Whilst supportive of the government, he nevertheless provided challenge to ministers from a socialist perspective. In late May 1940 he spoke on the Finance Bill, telling the Conservative Chancellor, Sir Howard Kingsley Wood:

Hon. Members from these benches who have entered the Government have not hesitated to demand sacrifices from the workers in industry—not merely reasonable sacrifices, but unreasonable sacrifices—and the workers are going to make those sacrifices. Those of

my party who are not in the Government will equally not hesitate to
agree to heavy calls being made on the workers, and to sacrifices of
time, energy, and money, to meet the cost of the war. But when we
do that, we make two conditions. The first is that while those sacrifices are being made by the workers, persons with humble means,
the Chancellor shall at the same time go for big money and those
who have it.[6]

Having been elected to replace Lees-Smith in January 1942, he might
have expected to continue in the role for the rest of the war, but just
a month later there was a further change. Arthur Greenwood, who
remained Deputy Leader of the Labour Party and had been in government as Minister without Portfolio, was dismissed from the Cabinet.
As the most senior party figure out of office, he took over the role of
acting chairman of the parliamentary party, with Pethick-Lawrence
becoming vice chairman.

When Labour won the 1945 general election, Pethick-Lawrence was
appointed Secretary of State for India and given a seat in the House
of Lords as Baron Pethick-Lawrence. He led a cabinet delegation to
India to begin negotiations for its independence but found it a frustrating and exhausting experience. His tenure was ended by the arrival
in 1947 of Earl Mountbatten as the last Viceroy of India, who lobbied
for Pethick-Lawrence to be removed, prompting his resignation.

He remained active in the House of Lords for the rest of his life,
making well-informed speeches on a range of policy issues and cri-
tiquing the economic policies of the Conservative government from
1951 onwards. He died in 1961, seven years after his beloved wife Emmeline. The Pethick-Lawrences had been a formidable political partnership, and it is fitting that they are both memorialised with portraits

alongside their names on the base of the statue of Millicent Fawcett in Parliament Square, as supporters of the campaign for women's right to vote. Of the fifty-nine campaigners recorded on the statue, Fred is one of only four men.* Even the most hard-bitten Westminster journalists might at least concede there was nothing 'pathetic' about his support for that cause.

---

* The others include George Lansbury, whose commitment to the cause, as we have seen, was equally strong.

30

Arthur Greenwood

Labour, Acting Leader of the Opposition 1942–45

T his round of the pub quiz draws to a close with the last of the wartime acting Leaders of the Opposition. He is, however, best known (of course) for another incident in his career.

At the outbreak of the Second World War, the Prime Minister, Neville Chamberlain, came to the House of Commons to report on the grave situation following Hitler's invasion of Poland. During the emergency sitting on Saturday 2 September, he told MPs that Hitler had not yet replied to a final warning to withdraw German forces. The speech, though condemning Nazi aggression, stopped short of a declaration of war, and his ambivalence was received with dismay. The Labour leader Clement Attlee was absent, convalescing after prostate surgery, so it was his deputy, Arthur Greenwood, who had the task of responding:

> Mr Greenwood, on rising, was greeted with loud Opposition cheers and cries of 'What about Britain?' 'Speak for the working classes,' and 'Speak for England,' the last cry being raised by Mr Amery (Birmingham, Sparkbrook, U.), and taken up by the Opposition.[1]

This shouted comment from Leo Amery, now usually recorded as 'Speak for England, Arthur!' has entered Westminster folklore, for its strong implication that the Prime Minister was not representing the country's interests. Greenwood's subsequent speech was later to be seen as the high point of his career, as he delivered a heartfelt denunciation of the government's inaction, saying:

> I wonder how long we are prepared to vacillate at a time when Britain and all that Britain stands for, and human civilisation, are in peril. We must march with the French ... The moment we look like weakening, at that moment dictatorship knows we are beaten. We are not beaten. We shall not be beaten. We cannot be beaten; but delay is dangerous.[2]

It was not the last time that Greenwood would play a role in stiffening the resolve of the government to fight the Nazi threat, and it is for these important interventions that he is best remembered by history. This marks a distinct contrast with some of the previous Labour leaders we have considered, whose strong pacifism was an article of faith. It should be said that many of them were also strict teetotallers, another characteristic which Greenwood emphatically did not share. Indeed, his commitment to alcohol throughout his career was at times stronger than many of his political convictions.

Born in Hunslet in Leeds in 1880, Greenwood's father was a painter and decorator. The young Arthur attended local schools before winning a scholarship to Yorkshire College in Leeds, where he was awarded a degree and qualified as a teacher. He taught economics at Huddersfield Technical College before moving to the economics department of the University of Leeds. He was a socialist from an early age, having read the socialist paper *The Clarion* and Labour pamphlets as a schoolboy, and as an academic began writing his own left-wing papers on the need for educational reform.

Greenwood moved to London in 1914 and during the war became a civil servant in the Ministry of Reconstruction, whilst continuing to develop links to prominent Labour intellectuals, including Beatrice and Sidney Webb. He stood unsuccessfully for Parliament in 1918, before being elected in 1922 for Nelson and Colne in Lancashire. In the 1924 Labour government he was parliamentary secretary at the Ministry for Health, and in the 1929 government he returned there as the Minister for Health, which included responsibility for housing. His Housing Act in 1930 encouraged mass slum clearance and the replacement of poor-quality housing.

After the collapse of the Labour government in 1931, he was amongst those who lost their seats in the general election, but he returned the following year at a by-election as MP for Wakefield in Yorkshire. He helped draft the party's manifesto for the 1935 election and stood in the leadership election against Attlee, finishing third behind Herbert Morrison. His supporters then backed Attlee, ensuring he won. Morrison refused the party's deputy leadership, so it went to Greenwood instead.

When Labour entered the wartime coalition, Greenwood was made Minister without Portfolio His significant contribution came early on, during the dark days of late May 1940 when Winston Churchill was faced by those in the war Cabinet, led by Viscount Halifax, who wanted to seek negotiated terms with Adolf Hitler. Greenwood emerged as a vocal supporter of Churchill's resolve to fight on, and his support, along with that of Attlee, played a major part in helping the Prime Minister to face down Halifax and keep Britain in the war.

As the government got to work, Greenwood chaired the Cabinet's economic policy committee and was later given oversight of reconstruction policy. He was, however, seen as a fairly ineffectual minister and was sacked in February 1942, with Attlee's agreement. It was at this point that he took over the duties of acting Leader of the Opposition in the House. This meant he was the person who often replied to Churchill's set-piece speeches on the progress of the war.

Not long afterwards, he gave a practical demonstration of his own fighting spirit. Walking home after a late sitting of the House in the early hours of 2 July, he was set upon by a knife-wielding assailant. He gave the following dramatic account of the attack:

> It happened somewhere about the Tate Gallery. I was walking home from the House when I saw a man come rushing straight for me. I saw the gleam of the knife. It is difficult to reconstruct exactly what happened then. I hit out at him and I must have hit him pretty hard. He went down with his head on the running board of a car. He scrambled up and got into the car and got away. I went on home. The back of my hand is slit open.[3]

The job of questioning the government during a time of total war, at a time when the main parties were both working together in coalition, was a tricky balancing act, which strained the traditional role of opposition. In February 1944, Churchill gave an update on the progress of the war and towards the end of his speech observed that there was 'in some quarters, the feeling that the way to win the war is to knock the Government about, keep them up to the collar, and harry them from every side' – an approach he said he found 'hard to bear'. In his response, Greenwood gave a notably conciliatory reply to this point, saying:

> If we do, on occasions, sharpen the edge of criticism, my right hon. Friend must not think that we are doing it because we want to let

him down. It may well be that we are trying, in perhaps a rather stupid way, on this side of the House, to help the good cause.[4]

Away from the war, the issue of post-war planning began to be discussed, particularly following the Beveridge Report on the future of social welfare provision. A government White Paper on proposals for the National Health Service was published in 1944 by the Conservative Minister for Health, and as a former Minister for Health himself, Greenwood took a particular interest in the details. On reading his speech, I was struck by one passage, which appears commendably enlightened when viewed from the twenty-first century. He said:

I would like to see a little more prominent place, when the details are worked out, given to the question of mental treatment. Mental treatment seems always to have been the Cinderella of the health service. I know it is intended that it should be part of the scheme, but I hope there will be no delay in the matter because we are very much behind and very old-fashioned. When I abolished the term 'lunatic asylum' by Act of Parliament, I did it for a psychological reason. There is nothing disgraceful, nothing that can be shown up against one, if one happens to suffer from mental disease. It is not a crime, it is an illness, and there is many a man who has suffered from mental disease who is better than men who have suffered from gout at the other extremity. One feels that mental treatment has rather been neglected.[5]

It is perhaps a measure of the persistence of the stigma around mental health that a similar speech could equally well be made today, but for Greenwood to be making the point eighty years ago reflects particularly well on him. This is all the more poignant when we consider that

THE NOT QUITE PRIME MINISTERS

he himself suffered from alcoholism for most of his life. His drinking had become notorious, and it seems certain that it contributed to his poor performance in some of the ministerial roles he occupied and thus prevented him reaching higher office.

After the war, Attlee appointed him as Lord Privy Seal and then Paymaster General in the Labour government, as recognition of his continued seniority in the party. He played a role in supporting the creation of the NHS through his chairing of the Cabinet committee on social services, but by 1947 Attlee felt he was 'losing grip' and wrote him a diplomatically worded 'Dear Arthur' letter, which informed him:

> I am making some changes in the Government. It is in my view
> essential to look to the future of the movement and to bring on some
> of the younger members of the Party. This necessarily involves the
> retirement of some of the older men who have given long service to
> the movement. I have very reluctantly come to the conclusion that I
> should include you among the latter.[6]

Greenwood took his sacking gracefully, replying that he had appreciated the 'generous terms in which it is couched'.[7] This was particularly notable given Attlee's reputation for bluntness on such occasions, having reportedly once responded to a sacked minister who asked why he was being removed, 'Afraid you're not up to it.'

Greenwood was spared such indignity and remained a respected senior figure within the party. He was elected Chairman of the National Executive in 1952 and remained treasurer until the following year. When he died in 1954, there were generous tributes to him in the House of Commons from both Churchill and Attlee, with the latter saying, 'Perhaps there was never anybody in our movement who so widely earned the deep affection of all the members.'[8]

31

Herbert Morrison

Labour, Acting Leader of the Opposition 7–14 December 1955

'Of course! That's why the PM resigned. He's always hated Ray. He just hung on long enough to make sure that his deputy didn't get the leadership! Like Attlee and Morrison.' Wise words from one of my favourite politicians, Jim Hacker of the BBC television comedy *Yes Minister* and its successor, *Yes Prime Minister*. Hacker, despite being a graduate of the LSE, clearly knows his political history. He made his observation in the episode where (spoiler alert) he unexpectedly succeeds to the premiership after one of the obvious front runners is knocked out of contention. The scenario is indeed reminiscent of the position of Herbert Morrison, who was deputy leader of the Labour Party and for years the assumed heir apparent to Clement Attlee. It is now generally accepted that Attlee remained as leader just long enough to ensure that this succession did not occur.

But whilst he ultimately failed to secure the prize, Morrison did actually serve as leader of the Labour Party, albeit briefly. On 7 December 1955, six months after Labour had lost another general election, Attlee summoned a special meeting of the shadow Cabinet to inform them that he was resigning the leadership. On the same day, it was announced by Downing Street that he was being granted an earldom by the Queen. For the next week, before Labour MPs voted in the leadership election, Morrison became acting leader and took Attlee's place on the opposition front bench at question time.

Now that we have reached post-war British politics, the names of the opposition leaders on our list become more reliably familiar – to me, at least. I also have something of a local connection to Morrison, who lived for most of his career in Eltham, south-east London, as I have for the last twenty years. If you walk from the train station along Archery Road towards the high street, there is now a blue plaque on one of the houses on the right-hand side, marking Morrison's old house. An elderly acquaintance once told me they remembered the days when a policeman stood outside, guarding the senior Cabinet minister. This wasn't the only address in the area at which he lived, either: I soon discovered that he previously lived on Well Hall Road and, later in life, moved to Colepits Wood Road. In the years when I was a local councillor (before the electorate administered a cure) I represented all three of these addresses, and I sometimes wondered what it might have been like for my predecessors to find themselves canvassing him for his vote.

Morrison was a giant of the Labour Party during the middle of the twentieth century and could well have become Prime Minister. The fact that he did not was a considerable disappointment to him, despite having enjoyed a successful political career by any other measure. His achievements certainly made an impact on a young member of his family: his grandson Peter Mandelson, who would play a leading role in a future Labour government. He recalled, 'As a young boy, I would come to feel pride, respect and sometimes awe at my grandfather's political status and accomplishments.'[1] Mandelson's mother was

Morrison's only child, but their relationship was somewhat strained, and his visits to see them were fairly infrequent.

There were, however, a number of parallels between the two Labour politicians – both of whom served in high office under landslide-winning Prime Ministers. Morrison was born in 1888 in Stockwell, Lambeth, where ninety-one years later Mandelson took his first steps in elected politics as a Labour councillor. Morrison's father was a police constable and a Conservative supporter, and the young Herbert rebelled strongly against this background. After leaving school at fourteen and working as an errand boy, he became a supporter of the radical Social Democratic Federation and the Independent Labour Party. He was a conscientious objector during the First World War and worked in a market garden for its duration.

He carved out a long career in local government, which began when he became Mayor of the Metropolitan Borough of Hackney, 1920–21. He was then elected to the London County Council (LCC) in 1922, which would become a lifelong association. He then briefly entered the House of Commons the following year as MP for Hackney South, before losing the seat in 1924.

He was back in the Commons in 1929 and became Minister for Transport in the second Labour government. In this role, Morrison developed a reputation as an effective administrator, pushing through a landmark piece of legislation in the form of the Road Traffic Act 1930, which abolished speed limits for cars, introduced the first Highway Code and created new offences of dangerous and reckless driving. He also attempted to reform public transport in London by proposing the creation of a new public corporation to bring together the provision of most passenger transport services in the capital. This failed to pass before the fall of the Labour government in 1931, but it was taken up by the succeeding National Government and led to the establishment of the London Passenger Transport Board, known as London Transport, in 1933.

Like many of his colleagues, Morrison lost his seat in the 1931 Labour wipeout and turned his attention back to the LCC, where Labour won an unexpected victory at the elections in 1934, making Morrison its first Labour leader. He set about an ambitious programme of reforms, from the creation of the green belt to the beginnings of slum clearance and the building of new homes and schools. One of his most prominent achievements was winning a long-running battle with central government over the financing of a replacement for the old Waterloo Bridge, allowing work to begin on the project, which would not be completed until 1945.

In the meantime, Morrison returned to Parliament in 1935 and contested the subsequent leadership election against Clement Attlee and Arthur Greenwood. Despite the support of a number of influential Labour MPs, his chances were damaged by having been absent from the previous parliament, and in the first ballot he trailed in second place with forty-four votes to Attlee's fifty-eight, with Greenwood on thirty-three. In the second round, Greenwood's support went almost completely to Attlee, who emerged victorious on eighty-eight votes to Morrison's forty-eight. Part of the reason for his rejection might have been the perception that he was more committed to his career as the leader of London's local government, but his use of a magazine article to attack the left of the party following the general election also made him some enemies.

Turning down nomination as deputy leader, he returned his attention once more to London politics and to sharpening Labour's campaigning techniques in the capital, using advertising agencies to create posters highlighting his administration's achievements. This effort was rewarded at the LCC elections in 1937, where Labour won more seats and retained control of County Hall. But Morrison had not given up on the leadership of the parliamentary party, and as the clouds of war gathered in the following years, his supporters began a media briefing campaign suggesting that he would be a more formidable opponent for the government. This culminated in a number of direct attacks on Attlee by the Labour MP Ellen Wilkinson, a close friend (and perhaps more) of Morrison, who wrote in 1939:

> I wonder what Mr Chamberlain would think if he were informed that in future he would have to face daily a Herbert Morrison, that superb political organiser, at last induced to give the Front Opposition Bench the gifts that have made him such an administrative success in the LCC.[2]

This effort was counterproductive, increasing suspicion of Morrison and bolstering support for Attlee, who received a renewed vote of confidence from Labour's National Executive Committee (NEC). When war came, Attlee made it clear that Labour would not join the government under Chamberlain, and Morrison played a part the following year in the events that brought down the Prime Minister, by making a highly critical intervention in the infamous Norway debate in May 1940, which brought about the government's downfall.

In the coalition government that was then formed under Churchill, Morrison was first appointed Minister of Supply but was only in that position for a matter of months before being promoted to Home Secretary at the start of October, just a few weeks into the Blitz. This crucial role played to his strengths of organisation and communication, as well as to his experience and contacts in local government. For the next five years he toured bombed cities, took control of and reorganised fire and rescue services, and skilfully navigated the many challenges of war on the home front. He also became a literal household name, with the indoor table-like 'Morrison shelters' (used as an alternative to the outdoor Anderson shelters during air raids) named after him.

Alongside his major role in government, he also continued to pay attention to the Labour Party's organisation, attending NEC meetings and policy committees to develop plans for post-war reconstruction. He suffered a setback when he was beaten by Arthur Greenwood in a contest to become party treasurer in 1943, but he remained a key figure in planning for the coming general election as the war ended, chairing the campaign and policy committees and producing the first draft of the manifesto. He succeeded Greenwood as deputy leader in May 1945.

As Labour stormed to its landslide victory in July 1945, Morrison plotted an audacious coup for the leadership. He had written to Attlee in advance to inform him that, in his view, the new parliamentary party should have the opportunity to elect a new leader and that he would himself be accepting nomination for the post. He wrote, 'I am animated solely by considerations of the interests of the Party, and regard for their democratic rights, and not by any personal unfriendliness towards yourself.'[3] A meeting was called at Labour headquarters at Transport House, where Attlee told his colleagues he was due to be called to the palace that evening following Churchill's resignation. Morrison repeated his call for a new leadership election and insisted that Attlee should not accept a commission to form a new government, with the threat that he and his supporters would refuse to serve if Attlee did so.

During the argument, Morrison was called away to answer a telephone call, and in his absence, Ernest Bevin told Attlee he must go to the palace straight away. He did so, seeing the king and accepting the premiership before heading to a victory rally at Westminster Central Hall, where amid wild cheering he announced, 'I have just left the

Palace.' This news came as an unwelcome surprise to Morrison, who had just told a colleague 'we cannot have this man as our leader', but it was too late.[4] The attempt had failed, and Attlee was Prime Minister. It is an extraordinarily dramatic story and one which I have long felt cries out to be dramatised in a lavish feature film. (If anyone reading this decides to take up the challenge, I'll settle for a cut of the proceeds and a cameo appearance as the Labour MP who tells Morrison the game is up.)

Having failed to secure the premiership for himself, Morrison continued agitating for a leadership election, whilst telling Attlee he wanted to be made Foreign Secretary. Instead, he was appointed Lord President of the Council, Leader of the House of Commons and de facto Deputy Prime Minister. He spent the next five years playing a key role in domestic policy, overseeing the government's nationalisation programme and chairing Cabinet committees. He also took pride in the organisation of the Festival of Britain on the South Bank in 1951, whose attractions included the Dome of Discovery. This provides another irresistible parallel with his grandson, with Mandelson becoming Minister for the Millennium Dome in the run-up to the year 2000.

Morrison did eventually get his wish to become Foreign Secretary, succeeding Bevin in March 1951, but he had little affinity with the job and his tenure was cut short by Labour losing the general election in October of that year. He was still seen by many as being Attlee's natural successor and might have taken over at that point had Attlee stood down. But crucially, Attlee did not, continuing on to fight the 1955 general election. By the time he did retire, following the 1955 election, there was a younger generation of Labour politicians on the rise, and the leadership slipped from Morrison's grasp for the last time.

Joining Morrison in the contest to succeed Attlee were two bitter rivals, Nye Bevan and Hugh Gaitskell, who represented the competing factions which divided Labour throughout this period. In a surprising bit of last-minute intrigue, Bevan offered to stand aside to allow Morrison to become leader, on the condition that Gaitskell did the same. The gambit failed, with Gaitskell rejecting the idea, and *The Times* reported on how badly it had gone down at Westminster, with MPs seeing it as 'no more than a device' to prevent Gaitskell from winning so Bevan could keep his own leadership chances alive. It went on to note:

> There is great sympathy with the claims of Mr Morrison to the leadership, but the predominant feeling is that his age is against him and that the time has come to elect a younger man who will be able to lead the party for a long time to come. Mr Morrison is 67 and Mr Gaitskell 49. The supporters of Mr Bevan believe that if Mr Morrison were to become leader for a few years, Mr Bevan – who is 58 – might so consolidate his position that he would have better prospects in a deferred contest with Mr Gaitskell for the leadership.[5]

Such calculations and plotting remain all-too familiar in leadership elections to this day. In the end, Morrison was pretty much humiliated, gaining just forty votes and finishing in last place behind Bevan on seventy and Gaitskell on 157. It was fewer votes than he had managed twenty years earlier, despite the parliamentary party being twice the size. He resigned as deputy leader and retired to the back benches, where he spoke rarely. He stepped down from the Commons in 1959 and was made a peer as Baron Morrison of Lambeth, using his last years to campaign against plans for the replacement of the LCC with the Greater London Council. In this he failed, but in a poignant coincidence the LCC was formally abolished at the end of March 1965, the same month that Morrison died. He was cremated at Eltham and his ashes scattered on the Thames in front of County Hall.

32

Hugh Gaitskell

Labour, Leader of the Opposition 1955–63

It is an incident straight out of a James Bond story. Arriving in a tropical island paradise, our hero embarks on a covert mission. Known as something of a ladies' man with a love for the high life, he leaves a secluded beachside villa in the company of a glamorous married woman, with whom he is having a clandestine affair. As they drive out of the gates of the property, a group of hostile operatives are on the lookout for them, and a high-speed chase ensues along the coastal roads. He shakes them off, drops off his lover and after hiding out for a time in a remote building, manages to make his way back to the villa, where to avoid the hostile forces on the lookout for him, he hides in the bushes outside until he can be rescued.

The man's name was Gaitskell: Hugh Gaitskell, and the James Bond references are no accident. It was 1960, and the Leader of Her Majesty's Opposition was in Jamaica, staying at Goldeneye, the villa owned by Ian Fleming. Gaitskell had been driving Fleming's wife Annie to go swimming when they spotted paparazzi photographers at the gate and panicked. He dropped her off at the post office, then fled, ending up at a hardware shop twelve miles away. Picking up an urgent message to call him there, a friend telephoned the shop and asked if Mr Gaitskell was there. The bemused owner is recorded to have given the superb reply, 'You mean de strange Englishman who is hiding behind de keg of nails?' Gaitskell's friend came to pick him up, but as they drove back to Goldeneye the photographers were still at the gate. Gaitskell refused the suggestion he should lie down in the back of the vehicle and instead announced 'I will hide here' and leapt out to hide in the bushes until Annie came to find him.

It is a glorious tale and one which might have reached a wider audience at the time. On being told what had happened, Fleming, no fan of Gaitskell, responded, 'Silly bloody ass. Good story though' and suggested cabling it to the *Sunday Times*. He was dissuaded, but it gives a good insight into what he thought of his wife's adventures with the Labour leader.[*] The episode is made all the more intriguing by the fact that Goldeneye already has a place in British political history, as the place where Anthony Eden had retreated to convalesce on doctor's orders after the Suez Crisis in 1956, just prior to his resignation. We therefore had a situation where it seems the creator of James Bond was making his house available to the Prime Minister whilst his wife made herself available to the Leader of the Opposition.

Hugh Gaitskell was the Labour Leader of the Opposition for seven years and stood a very good chance of becoming Prime Minister at the general election in 1964. His tragic early death in 1963 deprived him of that opportunity and instead propelled Harold Wilson into the Labour leadership, from which he went on to win four elections and serve as Prime Minister for a total of eight years. The question of how those years might have been different had Gaitskell lived remains a perennial 'what if?' of British politics. I sometimes hear people say that

---

[*] The whole extraordinary tale is told in Morris Cargill's memoir *Jamaica Farewell* (Lyle Stuart, 1978).

historians should not engage in counterfactual speculation, but with respect, I think that's nonsense. The value of such discussions is in how effectively they highlight the significance of key events and individuals and what they tell us about the importance of time and chance. When history takes a sudden and unexpected turn, it is inevitable we will wonder about the path not taken.

1963 was full of such political forks in the road. Gaitskell's death in January was followed in October by the resignation of the Prime Minister, Harold Macmillan, who believed he was dying (but wasn't). Then in November, President Kennedy was assassinated in the United States. In the space of a year, there was new leadership on both sides of the Atlantic and on both sides of British politics, all of it occasioned by uninvited reminders of mortality. Might Macmillan have gone on to defeat Gaitskell in 1964? Or might a second-term President Kennedy and new Prime Minister Gaitskell have formed a transatlantic special relationship that would have defined the 1960s and shaped the progress of the Cold War? We can only speculate, and we shouldn't feel ashamed of doing so.

Hugh Todd Naylor Gaitskell (a superb name) was born in Kensington in April 1906, into an affluent family of colonial administrators. He attended Winchester College and then Oxford, where he studied PPE – now a familiar trajectory for aspirant Prime Ministers. He joined the Labour Party around the time of the general strike in 1926, a transformative event in his life which saw him committing himself to the cause of socialism, declaring rather dramatically in a letter to an aunt, 'Henceforth my future is with the working classes.' Other members of his family were less than pleased, believing that he was 'betraying his class'.[1]

After graduating with a first, he worked for a year as a tutor with the Workers' Educational Association in the coalfields of Nottinghamshire, before being appointed as a lecturer in political economy at University College London. He remained there for eleven years, becoming head of department, and during this time made his first attempt at entering Parliament, standing unsuccessfully as the Labour candidate for Chatham in 1935. He became active amongst left-wing thinkers, helping to run the New Fabian Research Bureau and then the National Institute of Economic and Social Research and contributing to the development of Labour policy, particularly in Keynesian economics.

At the outbreak of the Second World War, he became a temporary civil servant working for Labour's Hugh Dalton at the Ministry for Economic Warfare and then the Board of Trade. In 1945 he was elected as Labour MP for Leeds South, and his experience of Whitehall and high-level contacts brought him rapid promotion. He became Minister for Fuel and Power in 1947, then when the Chancellor, Stafford Cripps, became ill in 1949 he was one of three young ministers who took over many of his responsibilities – the others being Harold Wilson and Douglas Jay.

After the 1950 general election he was promoted again to become Minister for Economic Affairs, bringing him into conflict for the first time with Nye Bevan over moves to curtail rising NHS spending. When Cripps resigned due to ill health in October, Gaitskell was appointed Chancellor at the age of forty-four. The dramatic promotion further antagonised Bevan and set the scene for their lengthy and damaging feud. The clash was sparked by Gaitskell's Budget in 1951, in which taxes were raised to pay for increased military spending on the Korean War, and NHS charges were introduced for dental treatment and spectacles. The row over the issue led to Bevan's resignation from the Cabinet, shortly followed by Wilson. Meanwhile, Michael Foot, then the editor of the left-wing *Tribune*, wrote an editorial comparing Gaitskell to Philip Snowden, Ramsay MacDonald's Chancellor in 1931.

Labour's loss of the general election in October 1951 brought Gaitskell's time at the Treasury to an end, and in opposition the battlelines had been drawn for the factional infighting between 'Bevanites' and 'Gaitskellites' that was to dominate the Labour Party during the next five years. Whilst Bevan sought to bolster his left-wing support in the party's constituencies, Gaitskell nurtured the support of the moderate left in the parliamentary party, with his house in Frognal Gardens, Hampstead becoming the centre of efforts to defeat the left. This came to a head in 1955, when Bevan was stripped of the Labour whip for voting against the leadership's position on nuclear weapons.

With another general election defeat in 1955, the debate over the future of the party intensified. Gaitskell argued strongly against calls for a more left-wing programme, insisting that elections are won in the centre ground of politics. When Attlee retired in December of that year, Gaitskell's support amongst Labour MPs was overwhelming, and in the leadership election he defeated Bevan by 157 votes to seventy, with Herbert Morrison, as we saw, trailing in a poor third with forty votes.

Long books can and have been written about Gaitskell's seven years as Leader of the Opposition, during which he made a concerted effort to modernise the Labour Party and redefine its mission for the second half of the twentieth century. His first challenge came with the Suez Crisis, when Eden misled the country over the UK's role in conspiring to invade Egypt to retake the canal. Gaitskell was outraged to find Eden had lied to him in private and called for his resignation, but he faced criticism himself for seeming to have shifted his position from one of support for the invasion.

His long feud with Bevan was eased during the following years, however, with his rival accepting the role of shadow Foreign Secretary in 1956 and breaking with much of the left the following year by rejecting unilateral nuclear disarmament. Their partial reconciliation allowed the party to enter the 1959 general election more united than before, but it suffered another major defeat, with the Conservatives under Harold Macmillan increasing their majority to over 100 seats. The rising prosperity of the country had played to the government's advantage, and the Conservatives had mounted a concerted publicity campaign to convince the electorate not to risk giving Labour control of the economy. Gaitskell's leadership was criticised as being too earnest and unexcitingly technocratic compared to the distinctive image of 'SuperMac', the Prime Minister. Macmillan himself gave a critical assessment of his opponent, commenting:

> The trouble about Mr Gaitskell is that he is going through all the motions of being a Government when he isn't a Government. It is bad enough having to behave like a Government when one is a Government. The whole point of being in opposition is that one can have fun and lend colour to what one says and does. To be colourful; that is the opportunity opposition gives you.[2]

The criticism is perceptive about the art of opposition, and certainly Labour's ingrained aversion to using modern methods of political communication had inhibited them from projecting a dynamic image of their leader or their policies. But it is ironic that Gaitskell should be criticised for not being 'colourful' enough, given his private life could certainly be characterised in that way. As we saw at the opening of the chapter, he enjoyed the good life, frequently going out dancing and enjoying good food, lively conversation and the company of glamorous women. His affair with Ann Fleming was well known in Westminster and caused concern amongst his colleagues, who felt his high society lifestyle did not fit well with Labour politics. But the fact he exuded personal warmth and was excellent company won him many loyal friends and helped smooth over political disagreements.

The 1959 defeat shook confidence in his leadership, but he responded with boldness, diagnosing the party's problem not as a lack of hardline socialism but rather a lack of boldness in modernising its policies to appeal to the mainstream majority. In particular, he felt its dogmatic attachment to nationalisation of industry was off-putting to voters, and he sought to break the attachment by ditching Clause IV of the party's constitution, which enshrined this aspiration. Faced with a predictable rebellion from the left and from several trade unions, he ultimately dropped the proposal, but it signalled his modernising intent.

More confrontation was to follow when he sought to oppose moves from the left of the party to adopt a position in favour of unilateral nuclear disarmament. This gave rise to one of his best-remembered speeches, in which he unleashed a heartfelt plea to the party to back him and the majority of his parliamentary colleagues, asking, 'Do you think that we can become overnight the pacifists, unilateralists and fellow travellers that other people are? How wrong can you be? As wrong as you are about the attitude of the British people.' As *The Times* noted, 'It was a terribly difficult speech Mr Gaitskell had to make, and in the 55 minutes he stood in the limelight he was fighting every inch of the way with the integrity and honesty the parliamentary party have learnt to expect from him. He evaded nothing.'[3] Amid a chorus of heckles and boos from left-wing delegates, he concluded with the most famous of lines:

There are some of us ... who will fight and fight and fight again to save the Party we love ... to bring back sanity and honesty and dignity, so that our Party with its great past may retain its glory and its greatness. It is in that spirit that I ask the delegates who are still free to decide how they vote to support what I believe to be a realistic policy on defence ... and to reject what I regard as the suicidal path of unilateral disarmament, which will leave our country defenceless and alone.[4]

It was a stunning piece of oratory, and as he finished he was greeted by wild cheering from two thirds of the audience and the singing of 'For He's a Jolly Good Fellow', whilst his opponents booed. The party's divisions were on open display. When the votes came in, the leadership was defeated, but the margin was narrower than had been feared, with the trade union votes being decisive. Meanwhile, nearly two thirds of constituency delegates had backed him. It was a hollow victory for the left, and the parliamentary party disregarded the result. The following month, Wilson challenged him for the leadership of the party and was defeated by 166 votes to eighty-one, securing Gaitskell a renewed mandate for his leadership.

There were other notable events during the remainder of his leadership, not least his last conference speech in 1962, in which he declared that membership of the European Common Market would be 'the end of a thousand years of history'.[5] But it is his fight to reform and modernise the Labour Party that stands out as his most significant legacy and a forerunner of many later battles along similar fault lines. As the Conservative government grew tired and unpopular, it seemed his fight for the centre ground might take him and the party back to Downing Street.

Then in early January 1963, shortly after returning from a visit to the Soviet Union for talks with Nikita Khrushchev, he fell ill after contracting a virus and was admitted to Middlesex Hospital in London. For several weeks the media charted his progress as he fought what is now believed to have been a flare-up of the autoimmune disease lupus. On 15 January his condition was reported to have worsened, and a statement issued via the Labour Party said it was 'now giving rise to some anxiety'.[6] The next day, a medical bulletin described the outlook as 'very grave', whilst a Labour spokesman said their leader's condition was 'critical but not hopeless'.[7] On 17 January he suffered renal failure, and a kidney machine was brought to the hospital to treat him. But to no avail: at 9.12 p.m. on Friday 19 January, he died of heart failure.

The death of the Leader of the Opposition at the age of just fifty-six triggered a wave of shock and mourning. Even his enemies in the party and his political opponents were moved by the tragedy. Inevitable conspiracy theories have since circulated suggesting his death was some kind of convoluted Soviet plot, but these are perhaps better suited to a James Bond novel than to reality. What is clear is that a highly consequential Labour leader, standing on the brink of power, was cut down in his prime. Fate has played some cruel tricks on politicians, but this was a particularly devastating one.

During his 1960 stay in Jamaica, Gaitskell had escaped the press long enough to have been taken on an idyllic trip to Port Antonio, rafting down the river and stopping to swim in clear pools and eat freshly cooked fish. His host, Morris Cargill, recalls asking him during a relaxed moment how an honest man with an open mind could put up with the 'bullshit and boredom' of politics and whether he really wanted to be Prime Minister. Gaitskell reportedly replied, dabbling his feet in the river:

> I think that politics, like marriage, is something people should go into when they are young before they have learned the disadvantages … But I must confess that I have a craving to be Prime Minister of England. Yes, I really want to be. To be Prime Minister of England is such an immense honour.[8]

His early death denied him that opportunity, but it also frustrated his aims of reforming the Labour Party and in doing so, changed the course of political history. Whilst the story might have been embellished for publication, he reportedly went on to tell Cargill that he had a 'negative reason' for wanting to make it to No. 10, saying, 'I must stop that bastard Harold Wilson from becoming Prime Minister.'[9]

33

George Brown

Labour, Acting Leader of the Opposition
18 January–14 February 1963

The death of Hugh Gaitskell brought mixed emotions for many Labour figures. First there was shock and personal sadness, but, being politicians, there were also political calculations to be made. Tony Benn, who had been highly critical of the late leader, recorded in his diary, 'His death seems a disaster because it looks as if George Brown will succeed him and for a number of reasons he is totally unsuited to be Leader of the Party.'[1] The prospect of George Brown succeeding to the leadership also alarmed allies of Gaitskell, who were more blunt about their misgivings, with Anthony Crosland asking, 'Are we going to be led by a neurotic drunk?'[2]

For the moment at least, they were. Until the leadership contest was held, Brown was now acting leader of the party. A centrist ally of Gaitskell, he had been elected deputy leader following Nye Bevan's death in 1960 and had been re-elected in the two following years, despite being challenged by candidates of the party's left. In the first of these challenges, in 1961, he easily defeated Barbara Castle, but a year later he had faced tougher competition from Harold Wilson, who ran him closer, winning

103 votes to Brown's 133. Now, just two and a half months later, the two of them were again in competition, this time for the leadership itself.

Clearly, questions of policy and political ideology would be important. Wilson was a man of the party's left, who had challenged Gaitskell for the leadership in 1960, whilst Brown was from the Gaitskellite right of the party. On the face of it, this pointed to victory for the incumbent deputy, who could be expected to inherit Gaitskell's support and present himself as the unifying continuity candidate. But as the responses of his colleagues showed, there was more than that at issue.

Brown's reputation for drunkenness and erratic behaviour had become well established and was serious enough to cause a number of his natural supporters profound concern. Many of them voted for James Callaghan in the first round of voting, leaving Brown trailing behind Wilson. In the final ballot, with Callaghan eliminated, Wilson picked up the bulk of his votes and defeated Brown by a comfortable margin. In the years that followed, as Brown continued to serve as deputy leader and in senior ministerial positions in Wilson's government, the worries about his temperamental suitability for high office were largely borne out.

Brown was born in Lambeth in 1914 into a working-class family, in which his father was a staunch trade unionist. He left school at fifteen and joined a firm in the City as a clerk but was sacked for encouraging colleagues to join a union. After working as a fur salesman, he became a trade union organiser in the late 1930s and became active in constituency Labour politics, making a notable speech at the 1939 party conference condemning the actions of the extreme left.

During the Second World War he sought to join the RAF, but the Minister of Labour, Ernest Bevin, kept him and other trade union officials in their jobs assisting with industrial relations. In the 1945 landslide Labour victory, he was elected to Parliament for the seat of Belper in Derbyshire, which he gained from the Conservatives. He served as parliamentary private secretary to the Chancellor, Hugh Dalton, and was then appointed as a junior agriculture minister. When Ernest Bevin died in 1951, Brown was made Minister for Works in the reshuffle (outside the Cabinet) and served for the six months until Labour's defeat in the 1951 election.

In the fractious struggle between the Bevanites and Gaitskellites during Labour's period of opposition, Brown was very strongly on the Gaitskellite wing and became a close ally of Gaitskell himself, who perhaps found the pugnacious trade union MP a refreshing and useful contrast to the intellectual Hampstead set who comprised his political circle of supporters. Brown busied himself in the fight against Bevan, and when Gaitskell won the leadership, Brown was elected first to the shadow Cabinet and then, in 1960, to the post of deputy leader. Though he defeated the attempts by Castle and Wilson to displace him, he remained a polarising figure, with concerns about his political stance combined with growing chatter about his drinking.

After Gaitskell's death, Brown could have projected himself as his natural successor and a party unifier, making the most of his position as acting leader during the contest. Instead, he was said to have campaigned too aggressively, with his 'arm-twisting' going down badly with colleagues – as did the crass campaign slogan deployed by one of his backers, who is said to have told MPs, 'To keep the spirit of Gaitskell alive, vote for Brown.'[3]

It was Wilson who surprisingly emerged as the unifying candidate, carefully reassuring Gaitskellites that his election would not reopen old divisions. Brown, by contrast, was far from magnanimous in defeat, refusing to confirm whether he would continue as deputy and disappearing off to Scotland for five days to nurse his grievances, presumably with the aid of a few bottles of Scotch. When he returned from what was widely seen as a sulk, he asked to be shadow Foreign Secretary, but Wilson had already appointed Patrick Gordon Walker, and Brown had to settle for shadow Home Secretary.

When Labour entered government the following year, Wilson made him Deputy Prime Minister and Secretary of State for the new Department of Economic Affairs. In office, he played an important role in developing the government's 'National Plan', but in 1966 a financial crisis split the Cabinet. Brown sent a resignation letter to Wilson, only to publicly retract it hours later, after meeting the Prime Minister, and tell reporters waiting outside No. 10, 'We've decided at the end of the day that my duty is to stay with my colleagues in the Cabinet.'[4] Later accounts suggest that the letter had been an attempt to bounce Wilson into making concessions and that Brown had retracted it when his bluff was called.

Shortly afterwards he was moved to become Foreign Secretary, the job he had coveted, but his tenure was marked by increasingly erratic behaviour, exacerbated by his drinking. The frequently cited tale of him drunkenly propositioning the Cardinal Archbishop of Lima at a diplomatic reception is sadly unsubstantiated (and bears all the hallmarks of being apocryphal), but there were plenty of other public embarrassments. These led *Private Eye* to coin the phrase 'tired and emotional' to describe his behaviour – a euphemism which has proved a more enduring legacy than many of Brown's other achievements in office. Even *The Times*, which was supportive of his skills and moderate politics throughout his career, had to concede his flaws when seeking in an editorial to argue 'the case for George Brown':

No one has ever been met who behaves like Mr Brown, and while his behaviour is often endearing it is sometimes extremely offensive … Indeed, he is impossible; he is 'too much'; one would not invite him to cucumber sandwiches with one's maiden aunt – but he is a remarkable man with some of the qualities and all the courage of a great statesman.[5]

His erratic habits of threatening resignation and behaving boorishly whilst drunk combined to bring about his downfall. On 14 March 1968, another currency crisis prompted Wilson to take emergency measures, including declaring the next day a bank holiday in order to close down the London foreign exchange market. As events unfolded into the evening, the Foreign Secretary could not be located, and the clear implication that he was drunk was reinforced by reports that he was only 'so-so' when officials had last seen him. A meeting of the Privy Council was convened without him at 12.15 a.m. to declare the bank holiday.

When he discovered what had occurred, Brown reacted furiously, gathering together a group of other Cabinet ministers who had also been excluded from the emergency discussions and heading over with them to confront Wilson at Downing Street. At this meeting, in the early hours of the morning, Brown did a poor job of protesting his sobriety, engaging in 'a good deal of incoherent shouting' at the Prime Minister for not having contacted him and widening his attack to denounce Wilson's style of government. When the Prime Minister insisted he had tried to contact him, Brown refused to believe him. Wilson recorded later:

> He accused me of lying and I was not having that … He got up in the most abusive way and I told him to sit down and that I was not having him refusing to accept the truth of what I had said. He was shouting resignation threats, attacking the decision taken, and then he came round the table to leer at me and said we had made a great blunder tonight…[6]

Others present said that Brown stood 'breathing flame and fury down Harold Wilson's neck', and it looked for a moment as though the country's chief diplomat was about to punch the Prime Minister.[7] Instead, he stormed out of the Cabinet room and slammed the door.

As resignations go, it was about as dramatic as it could have been, and this time there was no going back. When Brown sent an ambiguous letter the next day suggesting that they 'part company', Wilson refused to play the usual game of dissuading him and simply accepted the resignation.

It was a farcical end to Brown's career, and he never held office again. He lost his seat at the 1970 election and went to the Lords as Lord George-Brown.* Six years later he left the Labour Party in protest at trade union reform, but his announcement was overshadowed when he fell over and ended up in the gutter in front of newspaper photographers. *The Times* the next day printed an editorial which denounced those papers that printed the pictures and expressed sympathy with his position:

> Perhaps Lord George-Brown had been drinking. If we had severed the loyalties and service of a lifetime and felt emotions of the depth and passion that Lord George-Brown feels, we would not expect to be altogether sober ... the truth is that when it comes to the heart of the matter, to the courage that supports a nation, Lord George-Brown drunk is a better man than the Prime Minister sober.[8]

Such sympathies were rare, and most viewed him as an irrelevant and sad figure of fun, which is how he is remembered today. The damage that alcohol did to his career and reputation ultimately did the same to his body, and he died of liver disease in 1985.

---

* The unusual title arose from his desire to be known after his elevation as 'Lord George Brown' (an affectation that has since become prevalent in reference to life peers) rather than the proper form of 'Lord Brown'. After negotiations with a disapproving Garter King of Arms, he was finally allowed to adopt the hyphenated 'George-Brown' as his title, on the condition he first change his surname by deed poll to 'George-Brown', which he duly did. He thereafter became George Alfred George-Brown, Baron George-Brown.

34

Robert Carr

Conservative, Acting Leader of the Opposition
4–11 February 1975

Back to the pub quiz trivia now, for what will be a rather short chapter on another short-serving leader. The question 'Who preceded
Margaret Thatcher as Leader of the Opposition?' is one which I believe even the most nerdy of political students would be unlikely to
answer with the name 'Robert Carr'. Frankly, the question 'Who was
Robert Carr?' would probably be equally challenging to them. Unlike
George Brown and other temporary incumbents, he does not appear
on any list of Leaders of the Opposition that I have seen (including
the internet's go-to oracle, Wikipedia). But this is my book, my rules.

We are leaping ahead twelve years from Brown's brief tenure as
Labour leader to the resignation of Edward Heath as Conservative
leader in February 1975, after he was outpolled by Margaret Thatcher
in the first ballot of the party's leadership contest. Instead of waiting
for the final outcome, he immediately began what became known as
his 'long sulk', later writing that he had 'arranged for Robert Carr to
handle the front bench of the party until the election of a new leader
was confirmed', a move which 'enabled the party to fulfil its obligations

as Her Majesty's Opposition' during the interim.[1] Whilst *The Times* noted that Heath 'continues nominally as Opposition leader', it explained that 'in fact he has asked Mr Robert Carr, the shadow Chancellor of the Exchequer, to undertake his duties in the House'.[2] And indeed, it was Carr who stood in at Prime Minister's Questions two days later, with Heath absent.

But who was he? Ironically, he began life in Finchley, later to be represented in Parliament by Thatcher. Born there in 1916, he was bound for Westminster at a young age – the school, that is – and then went to Cambridge to study natural science, law and economics. He joined the family manufacturing firm as a management trainee and continued to work there during the Second World War, after a lung disorder prevented him serving in the military.

After the war, Carr became a Conservative activist in Barnet and was shortlisted for the parliamentary seat in 1946, coming second to Reginald Maudling, a fellow One Nation Conservative, to whom he remained close. He was then selected for Mitcham in south London and won the seat in 1950, holding it until it was abolished in 1970, at which point he moved to neighbouring Carshalton.

Arriving in the Commons, his maiden speech impressed the Foreign Secretary, Anthony Eden, who appointed him as his parliamentary private secretary in 1951. Eden retained him in the role when he became Prime Minister in 1955, until Carr was promoted to become a junior minister at the Ministry of Labour. He remained in that post under Harold Macmillan but resigned in 1958 to return to the family firm as chairman for a few years, before re-entering government in May 1963 as Secretary for Technical Co-operation, responsible for overseas aid.

In opposition, he backed Reginald Maudling in the Conservative leadership election in 1965, but when Edward Heath won, Carr was appointed spokesman on aviation, before being promoted to shadow Minister for Labour in 1967. When the Conservatives won the 1970 general election, he joined the Cabinet as Secretary of State for Employment, navigating the minefield of industrial relations of those years. His Industrial Relations Act provoked strikes, protests and even terrorist attacks by anarchist group The Angry Brigade, who left two bombs outside his house in 1971, blowing in his windows and nearly killing his wife.

He was then moved to become Leader of the House of Commons and, later, Home Secretary, replacing his friend Maudling, who was forced to resign in 1972. He pursued a liberal agenda, welcoming Ugandan refugees fleeing Idi Amin's regime, a stance for which he was attacked by Enoch Powell.

After the Conservatives lost the election in 1974, Carr was made shadow Chancellor. And so it was that he was an obvious contender to become acting Leader of the Opposition for a week in February 1975, before Margaret Thatcher took over. In a final irony, Thatcher had been demoted to become shadow Chief Secretary to the Treasury after the election, so Carr was her boss during the leadership election. As a One Nation moderate, he was no fan of her politics, and the feeling was clearly mutual as she failed to offer him a senior position, despite him making clear that he would have liked to be shadow Foreign Secretary. Denied that move, he essentially retired from politics, accepting a peerage and resuming his business career. He did however lend his support to the One Nation cause in the party by becoming a founding member of the Tory Reform Group later that year.

He served as a director of a number of companies in the years afterwards, including Cadbury Schweppes, Securicor and Prudential Assurance, and lived on into a ripe old age, dying at the age of ninety-five in 2012.

35

Michael Foot

Labour, Leader of the Opposition 1980–83

First of all, it was not actually a donkey jacket. If you know the story, this might appear pedantic, but in any case, let me set the scene. One of the defining images of Michael Foot's leadership of the opposition was him standing at the Cenotaph in November 1981 alongside the Prime Minister, Margaret Thatcher, as they prepared to lay wreaths on behalf of the nation on Remembrance Sunday. His choice of outfit prompted a backlash of critical comment, including from our friends at *The Times*, who observed the following day:

> The top brass of the Royal British Legion were not amused by Michael Foot's shambling performance at yesterday's Remembrance Day service at the Cenotaph in Whitehall. Dressed as if he had just returned from walking his dog on Hampstead Heath, in green donkey jacket, sneakers and Paisley tie, Foot looked distinctly ill at ease sandwiched between the Prime Minister and David Steel (in morning dress).[1]

The report also quoted the Labour MP for Derby South, Walter

Johnson, describing his leader as looking like 'an out of work navvy' and as showing 'gross discourtesy' to fallen servicemen and their families. But as the furore raged in the pages of the right-wing press, Foot was being done something of an injustice. In fact, the coat was a rather expensive garment, newly purchased from Harrods, and not everyone took such a negative view of it. Foot told friends that, at the drinks reception after the service, the Queen Mother had complimented him on it, saying it was 'a smart, sensible coat for a day like this'.[2] As he later recalled in the House of Commons, 'Ever since, I have always admired her taste more than I have that of my colleague who complained.'[3] Readers who wish to judge the matter for themselves can do so by visiting the People's History Museum in Manchester, to which Foot donated the coat, and where it remains proudly on display.

Alongside the unintentionally iconic coat, Michael Foot's contribution to British political folklore is tied to his disastrous performance at the 1983 general election, when Labour fell to just 27.6 per cent of the popular vote, lost sixty seats and gifted Thatcher a landslide majority of 144 seats. The blame for this was put squarely on Foot's leadership and on the left-wing manifesto dubbed 'the longest suicide note in history' by Labour MP Gerald Kaufman. Foot's tenure is now considered an exemplar of failure in opposition, which it certainly was, but it came at the end of a much more substantial and productive career.

Foot was born in 1913 in Plymouth, into an established political family. Their politics were progressive, and his father Isaac, a successful solicitor, later became Liberal MP for Bodmin and was briefly a minister in Ramsay MacDonald's National Government in the early 1930s. From him, Michael inherited a lifelong love of books, history and literature – as well as politics.

It was an intellectually stimulating and competitive household in which to grow up, and several of his siblings went on to have notable careers in public life. Of his three elder brothers, Dingle Foot would become a Liberal (and later Labour) MP and serve as Solicitor General; Hugh Foot would become governor of Cyprus and later a life peer and Foreign Office minister; and John Foot would also end up in the House of Lords as a Liberal peer. He also had two sisters, Margaret and Jennifer, and a younger brother, Christopher. Most of the children were given the middle name Mackintosh, the maiden name of their mother Eva – a proud matriarch, who strongly encouraged her children to strive for success. These expectations were however focused mainly on the boys, a not-uncommon attitude for the time, but one which Michael seems to have found unjust.

Academically gifted, he excelled during his time at boarding school, and he followed in his brothers' footsteps to Wadham College, Oxford, where he studied PPE. He developed his political activities at university, becoming president of the Liberal Club and later president of the Oxford Union. One of his close friends was John Cripps, son of the Labour politician Sir Stafford Cripps, and through this connection he was found a job after graduation, working as a clerk in a shipping company in Liverpool. The work was dull, but the experience of living in a working-class industrial city solidified his increasingly socialist views, and he joined the Labour Party in 1935.

That same year, he was chosen as the Labour candidate for Monmouth but lost heavily in the general election. He remained active in Labour politics, having become close to Stafford Cripps, and developed a close friendship at this time with a young socialist named Barbara Betts, later to become Barbara Castle. Meanwhile, he had embarked upon a career in journalism, writing for the *New Statesman* and then for *Tribune*, which launched in 1937 with backing from Cripps. Foot had also become close to Nye Bevan, who introduced him to the right-wing newspaper owner Lord Beaverbrook. Despite their very different politics, Beaverbrook was intrigued by the bright young socialist writer and began inviting him to his lavish country house parties, where influential senior Conservatives and establishment figures mixed with authors and other assorted intellectuals. Impressed by him, Beaverbrook recruited Foot as a feature writer on the *Evening Standard* and promoted him to editor in 1942.

Foot had volunteered for the army at the outbreak of the Second World War but was rejected on account of his asthma. He was no pacifist, as is clear from his involvement in a significant publication that appeared in July 1940. Entitled *Guilty Men*, it was a satirical tract written under the pseudonym 'Cato' which excoriated the pre-war proponents of appeasement. Foot was the lead author, alongside fellow journalists Peter Howard and Frank Owen. It was a huge success, selling 220,000 copies, and shaped the narrative around Neville Chamberlain and the Conservative governments of the 1930s for years to come.

In 1945, Foot was elected as Labour MP for Plymouth Devonport, and as a new MP allied himself with other left-wingers such as Richard Crossman and Barbara Castle, in what became known as the 'Keep Left' group. He married the socialist film producer Jill Craigie in 1949, forming a strong political and personal partnership that would last for the next fifty years.

He remained close to Bevan, becoming a loyal supporter of the Bevanite faction in the years of Labour infighting that followed Bevan's resignation in 1951. He suffered a setback when he lost his seat in the 1955 election, and with Gaitskell now Leader of the Labour Party, Foot occupied himself with the growing anti-nuclear movement, as a founder member of the Campaign for Nuclear Disarmament. He was thus devastated when Bevan, now a member of the shadow Cabinet, declared himself in favour of retaining nuclear weapons in 1957. The split from his hero was painful and included a furious row at Foot's flat, during which Bevan smashed one of Jill's antique chairs. They were reconciled shortly before Bevan's death in 1960, and it was with his former mentor's blessing that Foot succeeded him as MP for Ebbw Vale at the resulting by-election that year.

Back in Parliament, Foot resumed his activism as part of the Labour left and had the whip withdrawn in 1961 for voting against the army estimates. He was then nearly killed in a car accident in October 1963, which left him and Jill with serious injuries. From then on, he walked with a stick, and others also noted that he became a more settled character – less dogmatic and more mellow. Despite this, and despite the accession of the more left-wing Harold Wilson to the Labour leadership, he remained outside the government when Labour returned to power. He turned down a suggestion from Wilson the following year that he might accept office, citing his disagreement with the government's position on the Vietnam War. Instead, he remained the unofficial leader of the left in the Labour Party, continuing to campaign on various causes both as an MP and a journalist. These included opposition to the UK's membership of the European Common Market and an unlikely alliance with Enoch Powell to thwart attempts at House of Lords reform. During this time he also continued work on his authorised biography of Bevan.

The dawn of the 1970s heralded a late entry into the political mainstream for Foot, as Labour unexpectedly lost the general election, and he was elected to the shadow Cabinet in opposition. In 1972, he stood for the deputy leadership of the party but was defeated by Edward Short. After Wilson led the party back into power in 1974, Foot entered government for the first time at the age of sixty, as Secretary of State for Employment. This appointment was intended to appease the left of the party and the increasingly militant trade unions, and in this it was fairly successful, with his credentials lending him the stature to negotiate the government's 'social contract' and agreements on wage restraint. He also pushed through a number of flagship pieces of employment legislation, including the Health and Safety at Work Act and the Employment Protection Act, which, amongst other things, introduced statutory maternity pay and established the Advisory, Conciliation and Arbitration Service (ACAS).

During the 1975 referendum on continued membership of the European Economic Community, he allied himself with left-wing colleagues such as Tony Benn and Barbara Castle in supporting the No campaign. His main reason was what he saw as a threat to the sovereignty of Parliament, writing dramatically in *The Times* that:

> Whatever the outcome on June 5, historians looking back, and starting soon I believe, will be amazed that the British people were urged at such a time to tamper irreparably with their most precious institution; to see it circumscribed and contorted and elbowed off the centre of the stage ... It is as if in 1940 we had set fire to the place, as Hitler did with his Reichstag.[4]

Proponents of Godwin's Law might have something to say about that last sentence, and it is indeed jarring to see a Nazi comparison used by the author of *Guilty Men*, though this is perhaps why he used it. In any case, such arguments were not persuasive enough to avoid a resounding win by the Yes campaign the following month. This appeared to settle the matter, at least for the time being.

When Wilson unexpectedly resigned as Prime Minister in 1976, Foot stood in the leadership contest to succeed him and led in the first ballot, six votes ahead of James Callaghan. This lead was overturned as the other candidates withdrew or were eliminated, and in the final run-off, Callaghan defeated Foot by 176 votes to 137. Foot had, however, strengthened his place as a major figure in the party and was rewarded with a leading position in government. Callaghan made him Leader of the House of Commons and Lord President of the Council, and he was now widely considered to be the de facto deputy Prime Minister. His status was further reinforced when a few months later he succeeded Edward Short as deputy leader of the party, defeating Shirley Williams in the contest.

During the next three years, Foot played a central role in helping navigate the most serious challenges the government faced and, on a day-to-day basis, seeking to manage its diminishing majority in the House. He was instrumental in negotiating the pact with the Liberals that stabilised the government from March 1977, but his other major responsibility would eventually lead to the downfall of the government, as he oversaw the devolution proposals for Scotland and Wales. When the referendums there failed to achieve the required endorsement, the Scottish National Party withdrew their support, and the Government's days were numbered. As Leader of the House, it fell to Foot to wind up for the government at the end of the fateful debate at the end of March 1979, held over the motion of no confidence in the government proposed by the Conservatives. It was one of the best performances of his career, but it was not enough, and the government was defeated by a single vote.

After the Conservatives under Thatcher won the ensuing election, Callaghan stayed on for eighteen months as leader, during which the party began to fall into bitter factionalism between its left and right wings. When he resigned, Foot stood again for the leadership, but it was widely expected that the more centrist Denis Healey would win. The former Chancellor did indeed poll highest in the first ballot of MPs, but his lead was not as large as had been expected, and in the second ballot, Foot picked up enough votes from the eliminated candidates to secure a narrow victory over Healey by ten votes. The left of the party was jubilant, but those on the right were dismayed, and the reports of his victory were interspersed with speculation about the prospect of figures such as Roy Jenkins, Shirley Williams, Bill Rodgers and David Owen splitting off to form a new party. Foot himself was asked about such rumours and replied, 'I do not think it is going to happen.'[5]

It did happen. Just over two months later, the 'Gang of Four' left Labour and founded the Social Democratic Party (SDP). This was in many ways the defining event of Foot's leadership, as moderate figures reacted to the increasing influence of the far left in the party, now personified by Tony Benn. Foot himself was seen as a less extreme figure, but commentators noted that he lacked the skills or inclination to resist the march of the Bennites. An editorial in *The Times* about his election was captioned 'An Unmitigated Folly', and asserted that:

> The only hope for Labour was a leader who would devote his energies to pulling the party back from catastrophe, even at the cost of much personal unpopularity for a while. If that task was achieved, then the prospect of a return to office with more realistic policies might well bind the party together under a leader who had won the respect of the country for his courage. Mr Foot is not the man for either of these tasks.[6]

Whilst the lead column of a right-leaning newspaper is not exactly unbiased, the analysis is convincing and was largely vindicated by subsequent events and the outcome of the 1983 election. But despite all this, it is worth pointing out that for the first year of his leadership, Michael Foot led a Labour Party that was ahead of the Conservatives in the opinion polls by up to fourteen points. However unlikely it appears now, he was a potential Prime Minister. But by the end of 1981, the SDP/Liberal Alliance had surged to overtake Labour, with one poll in December giving them 50 per cent of the vote and Labour and the Conservatives just 23 per cent each. It looked for a time as though party politics really might have been utterly transformed. Then, in the wake of the Falklands War and an economic recovery, the Conservatives regained a significant lead and held it consistently until the general election.

Labour's landslide defeat at that election will for ever be linked to Michael Foot's name and to images of his shambling public appearances. That he was fundamentally unsuited to the role and the wrong person to take on that particular challenge at that time is easily argued. But he cannot take all the blame for the conditions facing Labour at the time. He faced a concerted insurgency from the hard left and the Militant Tendency, against which he had begun to fight back, having no sympathy with their brand of revolutionary class warfare. But this battle would take years, and in the meantime, it made Labour look chaotic and unelectable.

After the defeat, Foot remained in Parliament until 1992 and busied himself writing books on Lord Byron and H. G. Wells, as well as on politics. He continued campaigning and writing well into his nineties, and when he died in 2010 there were warm tributes from across the political spectrum. Had his frontline political career ended in 1979, he would now be remembered as a principled, highly intelligent man of the left, with a distinguished record of significant achievements as both a politician and author. It was only the misfortune of becoming Leader of the Opposition that has reduced him in most people's minds to a donkey jacket of history.

36

Neil Kinnock

Labour, Leader of the Opposition 1983–92

We now reach the point in the book where I feel obliged to declare an interest, as we arrive at the first leader with whom I can claim a personal acquaintance. I first met Neil Kinnock when I interviewed him for my PhD thesis, after which he kindly agreed to become an honorary president of the Centre for Opposition Studies. In that capacity, I have been in contact with him from time to time, and he has spoken at a number of our events. I always enjoy catching up with him and find him hugely entertaining company. He is also the first Leader of the Opposition I can remember from my childhood, as a regular fixture on the TV news – and indeed in puppet form on *Spitting Image*. Kinnock was an integral part of the cast of characters who defined 1980s politics, alongside Margaret Thatcher, President Reagan, Norman Tebbit, Nigel Lawson and other such figures.

At an event I organised in 2017, we invited a small audience to the House of Lords to hear Kinnock in conversation with Professor Peter Hennessy. They made an excellent double act, and Neil told some splendid stories, but he began with a bittersweet joke:

I must be something like the only person in history to be able to give a very precise date to the span of their mid-life crisis. Mine lasted from about five o'clock on 2 October 1983 to about two o'clock on 18 July 1992. That was my period as Leader of the Labour Party. And parting was such sweet sorrow...

It was said with a grin and greeted with warm laughter, but it clearly contained an essential truth about his attitude towards the experience. In his more self-critical moments, Kinnock has also described his eight and a half years as Leader of the Opposition as 'purgatory' and said that having failed to win two elections, he considers himself a 'personal and political failure'. Many would consider that last observation unduly harsh, given the contribution he made to improving Labour's electoral position, and I have myself debated this point with him. But he remains cheerfully adamant that at the end of the day his record as leader was one of ultimate failure because 'if you lose two elections, you'd be a bloody idiot or appallingly arrogant not to think that'.

When he became leader in 1983, he was seen as a protégé of the outgoing leader, Michael Foot, to whom he had been close for many years. There was a sense here of a passing of a baton which had in turn been passed to Foot by his own mentor, Nye Bevan. Kinnock had, like Bevan, been born in Tredegar in South Wales, into a family of coal miners. He had grown up steeped in the same working-class Welsh Labour tradition as the legendary founder of the NHS, who dominated the local political landscape as the constituency MP for Ebbw Vale. As a child, Kinnock had been taken to hear him speak at the Tredegar Workmen's Institute and later read his book *In Place of Fear*, which inspired him in his commitment to socialism. When Bevan died in 1960 and Foot was selected as the Labour candidate in the by-election, Kinnock was one of the most enthusiastic young Labour activists supporting his campaign. Their friendship began properly in the years that followed, founded on their mutual reverence for Bevan and his legacy.

By this time, Kinnock was a student at what is now Cardiff University, having become (as he famously later put it) 'the first Kinnock in a thousand generations to be able to get to university'.[*] His parents had made sacrifices to support him, as he passed the eleven-plus exam and won a place at Lewis School, Pengam, a respected grammar school often referred to as 'the Eton of the Valleys'. After gaining A-Levels in English, history and economics, he was accepted to study history and industrial relations at Cardiff. As well as developing his political skills in debates at the students' union, he also met the love of his life, Glenys Parry, with whom he formed a formidable personal and political partnership. Together they went on protest marches and joined the re-election campaign of one of the city's Labour MPs, James Callaghan, in the 1964 general election.

On leaving university, he was set on a political career and spoke about wanting to stand for Parliament. In the meantime, he trained to become a teacher and took a job in 1966 as a tutor for the Workers' Education Association in East Glamorgan. He and Glenys were married the following year and shortly afterwards moved to the village of Blackwood, where they became active members of the local Bedwellty constituency Labour Party. Then, in early 1969, the sitting MP for the seat announced his retirement on the grounds of ill health, and after a lively campaign and a dramatic selection meeting, Kinnock was selected as the new candidate for the seat.

As one of the safest Labour seats in the country, his road to the

---

[*]   A line so good that it was then taken up by a US presidential hopeful by the name of Joe Biden, who notoriously adapted it and the section of speech that followed it during a televised debate whilst campaigning for the Democratic nomination in 1987. The resulting plagiarism scandal helped end his bid for the White House.

House of Commons was now assured, and he was duly elected as an MP the following year at the age of twenty-eight. His election campaign contained an ironic nod to the changing balance between moderates and left-wingers in the party and in the unions. Prior to the election, the Transport and General Workers' Union had revised its list of sponsored candidates for the election, and Kinnock was successful in winning their backing and the financial support that went with it. One of those who was removed from the list was the former deputy leader George Brown, who went on to lose his seat at Belper. Some months later, Kinnock was having a drink in Parliament with a group of veteran left-wing MPs when the now Lord George-Brown came up and began drunkenly insulting them. Seeing a new face, Brown asked who this young 'whippersnapper' might be. 'I am the man who knocked you off the TGWU sponsored list,' replied Kinnock, 'and now I'm absolutely bloody delighted that I did.'[2]

During his first term as an MP, he developed a reputation as a fierce left-wing critic of the Tory government but also as something of a rebel against his own party's leadership, which continued when Labour returned to office. He remained close to Michael Foot, who had now entered the Cabinet, and agreed to serve for a year as his parliamentary private secretary, though neither of them really thought the position was necessary. Stepping down from the post in 1975, he wrote that twelve months of being 'neither government fish nor fully backbench fowl' was long enough and that he wanted the freedom to make his views clear on a number of issues of concern.[3] This he certainly did, frequently attacking the government's economic policy and even abstaining in a vote of confidence in the government in March 1976.

When Harold Wilson retired shortly afterwards, Kinnock actively supported Foot's bid to replace him but found the leadership contest amongst Labour MPs dispiriting. In a foreshadowing of later constitutional changes, he suggested in a letter to *Tribune* that in future the franchise should be widened to include constituency parties and trade unions. When Callaghan won the contest he sought to bring Kinnock inside the tent, offering him a junior ministerial post at the Department of Prices and Consumer Protection, where he would have worked under Roy Hattersley. Kinnock turned it down, saying he would prefer to go to the Department for Energy with responsibility for the coal industry – something Callaghan was not prepared to offer.

Instead, Kinnock continued as a left-wing critic of the government and focused increasingly on political activity outside of Parliament, travelling the country to speak to constituency parties and trade union branches. His increased prominence within the Labour movement resulted in his election to Labour's National Executive Committee in 1978, in a sign of the increasing shift to the left amongst grassroots members. He continued to travel the country during the run-up to the 1979 general election, in what would prove to be his last period as an outsider within the parliamentary party. Following Thatcher's victory, he would take a different course.

With Labour in opposition, Kinnock began to separate himself from the increasingly hard-left movement in the party. He put himself forward for election to the shadow Cabinet, finishing fourteenth in the ballot. Whilst only the first twelve were guaranteed a place, Callaghan used his discretion to appoint Kinnock as shadow Education Secretary, a significant position. When Callaghan stood down, Kinnock initially tried to dissuade Foot from standing in the leadership contest, fearing it would take too much of a toll on his old friend. However, when Foot stood, he loyally backed him and was kept on in his frontbench role under his leadership. Like Foot, he became increasingly frustrated by the activities of the Bennite hard left and their attempts to impose greater control by the party membership over the parliamentary party. Whilst he had long supported the move to widen the franchise in leadership elections, he was dismayed by the inward-looking and self-indulgent priorities of Tony Benn and his followers, which he believed were distracting from the need to focus on opposing the Thatcher government.

The Labour Party was now divided between the hard left of Benn and the soft left represented by Kinnock, and the personal enmity between them grew ever-more visceral. One effect of the landslide defeat of 1983 was the removal of Benn from Parliament, having lost his seat. As a result, Kinnock was able to claim the mantle of being the party's leading left-wing figure, and within hours of Foot's resignation as leader, Kinnock emerged as the clear frontrunner to succeed him. The first Labour leadership election using the new electoral college resulted in a landslide win for Kinnock, who polled 71 per cent of the vote. Roy Hattersley, who trailed in second place with 19 per cent, became deputy leader in the concurrent contest for that role.

On taking over as Leader of the Opposition, Kinnock recalls thinking, 'Well, I can't complain from here on in – I've just got to bloody well get on with it.' He despaired about the state of the party's policy stances and reputation, realising it would be a long slog back to power and would probably take more than one parliamentary term. One of his closest friends told him it would be a 'two-innings match', and he privately agreed.

What he had not anticipated at that time was that much of this first innings would be taken up by the turmoil and division of the miners' strike, which began in the spring of 1984. It was a painful issue for Kinnock, a proud son of the Welsh coal mining community, who had a natural sympathy for their cause. But he grew increasingly angered by the behaviour of Arthur Scargill, the militant leader of the National Union of Mineworkers, whose tactics handed Thatcher's government propaganda victories and ultimately doomed the strike to failure. Even today, Kinnock's loathing of Scargill remains undimmed for the damage he believes he did to the Labour movement and the miners' cause during that time.

In the aftermath of this traumatic episode, Kinnock redoubled his efforts to counter the entryism of the Militant Tendency in the party. This culminated in his impassioned speech at the 1985 Labour Party conference, in which he directly attacked the Militant-dominated leadership of Liverpool City Council for their dogmatic battle over the setting of their budget, which had resulted in the 'grotesque chaos of a Labour council – a *Labour* council – hiring taxis to scuttle round the city handing out redundancy notices to its own workers'.[4]

Accompanied by the boos of Militant supporters and the enthusiastic cheers of other delegates, the speech has gone down in history as a defining moment in the battle to return Labour to electability. It still stands as an exceptional piece of oratory, more powerful even than Gaitskell's 'fight, fight, fight' speech a quarter of a century before. It also encapsulates what became the mission of Kinnock's leadership, as he decried unrealistic promises and highlighted the need to win a general election. As *The Times* reported the next day:

> After the ovation delegates … spilled out of the hall in delight, congratulating each other on the discovery that they had a leader. There was enormous excitement and relief that someone had given voice to their feelings … They hoped that Labour's millions of lost supporters had seen it all on television and would return to the fold.[5]

His modernisation project in this phase of his leadership was symbolised by the adoption of the red rose as the party's new logo and the professionalisation of its communications operation under the guidance of Peter Mandelson, as its new director of publicity. At the 1987 general election, a slick party election broadcast directed by Hugh Hudson was dubbed *Kinnock: The Movie* and featured shots of Kinnock and Glenys walking in the hills of Wales, intercut with extracts of his speeches. The result of the election was disappointing, with Labour wining just twenty more seats, but the course had been set.

Over the next five years, Kinnock set about a concerted effort to drag the party's policy platform towards the centre ground. He instituted a policy review, which dropped the party's commitment to unilateral nuclear disarmament and reformed the party's structures to reduce the influence of the hard left. Such moves led to predictable calls of betrayal from the left of the party, but he was unrepentant. After defeating a leadership challenge by Benn in 1988, Kinnock led the party to victory at the 1989 European Parliament elections, the first time in fifteen years the party had finished in first place in a national election. As the Conservative government of Thatcher lost support, he exploited the unpopularity of the poll tax and saw Labour take a sustained lead in the opinion polls.

The resignation of Thatcher and her replacement by John Major in November 1990 gave the Conservatives a bounce in the polls and they retook the lead, but Labour edged ahead again during much of 1991 and entered 1992 in close competition with the government. A hung Parliament with Labour as the largest party was thought to be the most likely outcome of the general election that had been called for 9 April, and Kinnock stood on the brink of becoming Prime Minister. During the last week of the campaign, Labour's lead was put at between one and six points, but in the event, Major won a surprise victory, defeating Labour by 7.5 points and winning an overall majority of twenty-one seats. The polls had been wrong.

For Kinnock it was a devastating blow after more than eight years of dragging Labour from the brink of annihilation to the brink of power. In retrospect, his efforts can be seen as laying the foundations for Tony Blair's landslide win five years later, but at the time there was no such consolation, and Kinnock resigned the leadership. Reflecting on his contribution, he remains self-effacing:

Ultimately, the only test of a good opposition is to stop being in opposition. We came much closer in 1992, but any sportsperson who's failed to win a world championship by a few points understands what I felt then more than anybody. I coined a phrase once about the difference between Tony Blair and myself – I made the party electable; he got the party elected. And there's a hell of a difference.[6]

37

John Smith

Labour, Leader of the Opposition 1992–94

'John Smith (leader of the Labour Party) died today.' Those were the stark words I found written on a note which my mother had left for me to find when I returned home from school on the afternoon of 12 May 1994. In the days before smartphones and social media, news could not be assumed to have reached people, and she had clearly written it after popping home during her lunch break and watching the one o'clock news.

I immediately turned on the television and saw coverage of the tribute being paid in the House of Commons by the Prime Minister, John Major, who spoke movingly of Smith as 'an opponent, not an enemy' and a man with 'no malice'. His death, Major said, was 'the waste of a remarkable political talent; the waste of a high and honourable ambition to lead our country; the waste of a man in public life who, in all his actions, retained a human touch'.[1]

The atmosphere in the House of Commons was sombre and emotional. Margaret Beckett, now acting Leader of the Opposition, struggled to contain her emotions as she gave her tribute to 'a man of formidable intellect, of the highest ethics and of staunch integrity', and other MPs were openly weeping.[2] Smith's death, unlike that of

Hugh Gaitskell three decades earlier, had come suddenly and without warning. Westminster was genuinely shocked, as it came to terms with the removal from the scene of a Leader of the Opposition who had been widely expected to win the next general election and become Prime Minister. It was a personal tragedy but also a hugely consequential political event. Just as Gaitskell's untimely death had brought Harold Wilson to the premiership, so Smith's would now bring Tony Blair to Downing Street.

In 1999, as Blair began his second year in government, Channel 4 broadcast a documentary entitled *If John Smith Had Lived*, in which Andrew Marr examined the counterfactual scenario by interviewing leading Labour figures about how a Smith government might have differed from Blair's. It began with Marr showing headlines from the newspapers on the day after Smith's death, including the *Daily Mirror*'s 'The best Prime Minister we never had' and *The Independent*'s 'The man who would have led Britain'. The shock at his premature death had been, Marr said, 'A bit like Princess Diana for grown-ups.'

Smith was born in Argyll, Scotland in 1938, the son of a school teacher, Archie Smith, who shortly afterwards became headmaster of Ardrishaig Primary School, which his son attended. Smith then went on to Dunoon Grammar at the age of fourteen and from there to Glasgow University, where he took degrees in history and then law. He had joined the Labour Party aged sixteen and became an accomplished speaker at the university's debating society. On graduation, he became a solicitor and then an advocate at the Scottish Bar, also working as a libel lawyer.

As a moderate, he was an admirer of Gaitskell's leadership, and after a number of unsuccessful election campaigns in safe Tory seats, he was eventually elected to Parliament in the 1970 election as the Labour MP for North Lanarkshire, later renamed Monklands East. Unlike his fellow new MP Neil Kinnock, he was a loyal backbencher and described himself as 'an instinctive party man'.[3] Despite this, he rebelled against a three-line whip to support Britain's entry into the European Economic Community, having become a committed supporter of the European project.

When Wilson returned to office, he offered Smith the post of Solicitor General for Scotland, but Smith declined, not wishing to be pigeonholed as a legal specialist. Instead, he accepted a role as unpaid parliamentary private secretary at the Scottish Office and after the October 1974 general election was appointed as a junior minister at the Department of Energy under Eric Varley and then, from 1975, Tony Benn. When James Callaghan succeeded Wilson, he promoted Smith to Minister of State for the Privy Council Office, working under the Leader of the House of Commons, Michael Foot. In this position he won praise for his role in helping steer through the ultimately unsuccessful legislation to establish devolution in Scotland and Wales, a cause he strongly supported.

Made a privy counsellor in April 1978, he was promoted in November of that year to President of the Board of Trade, becoming the youngest member of the Cabinet at the age of forty. However, Smith was only in office for six months before the fall of the government returned Labour to opposition, after which he was elected to the shadow Cabinet, where he would serve continuously until his death. He supported Denis Healey's bid for the leadership in 1980, and was clearly on the right of the party, but was not tempted to join the breakaway of the Social Democratic Party in 1981, remaining tribally loyal to Labour despite his distaste for the Bennite left. Having initially shadowed his old job at the Board of Trade, he was moved to become shadow Energy Secretary in 1982.

When Kinnock became leader, Smith was appointed shadow

Employment Secretary for a year, before going back to his more familiar portfolio as shadow Trade and Industry Secretary from 1984 until
the 1987 general election. He became a formidable performer in the
House of Commons and played a notable role in the infamous debate
over the Westland affair in January 1986, using all his lawyerly skills to
prosecute the case against Margaret Thatcher over the leaking of the
Solicitor General's letter and prompting the Prime Minister to intervene on him to defend herself. As he later recalled, '*She* interrupted me,
eyes blazing, she was so angry! I was delighted because it seemed to
me to be a sign of weakness.'[4] Whereas Kinnock had been accused of
letting Thatcher off the hook with his performance that day, some felt
that had Smith led the charge, she might not have survived.

After the 1987 general election, Kinnock appointed Smith shadow
Chancellor, where he developed Labour's fiscal policies through the
'economic equality' strand of the party's policy review. Smith also
championed the introduction of a national minimum wage, despite
heavy opposition from some trade unions. The main proposals that
emerged from the review were published in a 1990 policy document
that rejected a return to punitive tax rates and accepted the operation
of a market economy but sought a rise in overall taxation to pay for
improvements in public services. Specifically, increases in child benefit
and pensions would be paid for by abolishing the upper limit on national insurance contributions and raising the top rate of income tax
from 40 to 50 per cent.

The unveiling of these tax policies two years before the general
election gave the Conservatives the opportunity to mount a concerted
attack on Labour, suggesting that the party had up to £35 billion of un-
funded spending commitments that would have to be paid for by even
higher tax increases. In the face of this campaign and concerns from
Labour's own polling and communications experts, Smith was put

under pressure to modify the plans, and this led to ongoing tensions with the leader's office. Smith and Kinnock were never particularly close, and on a number of notable occasions the leader's propensity to intervene in economic policy led to furious clashes between them.

In the mythology that has arisen about the Conservatives' unexpected victory in the 1992 general election, much attention has been focused on the shadow Budget which Smith outlined at the start of the election campaign, presented as a way of demonstrating Labour's readiness for office by detailing its intended Budget measures. Whilst the shadow Budget did lead to renewed attacks from the Conservatives and right-wing newspapers, these merely reinforced the existing campaign against Labour's tax plans, which had famously resulted in the 'Labour's Tax Bombshell' poster. This poster had been launched by the Conservatives in January 1992 – two months before the shadow Budget.

Despite ongoing arguments about the culpability of the shadow Chancellor for the election defeat, he was almost universally seen as the overwhelming favourite to succeed Kinnock as leader after the latter's resignation. With other possible contenders such as Gordon Brown and Robin Cook declining to oppose him, the only other candidate was Bryan Gould, the shadow Environment Secretary. When the result was announced it was a landslide for Smith, who won with 91 per cent of the vote.

Perhaps the most consequential of Smith's actions as leader came in the first few days after his election. In the shadow Cabinet elections held the week after he took over, two rising stars received the most votes: Gordon Brown and Tony Blair. They were rewarded by being appointed as shadow Chancellor and shadow Home Secretary respectively. Over the next two years they were to become increasingly frustrated by what they saw as Smith's lack of modernising zeal, but their prominent positions clearly marked them as future leadership contenders. Brown also laid down many of the foundations of what would later become New Labour's economic policy by instilling greater discipline over spending commitments and abandoning the proposed tax rises from the shadow Budget.

One area of modernisation which Smith did pursue was his commitment to abolish the trade unions' block vote in party elections and replace it with 'one member, one vote'. This significant change had been a pledge made by both him and Gould during the leadership contest, but it was not uncontentious. Smith's own deputy leader, Beckett, opposed the change, whilst Blair believed it needed to go further. Nevertheless, the narrow victory at the 1993 party conference was a boost to Smith's leadership and was an essential building block for later reforms under Blair, which would have been much more difficult without the change.

The signature reform of Blair's subsequent leadership was the rewriting of Clause IV of the party's constitution, which had committed the party to public ownership of industry. The suggestion of changing it, however, had first been raised under Smith's leadership, most prominently in a pamphlet published by Jack Straw. Whilst Smith had privately conceded that he felt the clause was outdated, he shied away from tackling it, and during a heated discussion with Straw over the issue, Smith angrily threw his colleague's pamphlet after him as he left his office. Once he had secured the one member, one vote reform, his appetite for further modernisation of the party diminished further.

Meanwhile, the Conservative government was beginning to tear itself apart over Europe during debates on ratification of the Maastricht Treaty, and Smith – though supportive of the treaty and of greater European integration – skilfully exploited the government's troubles by allying with Conservative rebels to make the passage of the legislation as painful as possible. The UK's ejection from the Exchange Rate Mechanism (ERM) on Black Wednesday in September 1992 had destroyed the Conservatives' reputation for economic competence, and growing allegations of sleaze added to the sense of a government in terminal decline. Smith had made his first major speech as leader following the ERM debacle, memorably condemning Major as 'the devalued Prime Minister of a devalued government', and he continued with effective performances in the Commons, exploiting Major's woes.[5] Labour's lead in the opinion polls steadily grew to around twenty points by the spring of 1994.

It was increasingly clear that Labour was on course for victory at the next general election, and in early May 1994, Smith was being kept busy campaigning for the imminent local and European elections. On the morning of Thursday 12 May he was due to travel to Basildon on a campaign visit, but at 8.05 a.m. he suffered a massive heart attack at his flat in London's Barbican. Paramedics arrived within minutes, and he was taken to St Bartholomew's Hospital, but all attempts to revive him failed, and he was pronounced dead an hour later.

The previous evening, he had attended a fundraising dinner at the Park Lane Hotel and made what turned out to be his last speech. Beckett, in her tribute in the House of Commons, recalled the event:

He was in fine fettle and in high spirits. He spoke not from a text but from notes, and when he sat down I congratulated him especially on his final sentence—spoken, as it was, off the cuff and from the heart. They were almost the last words I heard him say. He looked at the assembled gathering, and he said: 'The opportunity to serve our country—that is all we ask.' Let it stand as his epitaph.[6]

38

Margaret Beckett

Labour, Acting Leader of the Opposition May–July 1994

With John Smith's sudden death, Labour unexpectedly found itself with its first female leader. Under the party's constitution, Margaret Beckett, as deputy leader, automatically succeeded to the post pending a leadership election. On the morning of 12 May, she had been at home getting ready for the day when she received a phone call from Larry Whitty, the General Secretary of the Labour Party, to tell her Smith had suffered another major heart attack. She recalls she 'immediately went into protection mode' and began talking about the need to keep things calm and give him space to recover. Her husband Leo, who had picked up the phone, interrupted her to say, 'Margaret, I think he's already dead.'[1]

It was, she said, 'the most tremendous shock'. She headed into Parliament and went to the leader's office, where she tried to comfort the shellshocked staff there. She also had to find the words for her tribute in the House of Commons that afternoon, which she knew would be an emotional ordeal:

> It was one of the most difficult things I ever had to do ... What I
> do remember is that I wrote it – I went into the office, and I wrote

it – and then I just said it over and over and over again, and the first time I managed to say it without bursting into tears was in the House.[2]

The events of the following weeks have entered political mythology, as the sudden vacancy forced the two main leadership contenders, Tony Blair and Gordon Brown, to settle the question of which of them should stand. The eventual agreement by Brown to stand aside and allow Blair a clear run laid the foundations of New Labour but also sowed the seeds of resentment which would poison relations between the two men throughout their time in government together. Whilst commentators have raked over that 1994 psychodrama ever since, less attention has been paid to the woman who was already leading the party at the time and who was in fact a candidate to remain doing so.

Born Margaret Mary Jackson in Ashton-Under-Lyne in 1943, her mother was a teacher whilst her father, a carpenter, suffered ill health throughout her childhood and died suddenly when she was twelve years old. The memory of the policeman knocking on the door that evening to tell them the news was something she would never forget:

> It was one of those Indian summers that we sometimes get in October. My father had gone out that morning to see my grandparents about a hall carpet which he was making for them – rug-making was his hobby. He had put on a lightweight suit and forgotten to transfer the contents of his pockets over from his winter jacket. When he collapsed and died in the street, nobody knew who he was. It took them till early evening to find us ... The worst thing was that my mother – who had always been a tower of strength, who had never complained, always did everything well – broke down completely. All the years he was sick my mother had nursed him, but when he died, he died alone.[3]

It was a tough upbringing, and money was short. She later recalled feeling isolated from other children by the family's poverty and the problems of coping at home after her father's death. Such hardships fuelled her political convictions, and the experience of growing up with chronic illness in the household made her passionate about the importance of the NHS. She later reflected, 'One of the advantages of an unhappy childhood is that it makes the rest of your life seem so happy.'[4]

After being educated at a succession of Catholic schools, she went to the University of Manchester Institute of Science and Technology, where she graduated in metallurgy and subsequently worked as an apprentice at Associated Electrical Industries. In 1970, she went to work at the Labour Party as a researcher on industrial policy, supporting the relevant shadow Cabinet minister, Tony Benn. She stood unsuccessfully as parliamentary candidate for Lincoln in February 1974 against Dick Taverne, who had defected from the Labour Party and won a by-election as the Democratic Labour candidate the previous year.

In October 1974 she stood again and this time narrowly defeated Taverne. Upon entering Parliament she was swiftly appointed as parliamentary private secretary to Judith Hart, the Minister for Overseas Development, from whom she learnt a lot about how to be an effective minister. In 1975 she was appointed as a government whip, and then in 1976 she became a junior minister as parliamentary Undersecretary at the Department for Education and Science. She replaced Joan Lestor, who had resigned over spending cuts, and her decision to accept the appointment opened her up to some criticism from colleagues on the left. She remained in office until the 1979 general election, when she narrowly lost her seat.

Out of Parliament and now married to Leo Beckett, the chairman of her local constituency party, she went to work as a researcher at

Granada Television and in 1980 was elected to Labour's National Executive Committee (NEC). A left-winger, she supported Michael Foot for the leadership in 1980 and backed Benn's candidacy for the deputy leadership in 1981. She was then selected for the Derby South constituency, which she narrowly won by just 421 votes at the 1983 general election.

Beckett became a member of the Campaign Group of left-wing Labour MPs and was closely aligned with their causes, backing Arthur Scargill during the miners' strike. But she gradually moved away from the hard left, serving as an opposition spokesperson for social security from 1984, then joining the shadow Cabinet in 1989 as shadow Chief Secretary to the Treasury. In this role she formed an effective partnership with Smith, her boss as shadow Chancellor, and was credited with instilling much-needed fiscal discipline on the front bench. She enforced a formula that became known as 'Beckett's Law' to restrict spending commitments to only those that could be afforded 'as resources allow'.[5]

When Smith stood for the leadership in 1992, the media reported that he would be teaming up with Beckett, who would stand for the deputy leadership. She, however, was not keen and ruled herself out of the contest. It was only when her announcement prompted a flood of calls from colleagues urging her to stand that she changed her mind and decided to stand, with Smith's support. She was the clear favourite, and a profile of her in *The Times* noted, 'The conversion of Margaret Beckett from hard-left trouble-maker into strict keeper of the public spending purse has been remarkable.'[6]

Her pitch for the deputy leadership was based on what she called her 'modernisation manifesto', which proposed a simpler, fairer tax system, an education charter and a 'citizenship commission' to look at reforms to the financing of political parties, including state funding and campaign spending caps. She also called for a 'poverty census' to determine the true extent of the problem in society. At her campaign launch she said the party needed a leadership team 'capable of combining idealism with competence, openness to new ideas with experience and common sense'.[7] When the results were declared, she won with 57 per cent of the vote, beating both John Prescott and Bryan Gould.

As deputy leader to Smith, Beckett was made shadow Leader of the House of Commons as well as Labour's campaign co-ordinator. She chaired the NEC's campaigns and elections committee and was left by Smith to take sole charge of the party's campaigning efforts, working alongside Sally Morgan, the campaigns director, and David Hill, the director of communications. This gave her a good insight into the importance of polling in shaping the party's political messaging and the delicate balance that needed to be struck between polling and policy development.

When Smith died, the party had just won the May 1994 local elections with 40 per cent of the vote, with both the Conservatives and Liberal Democrats on 27 per cent. The European Parliament elections were due to be held the following month, and following a pause in campaigning until after Smith's funeral, Beckett continued with her responsibility for the campaign, though now as acting leader. She also inherited Smith's private office team and all the responsibilities of being Leader of the Opposition, such as tackling John Major at Prime Minister's Questions and meeting foreign heads of state. This included a meeting with Bill Clinton when he was in the UK for the fiftieth anniversary commemorations of D-Day.

As the sitting deputy leader, Beckett could have remained in post until she faced re-election at the party conference in the autumn, but she decided to bring forward the deputy leadership contest to run alongside that for the leadership. More surprisingly, she decided to put her name forward as a candidate for both positions. She later said that the decision was based on her realisation since becoming acting leader that she had the capacity to lead the party and was not prepared simply to run for deputy.

Understandable though this decision was, she stood little chance of winning against Blair, and her decision also made it more likely that Prescott would win the deputy leadership from her. She acknowledged this was a possibility but was undeterred, launching her campaign with an appeal to her colleagues: 'Judge me on my ability to manage and unify our party and communicate its ideals to the British people.'[8] As the campaign wore on, she emphasised her left-wing credentials, including her long-standing membership of CND, in a move which alarmed her more moderate supporters. She also publicly expressed her frustration at being written off as a serious contender for the leadership after Smith's death:

> One of my women colleagues said to me 'They buried you with John.' There is no doubt that I disappeared from the frame as far as most media commentators were concerned. I cannot say I was over-surprised. I am standing because I am doing the job of leading the Labour Party. I believe I can continue to do it well ... I have no doubt that I am capable of doing this job well and winning the election for Labour.[9]

Despite such fighting talk, she failed to make a breakthrough in the contest. Blair won an overwhelming mandate with 57 per cent of the vote, Prescott was second with 24 per cent and Beckett trailed in third with just 18.9 per cent. She also lost out in the much-closer race for deputy, with Prescott beating her by 56.5 per cent to 43.5 per cent. It was a disappointing outcome which effectively left her without a job, as her positions in the shadow Cabinet and on Labour's NEC were both ex-officio as deputy leader.

Picking herself up after the defeat, Beckett was re-elected to the shadow Cabinet that autumn with the second-most votes, one place ahead of Brown, and was appointed by Blair as shadow Health Secretary. A year later she was moved to shadow Trade and Industry Secretary and was given that portfolio in government after the 1997 election. She remained in the Cabinet for the whole of the next decade under Blair's premiership, moving to become Leader of the House of Commons in 1998, then Environment Secretary for five years from 2001.

In 2006, following poor local election results, Blair reshuffled the Cabinet, and called Beckett into No. 10. She did not know what to expect, and when he told her he was appointing her Foreign Secretary, her response was 'one word, and four lettered'.[10] It was certainly a surprise but was fitting recognition of her reputation as a safe pair of hands and an effective minister. Whilst she only served for a year before being removed by the new Prime Minister Gordon Brown, she earned a place in history as the first woman to have held that office.

Whilst that is an achievement worth recognising, it is only one highlight of a lifetime's public service in the Labour Party and was not her last contribution. In the aftermath of the 2015 general election, she chaired the review that sought to learn the lessons of that defeat, and at the time of writing she remains both a Member of Parliament and a member of Labour's NEC, on which she has served since 2011 after previous spells going back forty-three years.

It seems appropriate to end by quoting the words of her late husband, Leo, who said after her defeat for the leadership in 1994, 'Margaret will be back. She loves her politics too much – and her party.'[11]

39

William Hague

Conservative, Leader of the Opposition 1997–2001

On 12 October 1977, the Conservative Party conference in Blackpool was treated to the first platform speech by a future leader. With Margaret Thatcher looking on approvingly from the stage, the sixteen-year-old William Hague stepped up to the microphone. As *The Times* recorded the next day:

> Looking somewhat like a baby Harold Wilson, but speaking with the authority and cadence of a baby Churchill, he electrified the conference with a stern summons to revive pure Conservatism ... There were gasps, then they cheered him to the roof.[1]

He became an instant celebrity, with Thatcher calling him 'the star of the show' and posing for photographs with him. This first encounter was a mixed blessing, as he bristled slightly when she told him in front of the cameras that he must now go and telephone his mother. He was interviewed for *News at Ten* and appeared on the BBC's *Nationwide* with the shadow Chancellor, Geoffrey Howe. Photographers followed him around the conference, and he later recalled the editor of the

Daily Mail walking around behind him saying, 'Hold the front page, I'm going to make this kid a star.'[2]

His appearance didn't go down well with everyone. Lord Carrington, the Leader of the Opposition in the House of Lords, was said to have been 'nauseated' by the performance and asked his colleague Norman St John-Stevas, 'If he is as priggish and self-assured as that at sixteen, what will he be like in thirty years' time?' Stevas replied, 'Like Michael Heseltine.'[3] Hague himself had been looking to the future during the speech, winning approving laughter from the assembled Tory faithful as he told them, 'It's all right for you – half of you won't be here in thirty or forty years' time. But I will be.'[4] He was to find over the years that not only would *he* still be around in several decades' time but so would the archive footage of his precocious debut. Perhaps the best advice he got during those heady few days was from Sir Keith Joseph, who advised him that what he needed now was 'a period of obscurity'.[5]

Returning to his comprehensive school, Hague was met by another crowd of photographers and journalists and was filmed walking into his classes. His contemporaries, predictably, took to mocking him by chanting the speech at him on the school bus, but things soon calmed down. Hague seems to have taken to heart Joseph's advice, which had been reinforced by his sensible mother Stella, and turned down numerous other media opportunities to concentrate on studying for his A-Levels.

His background appeared an unusual one for a future leader of his party. He was born in 1961 in Rotherham, situated in what he later described as the 'Socialist Republic of South Yorkshire'. The Conservative Prime Minister at the time was the patrician Harold Macmillan, shortly to be replaced by the even more aristocratic Earl of Home. However, times were changing, and the next three Conservative leaders would be grammar school pupils from more humble backgrounds.

Hague's paternal family, though not aristocratic, did have some degree of local notoriety in their suburb of Rotherham. As his biographer put it, 'The Hagues were a big name in Greasbrough' – his great-great-grandfather having been a builder who constructed most of the houses in the village, including the three-bedroom house in which William first grew up.[6] In 1870, Charles Hague had established a small family business producing soda water, which was passed on to successive generations as Hague & Sons, supplying a range of fizzy drinks. William's father, Nigel Hague, had taken over the firm and expanded it successfully into supplying beer and wine alongside their signature bottles of pop. The greater prosperity this brought allowed the family, when William was ten years old, to move to a rented six-bedroom house in the picturesque village of Wentworth. He grew up playing in the open fields and going on long walks with his golden retriever, Caesar. It appears an idyllic childhood.

After attending a local primary school, he won a scholarship to Ripon Grammar School, but he disliked it and ran away. His parents realised he was unhappy, and he was moved instead to Wath Comprehensive School, nearer to the family home. Intelligent and bookish, Hague prospered, achieving eight As at O-Level (and a B in Greek) and getting enthusiastically involved in the school's debating society. He had also become politically active, having joined the local Conservatives, and cut his teeth canvassing for the local elections in the rather unpromising territory of solidly Labour-voting mining villages. He also infamously got his mother to take out a subscription to *Hansard* for him and developed a fascination with parliamentary debates and the political issues contained in them.

In the school holidays he helped out with the family firm, working as a driver's mate for deliveries to the pubs and working men's clubs of South Yorkshire. Lugging crates and barrels kept him fit, but he also partook in liquid refreshment during the rounds, developing a taste for beer from the age of fifteen. This routine became the subject of much media attention when he was Leader of the Opposition, after he suggested in an interview for *GQ* magazine that it meant he had sometimes drunk up to fourteen pints a day.

The claim was widely mocked, but there are some corroborating stories of his teenage drinking exploits. Shortly after his party conference speech, he was booked to do a local radio interview in the evening but returned home after a day of deliveries somewhat the worse for wear, and his mother had to try to sober him up before his appearance. On another occasion, Hague and his friends had been in the pub on Christmas Eve before attending midnight mass at the neighbouring church. A drunken Hague announced he was going to give his own sermon during the service and was so determined to do so that his friends had to wrestle him to the ground to keep him out of the church.

His political interests had hardened into a desire to become an MP, and he confidently told friends he intended to fight an unwinnable Tory seat in his twenties, enter Parliament before he was thirty and become a minister shortly afterwards, and not marry until he had done so. However much he might have been teased about his lofty ambitions, his determination ensured that was exactly what he did. The only part of the plan which was not realised was the ultimate objective, which he had admitted to his music teacher at a party after his school's annual Gilbert and Sullivan performance. 'You know, Mrs Senior', he had told her, 'one day I'm going to be Prime Minister.'[7]

After gaining four As in his A-Levels, he secured entry to Oxford to study PPE at Magdalen College, where his prowess at debating made him a star of the Oxford Union, of which he later became president. There are many tales from those formative years, but, given this book's penchant for silliness, one in particular stands out, as relayed in his only published biography. One evening, the story goes, Hague and a friend ventured away from the dreaming spires to attend a party in north London with a group of medical students. Much alcohol was consumed, culminating in a variety of drinking games, dares and forfeits. Hague fell victim to the ultimate prank of the group of rugby-playing students, who stripped him naked and threw him out onto the street. As he was shivering in the cold in front of a crowd of strangers, a neighbour went to the door to complain about the noise from the party, giving Hague the chance to barge back in. Furious, the fully naked future statesman charged at the most obnoxious of his hosts and punched him to the ground.*

Graduating with a first, Hague moved to London and took a spare room in a flat in Clapham offered to him by Alan Duncan, a friend from Oxford who was now working for Shell, where Hague had also secured a job. During his time there he took a leave of absence during the run-up to the 1983 general election to become a speechwriter at the Treasury for the Chancellor, Geoffrey Howe, and Leon Brittan, the Chief Secretary. Both would later act as referees for Hague's application to the list of Conservative parliamentary candidates. After the election, he was headhunted by the management consultants McKinsey and left Shell to join them.

By the time of the next election, he was able to tick off another of the steps on his career to-do list, fighting his 'unwinnable' home seat of Wentworth at the 1987 general election, which Labour won by a majority of over 20,000. The following year, he got his chance at a more realistic prospect when Leon Brittan resigned from the Commons after being appointed a European Commissioner. Hague was

---

* During the writing of this book, I mentioned this anecdote to one of Hague's Oxford friends, who commented that it sounded most unlikely, but I think it falls into the category of stories that ought to be true, even if they aren't.

one of 365 applicants for the candidacy but triumphed in the final selection meeting in November over three others, including his friend Alan Duncan. Despite this rivalry, at the by-election in January 1989 Duncan loyally threw himself into helping the campaign, in which the Conservatives faced a strong challenge from both the Social Democratic Party and the Social and Liberal Democrats. In the end, Hague won by a majority of 2,634.

Once in the Commons, he was swiftly promoted. In 1990 he was appointed parliamentary private secretary to the Chancellor, Norman Lamont. Hague remained working for him for the next three years, his duties as a ministerial bag carrier being taken rather literally one Budget day, when he had to bring a bottle of whisky to the Commons for his boss to swig from during the speech. As they prepared to step outside No. 11 for the traditional photocall, Hague realised that the sight of an off-licence carrier bag would be rather unbecoming, so at the Chancellor's suggestion he instead placed the bottle inside the iconic budget box. With this done, however, there was no room for the actual speech, which Hague had to carry under his arm. As he later recalled:

> We went out in front of the cameras, and Norman held up the budget box, and I'm standing behind him thinking if that isn't locked properly this could be the most embarrassing occasion in the history of politics. And he's holding up a box containing a bottle of whisky, and everybody looking [sic] at the PPS behind, carrying this anonymous folder, and that's the budget.[8]

When Lamont was sacked in 1993, Hague was rewarded with his first ministerial job, as a junior minister at the Department of Social Security. He was promoted to Minister of State a year later and oversaw the introduction of the Disability Discrimination Act, which he now claims as one of his proudest achievements. In 1995, John Redwood resigned as Welsh Secretary to challenge John Major unsuccessfully for the leadership, and Hague was appointed to replace him, becoming at the age of thirty-four the youngest Conservative Cabinet minister of the twentieth century. At the Welsh Office his assistant private secretary was a bright Welsh civil servant called Ffion Jenkins, whom he asked to teach him the words of the Welsh national anthem. This was to avoid the embarrassment suffered by his predecessor, who had been caught on camera cluelessly attempting to mime along to it at a conference. The Welsh lessons sparked a romance, and they were married two years later.

The 1997 general election was a historic disaster for the Conservatives, who suffered their worst defeat since 1832. On the night the results came in, Hague (whose count was not until the following day) was at Conservative central office as one of the Cabinet ministers designated to give media interviews. As a succession of Cabinet ministers lost their seats, Conservative officials began to calculate that on the basis of some of the swings being seen, almost all the senior figures who might lead the party could be wiped out. Director of communications Charles Lewington recalled:

> We were instructed by the party chairman to go and locate William Hague ... and make sure he stayed. It was rather like a regimental headquarters of a terrible battle where all the senior officers had been wiped out, and the sergeants were deputed to go and tell the captain that at the tender age of thirty-five it was entirely possible that he would have to take command. It was an extraordinary moment.[9]

Whilst the worst fears of electoral annihilation were not realised, a number of senior leadership contenders were indeed knocked out of contention by the electorate, including Michael Portillo and Malcolm Rifkind. Michael Heseltine was also ruled out after suffering heart problems shortly afterwards. In the end, it came down to a contest between Hague and the former Chancellor Kenneth Clarke, after a dramatic few weeks of intrigue and plotting. Initially, Hague had agreed to stand aside and back Michael Howard in return for the deputy leadership, but he later changed his mind, after realising Howard would not win. The alliance with Howard had been discussed over champagne on the Monday after the general election, but they never shook hands on it – an omission which Hague now says was crucial. Had they done so, he would not have felt able to back out.

His leadership bid benefitted from the increasing Euroscepticism of the Conservative Party in Parliament and in the country, which made Clarke an unappealing prospect to them, and which prompted Thatcher to issue a very public endorsement of the man she had first applauded twenty years before in Blackpool. After winning, Hague set about modernising the party with a set of reforms labelled the 'Fresh Future', the most significant of which was a change to the voting system for future Conservative leaders, giving the final say to the party's grassroots membership.

Unfortunately for him, early press coverage was not sympathetic, and his attempts to project a youthful and more informal image in his first months in the job rather backfired. In early August 1997, whilst on a visit to Cornwall, he visited Flambards Theme Park for a photocall that has gone down in political history. Accompanied by his chief of staff, Seb Coe, he rode the log flume wearing a baseball cap with 'Hague' embroidered on the front. The resulting pictures opened him up to ridicule by the media, and his choice of headgear became a defining image of his leadership that has remained lodged in the public imagination. Another photocall later that month during a visit to the Notting Hill Carnival was similarly mocked.

These setbacks were early signs of the fundamental difficulty Hague was to experience throughout his leadership. Faced with the overwhelming popularity of Tony Blair and New Labour, he could make little progress in the polls, despite shining in the House of Commons and becoming a star performer at Prime Minister's Questions. He increasingly fell back to a core vote strategy of Thatcherite rhetoric and Eurosceptic pledges to keep the pound, which delivered a victory in the European Parliament elections in 1999 but was not enough to increase support at the general election. In 2001, the party duly fell to an almost identical landslide defeat, making a net gain of just one seat.*

He announced his resignation the following day and retired to the backbenches, an ex-leader at the age of just forty. Some have questioned since whether he was unwise to have sought the leadership so early. He dismisses this, believing that despite it being a 'very difficult experience' he was still right to have done it, personally and politically:

> I think all of the other candidates would have had a much harder job keeping the Conservative Party intact through that period than I had. I feel I did the night shift in leading the Conservative Party. But somebody had to do it. And it got it out of the system for me. You know, the experience of being leader of the party at a young age for four years and fighting an election absolutely got that out of my system for me. I had no remaining ambition to become Prime Minister.[10]

---

* For a slightly more detailed assessment of his time as leader, I might humbly suggest a look at the chapter I wrote on Hague in the book *Leaders of the Opposition from Churchill to Cameron*, edited by Timothy Heppell (Palgrave Macmillan, 2012).

Despite this ultimately unfulfilled ambition, it was not the end of his political career. He would go on to serve as Foreign Secretary and First Secretary of State in David Cameron's coalition government in 2010, having made the smooth transition from rising star to elder statesman. Looking back on that speech in 1977, he later conceded it would have made his career easier had he not done it, because 'if you do that as a teenager, they think you are a bit of a freak for the rest of your life'. Now, whenever any young aspiring politician asks his advice on making such a debut at an early age, his reply is simple: 'Don't do it.'[11]

40

Iain Duncan Smith

Conservative, Leader of the Opposition 2001–03

Iain Duncan Smith is not destined to be remembered as a successful or particularly remarkable Leader of the Opposition. This is perhaps a little unfair. He did, in fact, notch up a number of notable achievements from his tenure. He was the first Conservative leader to be elected by a ballot of the party's grassroots membership, and he remains the only one to be removed by a vote of no confidence from the party's MPs. He was the first and only post-war Conservative Leader of the Opposition not to have led the party into a general election and is the only Conservative leader except Austen Chamberlain never to have served in one of the great offices of state. In 2021, a survey of eighty-five academics with a specialism in British politics placed him bottom of the league table of all eighteen post-war Leaders of the Opposition.

Compiling a biographical sketch of him also suffers from the obstacle that he is, so far as I can see, the only Leader of the Opposition since the nineteenth century (discounting temporary incumbents) with not a single full-length book written about him. Despite this inexplicable omission, I shall do my best to amplify the life and achievements of the 'quiet man'.

He was born on 9 April 1954 in Edinburgh, the son of Wilfrid Duncan Smith, an RAF pilot, and his wife Pamela Summers, a ballerina. His birth certificate gives his name as 'George Ian Duncan Smith', but at some later point an extra 'i' was added to his second name, by which he began to be known. There is some suggestion that his father changed the spelling to emphasise his Scottish roots, or that it was incorrectly registered in the first place (Duncan Smith's office later gave journalists different explanations when asked about it).

After attending a number of different primary schools and a cadet college in Anglesey, he spent a year at the Università per Stranieri (University for Foreigners) in Perugia, Italy. His attendance there became the subject of some controversy during his leadership, when it emerged that his official biography on the Conservative Party website and his *Who's Who* entry both incorrectly stated that he had attended the medieval Università di Perugia, a more prestigious institution in the same town. The discrepancy was uncovered by the BBC's *Newsnight* in 2002, to the embarrassment of the then Tory leader.

Seemingly uncontested is the fact that Duncan Smith then attended the Royal Military Academy Sandhurst and was subsequently commissioned into the Scots Guards as a second lieutenant in 1975, being promoted to lieutenant two years later. He served in Northern Ireland and Rhodesia before retiring from the army in 1981. He then worked at GEC-Marconi, during which time he attended a number of short courses at the company's Dunchurch College of Management.

After standing unsuccessfully for Bradford West at the 1987 general election, he was selected as the Conservative candidate for Chingford on the retirement of Norman Tebbit and elected to the seat in 1992. As a committed Eurosceptic, Duncan Smith was a leading rebel against John Major's government during his first term as an MP, voting repeatedly against the Maastricht Treaty. Following the 1997 general election, he was appointed to the shadow Cabinet by William Hague as shadow Secretary of State for Social Security, later moving to become shadow Defence Secretary.

Following Hague's resignation, Duncan Smith's election as leader in 2001, after he defeated Michael Portillo to secure a place in the run-off against Kenneth Clarke in the ballot of party members, was something of a surprise. Portillo had been the favourite to become leader, having been denied the opportunity to run in 1997 after losing his seat. Since returning to Parliament at a by-election in 1999, he had been shadow Chancellor under Hague and had moved away from his right-wing reputation to embrace a modernising position as a champion of more socially liberal politics. His disclosure of homosexual relationships in his youth led to a particularly nasty smear campaign against him from figures on the party's right, including Tebbit, who attacked Portillo's 'deviance'. Such comments resurfaced in the leadership campaign, with Tebbit pointedly endorsing Duncan Smith as a 'normal family man with children'.[1] This homophobic dog-whistle combined with concerns on the right over Portillo's progressive policy positions to damage his prospects. In the final ballot of Tory MPs, Clarke secured fifty-nine votes, whilst Duncan Smith came in second with fifty-four, defeating Portillo by one vote and eliminating him from the race.

With Conservative Party members having the final say in the leadership election for the first time, Duncan Smith was now head-to-head with Clarke as the contest went to the country over the summer. Just as with Hague four years earlier, Duncan Smith's Eurosceptic credentials boosted his chances, but the toxic nature of the campaign continued, with accusations that he was being supported by members of the far-right Monday Club and the sacking of a member of his campaign team after expressing sympathy for the racist British National Party. In the end, Duncan Smith defeated Clarke in the final vote by 61 per cent to 39 per cent, but coverage of his victory was completely overshadowed by events in the United States.

The result was due to be announced on 12 September at a big event at the Queen Elizabeth II conference centre in Westminster, but in the aftermath of the 9/11 terrorist attacks the declaration was delayed for a day and scaled down into a smaller event at the party's headquarters. The defeated Clarke spoke briefly, expressing his hope that the new leader would lead the party to victory but sounding unconvinced. Duncan Smith then gave a subdued acceptance speech. Matthew Parris described the scene in a prescient sketch for *The Times*:

> Mr Duncan Smith spoke with dignity and deliberateness. His face was tense but composed, like someone lowering himself into slightly too hot a bath ... The room was not quite full. The journalists were not quite riveted. The losing side was not quite reconciled. The winners were not quite cock-a-hoop ... A band of UK Independence Party activists with their leader had joined Tories outside to cheer Iain Duncan Smith. Their cheers were as ominous as the Clarkeites' boos. Sooner or later, the new Tory leader knows that he must forfeit the company of one or the other.[2]

Duncan Smith began his leadership in the midst of a global crisis, and his first duty (or 'first debut' as one of his team told reporters) was to reply to Tony Blair's statement on international terrorism at the recalled sitting of Parliament.[3] The Leader of the Opposition offered the government unconditional support for its stance, stressing he stood 'shoulder to shoulder' with Blair in his response to the terrorist attacks.[4] This stance became a running theme of Duncan Smith's leadership, as he balanced domestic political opposition with support for Blair over military action in Afghanistan and later, Iraq.

As had been predicted, Conservative moderates remained unreconciled to the new leader and were particularly unhappy when his new frontbench team rewarded hardline Eurosceptics and right-wing former rebels. This included Bill Cash as the shadow Attorney General and Eric Forth as shadow Leader of the House of Commons. Leading supporters of Clarke's leadership campaign were excluded, and one backbencher complained, 'Iain had the support of one third of the parliamentary party and he has packed his entire team with that third.'[5]

This rather set the tone for the remainder of Duncan Smith's leadership. He faced continual criticism for his failure to make a breakthrough in the opinion polls or in the media. Whereas Hague had at least been able to cheer up his troops with his performances at Prime Minister's Questions, his successor was not effective at the Commons despatch box, nor a compelling platform speaker. Duncan Smith attempted to turn his limitations to his advantage in his 2002 party conference address by declaring, 'Do not underestimate the determination of a quiet man', but the line was roundly mocked and led to Labour MPs greeting his subsequent appearances at the despatch box with a loud 'Shhhhhhhhh!'[6]

In November 2002, he faced a rebellion by forty-three of his MPs after he imposed a three-line whip instructing his party to oppose the government's legislation to allow unmarried and same-sex couples to adopt children. He was openly attacked in the debate by Portillo, whilst John Bercow resigned from his position in the shadow Cabinet in protest. In the wake of the crisis, he called a press conference at Conservative Central Office on 5 November to make a 'personal statement' to the party:

> We cannot go on in this fashion. We have to pull together or we will
> · hang apart ... The Conservative Party wants to be led. It elected me

to lead it in the direction I am now going. I will not look kindly on people who put personal ambitions before the interests of the party. My message is simple and stark: unite or die.[7]

The appeal was not well received, with many MPs observing that it was a heavy irony for the serial Maastricht rebel to now be demanding unquestioning loyalty to his own leadership. He survived for another year, but ongoing questions about his abilities were compounded by the so-called 'Betsygate' scandal, which erupted in the autumn of 2003 as he faced a parliamentary standards inquiry into the use of public funds to employ his wife in the leader's office. The episode acted as a catalyst for the pent-up frustrations over the leadership, and with party donors withdrawing funding from the party, MPs were urged to act. In a turn of phrase typical of the unpleasantness of Westminster intrigue, a Conservative frontbencher was quoted as saying, 'The stench of death is all around us, but we have not quite decided how to dispose of the corpse.'[8]

They soon decided. In what would become a familiar process in later years, the required number of MPs submitted letters to the chairman of the 1922 Committee asking for a vote of no confidence. Duncan Smith responded defiantly, appealing for support and writing an article for *The Times* on the day of the vote, in which he noted that the previous day was the feast day of St Jude, 'the patron saint of impossible causes'.[9] Despite pledging to address the shortcomings of his leadership, he was unable to convince a majority of his colleagues to back him and lost the vote by ninety votes to seventy-five. In his statement accepting his dismissal, he referred several times to his position as the first leader to have been elected by the party's grassroots and ended by saying, 'I profoundly hope that the next leader to be elected in this manner will also be the next prime minister.'[10] Whilst it didn't occur in quite the way he envisaged, that hope was ultimately fulfilled, with the next leader to be elected in a full contest being David Cameron.

Like many of the failed leaders we have considered, Duncan Smith's troubled tenure does not reflect his only contribution to public life. A year later he established the Centre for Social Justice (CSJ) to pursue the social policy agenda that had begun to be developed under his leadership, and he was then appointed in 2005 to chair the social justice policy review under Cameron's leadership. When the party returned to office in 2010, Duncan Smith was appointed to the Cabinet as Secretary of State for Work and Pensions and oversaw the introduction of Universal Credit – one of the CSJ's flagship welfare policy proposals and one which has had a huge impact on the provision of welfare in the UK. It is a reminder that even in the most unpromising periods of opposition, the seeds of significant future policy can be sown.

41

Michael Howard

Conservative, Leader of the Opposition 2003–05

No, he did not threaten to overrule him. That, eventually, was the answer to the question which Michael Howard was infamously asked twelve times by Jeremy Paxman on the BBC's *Newsnight* in May 1997. During that interview, which took place during the Conservative leadership election, Howard was asked about a controversy from his time as Home Secretary, when it was suggested he had threatened to overrule the head of the prison service, Derek Lewis, to have the governor of Parkhurst Prison suspended from duty after the escape of three prisoners. He steadfastly refused to answer the question, later explaining that he could not recall whether he had done so, and instead clung to the line that he had not overruled Lewis. Seven years later, after he had become Leader of the Opposition, Howard was interviewed by Paxman again and finally gave the answer: 'As it happens, I didn't. Are you satisfied now?'[1]

By this time, Howard was perhaps able to laugh about the legendary interview, having now become leader of the Conservative Party. But at the time, his discomfort on television, combined with a series of personal attacks on him by his former junior minister at the Home

Office, Ann Widdecombe, is thought to have contributed to his failure in the 1997 leadership contest, in which he finished in last place.

Widdecombe's first salvo was reported in the *Sunday Times* on 11 May 1997, ten days after the general election defeat, where she was quoted as having told 'friends' that her former boss was 'dangerous stuff' and that there was 'something of the night' in his personality. She went on to tell those 'friends' that she believed Howard unsuitable to be leader of the Conservative Party and was 'determined to raise questions about his character' in the minds of Tory MPs.[2] The *Newsnight* interview took place two days later, and the following week, Widdicombe followed up with a detailed attack on his conduct at the Home Office in a debate in Parliament on 19 May.

The infamous 'something of the night' remark immediately entered the political lexicon and reinforced existing cartoon portrayals of Howard as a sinister vampire. Viewed today, such references are more than a little troubling, given they were directed towards the Jewish son of an immigrant from the Transylvania area of Romania. They seem at the very least a touch xenophobic and at worst, plain antisemitic.

Howard's father, Bernat Hecht, had arrived in the UK in 1937 after being invited to work as a cantor at a synagogue in Whitechapel, east London. He moved to Llanelli in 1940, escaping the Blitz, and married Hilda Kershion, whose Jewish family had come to Wales from what is now Ukraine in 1912. He began working for her family's draper business, and a year after their wedding, on 7 July 1941, their son Michael was born in Gorseinon Hospital, between Swansea and Llanelli. Many of Bernat's family remained in their home village of Ruscova, situated near the Ukrainian border in Romania, and later in the war they and other Jewish residents were rounded up and sent to Nazi concentration camps. His mother, Michael's grandmother, was amongst those who were murdered in the gas chambers of Auschwitz.

In 1947, Bernat applied for British citizenship for himself and his family, including Michael and his younger sister, Pamela. On the granting of the application, he anglicised his name to Bernard and changed the family name by deed poll to Howard. Their business flourished, and they soon owned two clothes shops in Llanelli, later opening another in Carmarthen. It was not a hugely political household, and Howard later suggested that neither of his parents had previously voted Conservative and were probably Liberals. He also recalled how his father had impressed upon him how much the family owed to their adopted country, a sentiment which Howard himself would later express as being at the root of his patriotism.

He attended the local primary school, moving to another at the age of seven, and was remembered by his teachers as bright and articulate. He passed the eleven-plus in 1952 and won a place at Llanelli Grammar School, where alongside his academic studies he became a keen football player – an act of rebellion in a school and area obsessed with rugby. He had also developed his interest in politics, with contemporaries recalling he talked of becoming a lawyer and an MP from the age of thirteen. In sixth form he took A-Levels in English, history and economics and joined the school's debating society. All this one might expect from a future Tory politician, but he also had more lively interests. At the age of sixteen he bought his first Elvis Presley record and became something of a wannabe rock 'n' roll star, forming a skiffle band with schoolfriends which played covers of songs by Bill Haley, Lonnie Donegan and, of course, Elvis. Howard was the singer, sporting a Teddy boy hairstyle, sideburns and drainpipe trousers with fluorescent socks. The thought of the future Home Secretary so attired and belting out 'Jailhouse Rock' is quite the image.

Despite his headmaster advising him to lower his sights to Welsh universities, Howard was determined to try for Cambridge and, after a number of rejections from his first choices of college, was finally accepted by Peterhouse to study economics in 1959. In common with another Welsh opposition leader, he was the first in his family to go to university, and he said the opportunity 'transformed' him. He became an active member of the Cambridge University Conservative Association (CUCA) and from his second year onwards spoke frequently at the Cambridge Union. During this time, he was part of what later became known as the 'Cambridge Mafia' of future Conservative Cabinet ministers, which included Kenneth Clarke, John Gummer, Norman Fowler, Leon Brittan and Norman Lamont. The group was bound together by a shared commitment to a modern One Nation strand of conservatism, and Howard recalls that Iain Macleod was their great hero at the time.

Although they became good friends, and remained so throughout their later careers, there was a good deal of rivalry within the 'Mafia' for advancement within CUCA and the Union. This led to a notorious controversy after Clarke, who had become chairman of CUCA, invited the fascist leader Sir Oswald Mosley to speak in a debate. Howard resigned from CUCA's committee in protest and publicly called for the invitation to be withdrawn. It caused a huge controversy, but both Howard and Clarke have since been accused of a degree of opportunism, given they were both seeking at the time to boost their profiles ahead of elections for the Union. In the wake of his dramatic resignation, Howard won greater support from the left and defeated Clarke in the contest to become Union secretary, putting him on course to become president, which he then did. Clarke had to wait a little longer.

Having switched from economics to law, Howard stayed on after graduation to take a master's degree in law whilst simultaneously studying for the Bar. He passed in December 1963 and began practising as a barrister, specialising in employment law. He continued to pursue his political ambitions and was selected as the Conservative candidate for the safe Labour seat of Liverpool Edge Hill at the 1966 general election. This was despite an awkward moment at his selection interview, where he declared his love for Liverpool Football Club, only to discover that the whole panel was comprised of Everton supporters. He later joked that being selected despite this was his greatest political achievement. Howard fought the seat unsuccessfully that year and, after failing to win selection for a more winnable seat, stood there again in the 1970 election. He achieved a much better result, with a swing to the Conservatives greater than the national average, but not enough to win the seat.

By this time, he had achieved some degree of national prominence as chairman of the Bow Group, having served since 1965 on its council and progressed through the ranks as its secretary and then political officer. The Bow Group in those days held annual elections and was rather like a Cambridge Union for adults, with many of Howard's contemporaries also taking officer positions and contributing to the writing of research papers.* One of Howard's causes at this time built on his work as an employment lawyer, calling for reform of industrial legislation by the removal of state benefits to strikers. This was the subject of an open letter he wrote to the new Conservative Prime Minister Edward Heath in 1970 and of his first speech to the Conservative Party conference that year.

Like many Conservatives of his generation, Howard was an enthusiastic backer of the UK's membership of the European Communities and served on the committees of the European Movement and the Conservative Group for Europe from 1970 to 1973. He backed

---

* The Bow Group continued as a membership body with elected officers until 2011, when its democratic structure was abolished and its incumbent chairman turned it into a right-wing pressure group.

continued membership of the European Communities in the referendum in 1975. That year he also married Sandra Paul, a well-known fashion model who had appeared on the cover of American *Vogue* in the 1960s and been married three times before. She had a twelve-year-old son, Sholto, from her first marriage to Robin Douglas-Home, a nephew of the former Prime Minister. It was a surprising match, with several of Howard's friends reportedly writing to advise him against it. But the marriage was to prove a success, with Sandra, by no means the typical Tory wife, strongly supporting her new husband's political ambitions.

Those ambitions appeared to have rather stalled during the 1970s, however. His legal career was going well, and he would eventually become a QC, but after his two elections in Liverpool he was unsuccessful for more than a decade in his attempts to win selection for a more promising Conservative seat. The closest he came was in the contest for Tunbridge Wells in 1974, where he tied in the final ballot with the eventual winner, Patrick Mayhew, who was then selected on the chairman's casting vote. In the run-up to the 1979 general election he failed to make the shortlist for Huntingdon (which selected John Major) and lost out in the final at West Derbyshire to Matthew Parris. In total, he applied for around forty seats without success. Whilst many of his contemporaries had been elected to Parliament, he had to wait until 1982, when he was finally selected for Folkestone and Hythe at the height of the Falklands War. At the 1983 election a year later, he won with a majority of 11,670 over the Liberal runner-up.

In the Commons at last, he had some catching up to do with the rest of the Cambridge Mafia, many of whom were already ministers, including two – Fowler and Brittan – in the Cabinet. He began his ascent with appointment as a junior minister at the Department of Trade and Industry in 1985, responsible for relations with the City of

London during the 'big bang' reforms the following year. After the 1987 election he was promoted to Minister for Local Government, where his tenure involved him in two issues that were to become lasting millstones around his neck. The first was the introduction of the community charge, swiftly dubbed the 'poll tax', which, though the impetus came from Margaret Thatcher, Howard was responsible for steering through Parliament. The second was his acceptance of a backbench amendment which became known as Section 28, during the passage of the Local Government Act 1988. This infamously decreed that local councils should not 'promote homosexuality' or allow schools to teach 'the acceptability of homosexuality as a pretended family relationship'. It became a totemic piece of homophobic legislation, which caused profound offence to many gay people. Howard later said he was wrong to have supported it, but the damage it caused to the reputation of the Conservatives on issues of gay equality was profound.

With a growing reputation for skilful handling of controversial issues, Howard was put in charge of overseeing water privatisation in 1989, before being promoted to Cabinet as Employment Secretary in January 1990, following the resignation of Fowler. In this role, he was responsible for legislation on trade union reform, including the banning of the 'closed shop' (the practice of making trade union membership mandatory for all employees). This was an issue on which he had been consistently campaigning for decades, based on his experience as an employment lawyer. Across the despatch box he faced another rising star barrister, Tony Blair, who as Labour's employment spokesman had recently given an early sign of his modernising credentials by reversing his party's commitment to the closed shop.

Howard remained as Employment Secretary when Major succeeded Thatcher as Prime Minister, before being moved, following the 1992 general election, to Environment Secretary. His year in that department coincided with the UN Earth Summit in Rio de Janeiro, in which he took a great interest, lobbying the United States to get them to participate and personally negotiating the wording of the agreement on reducing greenhouse gases to ensure it was successfully adopted by 143 countries. He remains proud of this work, though the outcome was criticised at the time for not including legally binding commitments.

Having secured his entry to the Cabinet on the departure of one of his Cambridge Mafia contemporaries, his next promotion was facilitated in the same way, when the sacking of his good friend Lamont as Chancellor prompted a reshuffle in which Howard was appointed Home Secretary. It was in this post that his public reputation was mostly made, for better or worse. He recounts the story of how his civil servants greeted him on his appointment by telling him that crime had risen consistently in previous years and that there was nothing he could do about it. He defied this established view and set about instituting a hard-line policy, where his prominent mantra was that 'prison works', and which resulted in a fall in recorded crime of 16.8 per cent. But his tenure was also marked by a number of high-profile prison escapes, which then prompted the controversy over his dismissal of the head of the prison service, Derek Lewis.

After the Conservative defeat at the 1997 general election, he stood for the leadership, but as we have seen, the attack on his record and character by Widdecombe, combined with William Hague's rejection of the offer to become his running mate, contributed to his defeat in the first round, where he came fifth out of five candidates. Under Hague's leadership he initially served as shadow Foreign Secretary but retired to the back benches two years later. It was only when Iain Duncan Smith became leader that he was recalled to the front bench as shadow Chancellor, a role in which he built his stature through impressive performances at the despatch box against Gordon Brown. When Duncan Smith lost the vote of no confidence in his leadership at the end of October 2003, Howard emerged as the consensus candidate to replace him, with other contenders including David Davis standing aside to allow him to become leader without a contest.

It was a surprising comeback but largely reflected the dire state of the Conservative Party at the time. There was a clear desire on the part of Tory MPs to bring some order to the chaos, and his accession was greeted with comments along the lines of 'the grown-ups are back in charge', as he brought greater discipline and professionalism to the opposition's operation. Here I should once again declare an interest, as one of his reforms to the party's organisation was to bolster the Conservative Research Department, recruiting a number of bright young advisers, including the future Deputy Prime Minister Oliver Dowden and, less notably, me.

Facing his former shadow, Tony Blair, in the Commons, he memorably contrasted his own meritocratic story with that of the privately educated Labour leader, telling him that 'this grammar school boy is not going to take any lessons from that public school boy' on the issue of university access.[3] Despite such backbench-pleasing performances, he struggled to make much progress in the opinion polls, and Labour made much of his past record in government, dubbing him 'Mr Poll Tax' and attacking him for political opportunism, particularly over the Iraq War. Attempts to project a more modern image to the country were undermined by media focus on the party's messages on tax and immigration, which seemed to show the party appealing once again to its core membership vote. At the 2005 general election, Howard led the party to another heavy defeat, albeit one which saw Labour's majority reduced from 166 to sixty-six. On the morning after the election he announced his intention to resign the leadership.

This was not quite the end of his contribution, however. Instead of standing down quickly, he remained in office until December, allowing for a long leadership contest which spanned the summer and the October party conference. He also reshuffled the shadow Cabinet, promoting two bright young protégés who had become close advisers to him during the run-up to the general election. One was George Osborne, whom he made shadow Chancellor at the age of just thirty-three, and the other was David Cameron, previously Howard's special adviser at the Home Office, who became shadow Education Secretary. The pair were part of what had become known as the 'Notting Hill set' of young modernisers in the party, and they mounted what was at first seen as an outside bid for the leadership, with Cameron as their chosen candidate. Whilst Howard had remained officially neutral during the contest, his actions in promoting the new generation and allowing them the time to make their mark proved decisive and set the conditions for Cameron to succeed where his three predecessors as Leader of the Opposition had failed.

42

Harriet Harman

Labour, Acting Leader of the Opposition May–September
2010 and May–September 2015

The next entrant on our list stands out for a number of reasons. As well as being one of only two women to feature, she is also the only one since the nineteenth century to have had two separate terms as leader. Like Margaret Beckett and George Brown before her, Harriet Harman assumed the leadership of the Labour Party on a temporary basis, having been deputy leader when the leadership became vacant. In her case, the two occasions where she was called upon to fulfil the duties of Leader of the Opposition were the result of post-defeat resignations rather than sudden deaths, but both involved dealing with a party grieving for its loss.

Her combined time as leader amounts to around eight months, which is certainly not the shortest tenure we have encountered, but it is still dwarfed by her wider experience on the political frontline. Having been in the House of Commons since 1982, she has in recent years been dubbed the Mother of the House as its longest continuously serving female MP.*

---

* A previous leader, Margaret Beckett, has actually served longer as an MP overall, having been first elected in 1974, but was out of the House between 1979 and 1983.

She was on the opposition front bench from 1984 to 1997, had two stints in the Cabinet and was deputy leader of the Labour Party in government and opposition for eight years.

Harman was born in 1950 in London's Harley Street, into a solidly middle-class household. Her father was a doctor, and her mother had been a barrister, later standing as a Liberal candidate at the 1964 general election. The family tree has a number of notable political connections – Joseph Chamberlain was her father's great-uncle, and her aunt married the Earl of Longford, a Labour peer. More pertinent to Harman's later political agenda, her great-grandfather's sister was the feminist and suffragette, Louisa Martindale.

Harman herself says her commitment to the cause of women's rights was fuelled by the experience of her mother, who, after practising the law for just a few years, had given up her career when she had children to become a housewife, as was widely expected of women at the time. The fact that her legal gown and wig ended up in the children's dressing-up box was a particularly poignant symbol that stuck in the mind of the young Harriet.

After being educated privately at St Paul's Girls' School in Hammersmith, she went on to study politics at the University of York. There, she steered clear of student politics, finding that it mostly divided itself between the extreme left-wing 'Trots' and the Tories, neither of which she wanted to be associated with. She also recalls one of her tutors telling her in her final year that she would get a better grade if she agreed to have sex with him, an offer she rejected in disgust.

On graduating, she trained to become a solicitor and took up work at the Brent Law Centre, where she met her future husband Jack Dromey and became involved in supporting a number of employment causes. She then moved on to become a legal officer at the National Council for Civil Liberties (NCCL), where she pursued a number of cases on behalf of women under the Sex Discrimination Act, as well as campaigning for new legislation for freedom of information and human rights.

She was adopted as the Labour candidate for Peckham in 1981. The following year, the incumbent Labour MP Harry Lamborn died, and she was elected to Parliament in the subsequent by-election. She was pregnant with her first child during the campaign and despite finding it difficult to juggle motherhood with her duties as an MP, felt it her duty to persevere to disprove the notion that women could not combine family life with a career. She described herself on one occasion as being the 'political wing of the women's movement'.[1]

In 1984, Neil Kinnock asked her to join the opposition front bench. She hesitated, feeling the pressure would be too great, but accepted the position after persuasion from Patricia Hewitt, her former boss at the NCCL, who was now Kinnock's press secretary. She was initially a social services spokesperson, moving to the Department of Health after the 1987 general election. When John Smith became leader in 1992, she was elected to the shadow Cabinet and was appointed shadow Chief Secretary to the Treasury. A year later, she wasn't voted into the shadow Cabinet after a number of perceived political mistakes, but Smith retained her in her post. In 1994, under Tony Blair, she received the fifth-most votes and was promoted to shadow Employment Secretary and then shadow Health Secretary.

In early 1996, Harman was embroiled in controversy when it emerged she and her husband were sending their son to a state grammar school, a move which opened her to charges of hypocrisy given Labour's opposition to selective schools. There were calls for her to resign from the shadow Cabinet, but she received support from Blair and remained in post, though she was moved to become shadow Secretary of State for Social Security ahead of the 1997 general election.

With Labour in power, she was appointed Secretary of State for Social Security, but her tenure was marred by growing tensions with her junior minister, Frank Field, who had been put in the department by Blair to 'think the unthinkable' on welfare reform. Backbench rebellions over benefit cuts to single parents also damaged her position, and she was sacked from the Cabinet after a year. She remained on the back benches until after the 2001 general election when Blair brought her back as Solicitor General, the first woman to hold the position. She was then made a minister at the Department for Constitutional Affairs following the 2005 general election.

When Blair resigned in 2007, John Prescott also stood down as deputy leader of the Labour Party, and Harman stood in the contest to succeed him. In a close vote, she narrowly beat Alan Johnson by less than 1 per cent in the final round, but despite her victory, Gordon Brown did not appoint her as Deputy Prime Minister. She later criticised this decision, questioning whether a man would have been treated the same way. Instead, she was made Leader of the House of Commons, Lord Privy Seal and Minister for Women and Equality. It was suggested to her during a reshuffle in 2009 that Lord Mandelson might be appointed as Deputy Prime Minister. She confronted Brown with her strong objections, telling him it would happen 'over my dead body'. Brown reluctantly dropped the plan, and Mandelson had to be content instead with the title of First Secretary of State.

Despite being denied the title, Harman stood in for Brown at Prime Minister's Questions when he was away and surprised commentators by putting in combative performances against the Conservatives' William Hague (who was deputising for David Cameron). As Minister for Women and Equality she also oversaw the introduction of the Equality Act 2010, which consolidated previous pieces of equalities legislation including the Equal Pay Act 1970, the Sex Discrimination

Act 1975 and the Race Relations Act 1976. It also placed public authorities under a duty to advance greater equality. For someone whose legal career had begun by pursuing such cases, it was a fitting piece of signature legislation, which reached the statute book in the last weeks of the Labour government.

After Labour lost the 2010 election, Brown decided not to put himself through the ordeal of becoming Leader of the Opposition, even on an interim basis. After resigning as Prime Minister, he immediately resigned as Labour leader, and Harman automatically became leader until the conclusion of the leadership contest. Unlike Beckett, she decided not to stand for the post herself. She later reflected that, as many women found, there was a general sense that she wasn't 'leadership material', but as she took on the job of Leader of the Opposition, she found, somewhat to her own surprise, that she was doing well:

> Going round the country, party members were saying, 'You're nailing it, we're so proud of you – why aren't you standing for leader?' And I was so relieved not to be cocking the whole thing up that I took it as a great compliment, but I didn't go that next step and think, 'They're asking me why I'm not going for leader – why aren't I?' I just never got to that point. I think if I'd stood, I definitely would've got it. Whether I'd have made a success out of it, well, we'll never know, but I think I would have got it.[2]

In the event, Ed Miliband became leader, somewhat ironically given that he had once been employed as Harman's aide. She remained as deputy leader during his tenure, taking on shadow Cabinet roles as shadow Secretary of State for International Development and then for Culture, Media and Sport. Harman also made clear to him that were Labour to come into power, she would expect to be made Deputy

Prime Minister. During the 2015 election campaign she embarked on a nationwide 'Woman to Woman' campaigning tour, focused on encouraging women voters to turn out, but her decision to use a bright pink minibus attracted criticism and mockery in some quarters.

When David Cameron's Conservatives won an unexpected majority, Miliband followed the precedent set by Brown and resigned the leadership with immediate effect. Harman was again acting Leader of the Opposition, but again decided not to stand in the contest herself and also announced she was stepping down as deputy leader. This time, her temporary leadership was not without controversy, as she suffered a backbench rebellion after whipping Labour MPs to abstain on the government's Welfare Reform and Work Bill. A total of forty-eight of them defied the whip to vote against it, including Jeremy Corbyn. It was a sign of things to come, with Corbyn and his supporters using the incident to highlight his left-wing credentials and boost his insurgent campaign to become leader, given that other leadership contenders had toed the line and abstained.

After the surprise result of the 2015 Labour leadership election, she handed over the reins to Corbyn with a prescient warning about the need for Labour to remain an electable force. In an interview with *The Times* published on the day of the result, she said:

> The whole point about the Labour cause is to give people representation and political power, it's not a think tank. There used to be an old left slogan: no compromise with the electorate. That is not a way to be progressive in politics because you can't make change.[3]

43

Ed Miliband

Labour, Leader of the Opposition 2010–15

As many politicians discover to their cost, a disastrous TV inter-view can cause lasting political damage or, in the case of Michael Howard, end their leadership ambitions. For Ed Miliband, however, one such interview launched him on the road to becoming leader of his party. In 1993, Harriet Harman appeared on Channel 4's *A Week in Politics*, in her role as shadow Chief Secretary to the Treasury. Driving to the studio with her five-year-old daughter in the back seat of her car, she was preoccupied with singing nursery rhymes and discuss-ing the different-coloured manes of her daughter's My Little Pony toys. Slowly, it dawned on her that she was utterly unprepared for the grilling she was about to receive, having not obtained any briefing on its subject matter. As she feared, it was a disaster. 'It wasn't just that I couldn't answer the questions, I didn't even understand them,' she wrote later.[1] The programme's interviewer, Vincent Hanna, had a carefully prepared line of attack which utterly floored the shadow min-ister, leaving her 'a puddle on the studio floor', in the words of his co-presenter, Andrew Rawnsley.[2]

The author of those questions was a bright 23-year-old researcher called Ed Miliband. He had gone to work on the show the previous year and impressed his bosses with his forensic briefings for its interviews. Some months later, Harman was looking for a new aide, and a colleague recommended that she approach Miliband. She called Rawnsley, who gave a glowing reference, and Harman duly hired her former tormenter to work in her office. Fourteen years later, they were serving in Cabinet together, and three years after that, she handed over the reins of the leadership to him and served as his deputy.

Miliband's narrow victory in the 2010 leadership election was a nail-biting finish to a contest that had divided not just his party but his family. His older brother, the former Foreign Secretary David Miliband, had been the favourite to win, and the spectacle of the two siblings fighting one another for the crown had dominated media coverage. When the younger contender unexpectedly prevailed, cameras surrounded the brothers at the declaration event as they shared an awkward embrace, and amateur psychologists speculated about the nature of the fraternal rivalry.

The Miliband brothers had grown up in Primrose Hill, north London. Their father was the renowned Marxist academic and author Ralph Miliband, whilst their mother Marion Kozak was a committed human rights campaigner and Labour activist. Both parents had arrived in the UK as Jewish refugees, with Ralph having fled from Belgium with his father during the Second World War and Marion having arrived from Poland shortly after it. Their escape from Nazi persecution formed the opening section of Ed Miliband's first conference speech as leader, in which he told their story:

> In 1940, my grandfather, with my dad, climbed onto one of the last boats out of Belgium. They had to make a heart-breaking decision – to leave behind my grandmother and my father's sister. They spent

the war in hiding, in a village sheltered by a brave local farmer. Month after month, year upon year, they lived in fear of the knock at the door. At the same time, on the other side of Europe my mother, aged five, had seen Hitler's army march into Poland. She spent the war on the run, sheltering in a convent and then with a Catholic family that took her in. Her sister, her mother and her. My love for this country comes from this story. Two young people fled the darkness that had engulfed the Jews across Europe, and in Britain they found the light of liberty. They arrived with nothing. This country gave them everything.[3]

Ralph Miliband's experiences had cemented both his hatred for fascism and his growing attachment to the ideas of Karl Marx. Just months after arriving in London at the age of sixteen, he had made a personal pilgrimage to Marx's grave in Highgate Cemetery and sworn a private oath to remain true to the workers' cause. These convictions were nurtured when he was accepted to study at the London School of Economics (LSE) under the Marxist academic Harold Laski. After interrupting his studies to serve in the navy during the war, he completed his studies at the LSE and secured a lecturing position there.

It was whilst teaching that he met Marion, a student, whom he then married in 1961 – the same year he published his most famous work, *Parliamentary Socialism: A Study in the Politics of Labour*. This provided a critique of the Labour Party, for what he saw as its lack of radical commitment to socialism and its attachment to the traditional institutions of the state. His disillusionment with Labour had led him to leave the party during the leadership of Hugh Gaitskell, but Marion remained a member. Whilst their father was the renowned academic thinker, it was their mother who provided the Miliband children with their introduction to political activism and the Labour movement, with her activities including support for the Campaign for Nuclear Disarmament and for the miners' strike in the mid-1980s. She was also a scholar in her own right, gaining a PhD from the University of Hull in 1976.

When Ed Miliband was born on 24 December 1969 at University College Hospital in London, he was therefore entering a household steeped in left-wing political thought and debate. He and David, who had been born four years previously, grew up surrounded by leading figures of the left, who would drop in for dinners and political discussions. These included Tony Benn, Tariq Ali and leaders of the South African anti-apartheid movement, such as Ruth First. First was assassinated by a letter bomb in 1982, just a few months after the twelve-year-old Ed had met her during one of her visits. The shock of her assassination had a profound effect on him, and he later ascribed to it his firm commitment that 'political causes matter'.[4]

After attending the nearby Haverstock School, a comprehensive in the middle of Camden, Miliband was accepted to study PPE at Corpus Christi, Oxford – the same subject and college as his elder brother had chosen. Before beginning university, he took a gap year and went to New York, where his father was teaching at City University. His mother also went out, and for a year the family lived together in Manhattan, whilst David was not too far away in Boston, studying for a postgraduate degree at the Massachusetts Institute of Technology. Ed secured an internship working for the public broadcaster PBS, then one with the left-wing magazine *The Nation*.

Returning to the UK, he began his degree at Oxford in 1989. During his time there he describes himself as having been a bit of a 'square', concentrating on his studies and his growing political interests. He became chair of the university's Labour Club in his first year and was elected president of Corpus Christi's Junior Common Room (JCR) in his second. From this position he mounted a high-profile campaign against a proposed 39 per cent rent increase for students at the college, which attracted regional television coverage and led to a partial victory, with the college delaying the full increase.

Miliband's political activity is sometimes given as the reason for him not getting the first-class degree that was widely predicted by his tutors. His finals took place shortly after the 1992 general election, and he had devoted considerable time over the previous year to campaigning for Labour both in Oxford and in London. He was deeply disappointed when the party lost to the Conservatives, but the experience made him more determined to pursue a political career. Emerging from Oxford with a respectable 2:1, he went back to New York for another brief internship at *The Nation*, then on his return applied for the job at *A Week in Politics*, which would bring him to Harman's attention.

He had been at Channel 4 less than a year when he accepted the role on Harman's team, and some of his colleagues thought he was selling himself short by giving up a promising career in television to work for a junior member of the shadow Cabinet. Such fears soon seemed to have been well founded, as Harman failed to be re-elected to the shadow Cabinet. She recalls that, as well as her personal humiliation, she was 'mortified' to have messed up Miliband's career, as it looked like he would now be out of a job only a month after joining her.[5] Luckily for them both, John Smith decided to keep Harman on as shadow Chief Secretary, despite the election setback.

Miliband swiftly made his mark as an effective researcher. In January 1994, he scored a notable hit on the Conservative government by forcing the Treasury to admit in a series of parliamentary answers that the tax burden was set to rise above the level left by the last Labour government in 1979. They ran the story past Gordon Brown, the shadow

Chancellor, who didn't seem too impressed and thought it would be of limited interest. Instead, the story dominated the Sunday newspapers, and Brown called Miliband to congratulate him and admit that he had been wrong – a somewhat unusual concession.

Having thus attracted the attention of Harman's boss, Miliband was soon seconded to work for him as a 'number cruncher' and remained with the shadow Chancellor's team after Tony Blair took over as Labour leader in May of that year. Despite the promotion, Miliband was still very much a junior member of the political team, with Ed Balls and Charlie Whelan being Brown's key aides at this time. A year into the job, he took time out to complete a master's degree in economics at the LSE, before returning as the election approached. Meanwhile, David Miliband had been appointed head of policy to Blair, putting the two brothers on either side of the Blair/Brown divide that was to characterise the New Labour years.

After the 1997 election, Miliband entered government as a special adviser to Brown but continued to be seen as 'the other Ed', as the clearly junior partner to Balls, who was frequently dubbed the 'deputy Chancellor'. The two were close colleagues but reportedly never became friends. Miliband was also less tribal in the ongoing battle between Brown and Blair, maintaining communications with his brother and other members of the Prime Minister's team.

After the 2001 election, he took another academic sabbatical, heading off to Harvard in July 2002 to teach economics for eighteen months as a visiting scholar. On his return to the UK in early 2004, Brown appointed him chairman of the Council of Economic Advisers, but he was by this time actively looking for a seat in Parliament. A year later, Miliband was selected to fight Doncaster North, where he was elected as the MP at the 2005 general election. Blair appointed him as Minister for the Third Sector in 2006, and when Brown succeeded as

Prime Minister, he promoted Miliband to Cabinet as Chancellor of the Duchy of Lancaster and Minister for the Cabinet Office. With his brother David now Foreign Secretary, it was the first time since 1938 that two siblings had sat in Cabinet together. A year later, he was promoted to Secretary of State at the new Department of Energy and Climate Change, taking a leading role in advancing the UK's commitment to reduce carbon emissions. He remained in post until the Labour government fell in 2010.

Miliband's decision to stand for the newly vacant leadership against his brother was the main focus of attention, but it was also notable that he was standing against Balls, his superior from their Treasury days. His victory over both of them represented his emergence from being not just 'the other Miliband' but also 'the other Ed'. His success owed much to his reputation for being more left-wing than his brother, and the label of 'Red Ed' was first applied to him during the contest. It was suggested he was sympathetic to his late father's Marxist views, and it was noted that, as a teenager, he had a summer job working for Tony Benn, as one of the veteran left-winger's 'Teabags' (The Eminent Association of Benn Archive Graduates). This, combined with his retrospective opposition to the Iraq War, helped him to be seen as the insurgent candidate against what he called 'the New Labour establishment', but he bristled at suggestions he was a throwback to the far left of the 1980s:

> I am not a Bennite. [I worked for him] when I was sixteen, for six weeks. It does show how political debate has narrowed in this country. I am someone who practises what a lot of people would see as social democratic politics, the need for a more equal society, decency at work. These are centre-ground positions, actually. It is a ludicrous caricature that I am either Michael Foot or Tony Benn.[6]

Nevertheless, the 'Red Ed' label was hard to shift in the right-wing press, and the Conservative Party did its utmost to continue embedding it in the public consciousness during his leadership. Miliband also never broke free of the perception that he had committed political fratricide by standing against and beating his brother, who then left frontline politics and eventually took a job in America. The relationship with Balls was also problematic, with Miliband initially refusing his former colleague his coveted role of shadow Chancellor, only conceding it after the resignation of Alan Johnson from the role in early 2011.

Whatever the criticism of Miliband's time as Leader of the Opposition, he was undeniably a serious contender to be Prime Minister. Labour held a lead over the Conservatives in the opinion polls for most of the 2010–15 government, and it was thought almost inconceivable that the Conservatives would be able to improve their position, leaving Miliband best placed to form a minority government even if Labour fell short of a majority. Whilst the party was polling well, however, Miliband's own popularity ratings were stuck in negative territory. He was seen by many voters as 'nerdy' and 'weird', an impression cruelly symbolised by an infamous photograph of him attempting to eat a bacon sandwich in 2014. An election stunt where he unveiled Labour's pledges carved on a large stone was also widely mocked.

Labour's loss in 2015 has been likened to that suffered by Neil Kinnock in 1992, the last occasion where an election that was predicted to result in a hung Parliament in fact resulted in a surprise majority for the incumbent Conservative government. This was something of an irony, given that Kinnock had been one of Miliband's earliest and most enthusiastic backers during the leadership contest and shared much of his political outlook. The two leaders could certainly compare notes on the experience of defeat, but also on their treatment by a hostile media, which focused on attacking their economic competence and personal suitability to be Prime Minister.

Following the election defeat, Miliband announced immediately that he would be standing down as leader, and the subsequent contest would provide a test of one particular part of his legacy. The controversy over the selection of a candidate in Falkirk in 2013 had led Miliband to commission a review of selection procedures in the party and its relationship with trade unions. Accepting its findings, he abolished the existing electoral college system for electing the leader, changing the process to a straightforward ballot of party members and affiliated supporters. That change was to have far more significant consequences than he or anyone else might have expected at the time.

44

Jeremy Corbyn

Labour, Leader of the Opposition 2015–20

At just before midday on 15 June 2015, a group of Labour MPs were crowded together in a medieval cloister in the Palace of Westminster. It was an evocative setting for some old-school palace intrigue, as the day's drama reached its climax. High noon was the deadline for nominations in the Labour leadership contest, and as supporters of the various candidates gathered in the offices of the Parliamentary Labour Party (PLP), Jeremy Corbyn's team were getting desperate. They were just two names short of the number needed to put their candidate on the ballot, but none of the MPs present wanted to sign until the others did. As the stand-off continued, Corbyn's long-standing ally John McDonnell began to beg. He later claimed to have literally got down on his knees to plead with them: 'Whether you support Jeremy or not, this is in the interests of democracy!'[1] At the last minute, Blackpool South MP Gordon Marsden relented, followed by former Cabinet minister Andrew Smith. As Big Ben began to chime, Corbyn's completed nomination papers were handed over.

It was a fateful moment, but one which might have been forgotten had the leadership election taken its expected course. When it was first reported in early June 2015 that Corbyn would put himself forward for the Labour leadership, the news had attracted little more than a couple of sentences in the newspapers. The main contenders were Andy Burnham, Yvette Cooper and Liz Kendall, and it was their campaigns that dominated media coverage. Labour's new leadership rules put the final choice in the hands of the party's grassroots members but still required that candidates should have the backing of thirty-five MPs to get onto the ballot in the first place, and it seemed highly unlikely that Corbyn would reach this threshold on his own merits. Another hopeful candidate, Mary Creagh, was forced to withdraw after attracting only a handful of backers.

By 11 a.m. on the day nominations closed, Corbyn was still nine backers short. The final hour was decisive and culminated in the tense last-minute scramble in the PLP offices. Before that, a number of Labour MPs had already responded to his appeal, including Margaret Beckett, Sadiq Khan and David Lammy – whilst making very clear they did not themselves support him. Beckett herself later conceded they had been 'morons' to have agreed, but at the time they were convinced by the democratic argument, as Lammy explained:

> While there is enough that Jeremy and I disagree on to mean that I won't be voting for him, I believe the choice of who becomes Labour's next leader should be made by Labour members and supporters, not by MPs. I have always been clear that the Labour party is a broad coalition, and it is important that Jeremy Corbyn's perspective is heard over the coming months.[2]

The argument for widening the debate helped Corbyn over the line, but the news was met with derision from many quarters. Ed Balls's former adviser Alex Belardinelli commented, 'This isn't a game.

Labour is supposed to be trying to elect a leader who can be a credible and winning candidate.' The academic Professor Tim Bale was quoted saying, 'If you're electing a leader, then the only people in the contest should be people who stand a cat in hell's chance of winning.'[3] The prevailing view was that Corbyn's candidacy was nothing more than an indulgent sideshow.

Corbyn had been a fixture on Labour's back benches for over thirty years by this point. First elected as the MP for Islington North in 1983, he was renowned for his unreconstructed views, which had seen him consistently support almost every conceivable left-wing cause and campaign, frequently rebelling against his party's leadership to do so.

His origins were comfortably middle class, with his father and mother working as a skilled engineer and a maths teacher respectively. Born in 1949 as the youngest of four boys in Chippenham, Wiltshire, the family moved when he was seven to Yew Tree Manor, a large seventeenth-century farmhouse in Shropshire. He was educated privately until the age of eleven, when he passed the eleven-plus and attended a nearby grammar school. Both his parents were members of the local Labour Party and were reported to have met in 1936 as students at the University of London, whilst attending a meeting about the Spanish Civil War. Their political activism was something Corbyn would later cite frequently in his speeches, including a story that his mother had been present at the Battle of Cable Street in 1936, when thousands of residents of London's East End, including many Jewish people and trade unionists, barricaded the streets to stop Oswald Mosley marching his British Union of Fascists through the area. This family history, which some suspect might have become somewhat embellished in the telling, later helped Corbyn burnish his left-wing credentials and deflect from his comfortable middle-class upbringing.

Whatever his parents' level of activism, Corbyn himself was certainly involved in left-wing politics from an early age, joining the Wrekin Young Socialists and the Campaign for Nuclear Disarmament and refusing on principle to join the school's Combined Cadet Force. Not having shown much academic prowess, he left school with two A-Levels at grade E, having failed a third, and was reportedly told by his headmaster, 'You'll never make anything of your life.'[4]

After some temporary jobs on a farm and a local newspaper, he applied to join the Voluntary Service Overseas programme, a Foreign Office initiative, and was sent as a trainee teacher to Jamaica, where he taught geography at Kingston College, an elite grammar school in the capital. There he formed an alliance with a prominent Marxist campaigner and, after leaving his teaching role, travelled through Latin America, visiting Brazil, Chile, Argentina and Uruguay and gaining a lifelong sympathy for Marxist and socialist campaigners in those countries.

On his return to the UK in 1971, he worked as a trade union official in north London and in 1974 was elected to Haringey Council, alongside his first wife, Jane Chapman, whom he married at the town hall two days after the election. During his time in local politics over the next nine years he became deeply involved with the organisation of the hard left, working with Ken Livingstone and others to seize control of the London Labour Party, expelling moderates and aiming to secure the leadership of the Greater London Council, which they succeeded in doing in 1981.

Having split from his wife, he also met and had a relationship during this time with Diane Abbott, who was to remain a close political ally. Their affair later became the subject of some fascination at Westminster, including the story that he had engineered an opportunity to show off his new girlfriend to a group of political friends by driving them back to his bedsit during a campaign session 'to collect more leaflets', only for them to walk in and find Abbott naked in his bed.[5] There were also reports of Corbyn and Abbott having taken a motorcycle holiday together in Europe, as well as having enjoyed the great outdoors with some bracing exercise in a field in the Cotswolds.*

In 1982, Corbyn was selected as Labour candidate for Islington North after the incumbent defected to the newly formed Social Democratic Party (SDP), taking with him many of the moderate members of the constituency party. At the following year's general election, Corbyn was elected to Parliament and aligned himself with the Socialist Campaign Group (SCG) of MPs, the hard-left faction whose de facto leader, Tony Benn, had just lost his seat. For the next nine years, Corbyn would be a leading organiser of the group, which opposed Neil Kinnock's efforts to steer the party away from the left and stood their own slates of candidates for shadow Cabinet and other party elections.

Corbyn's activities outside of Parliament were just as notable, as he continued to spend his time on protest marches, demonstrations and controversial political meetings. He was arrested outside South Africa House during a demonstration against apartheid in 1984 and again outside the Old Bailey in 1986 whilst protesting in solidarity with the IRA bomber Patrick Magee, who had been convicted of the Brighton bombing. Corbyn's unambiguous support for the IRA was one of his most controversial positions, and he had earlier attracted widespread condemnation and a reprimand from Labour's Chief Whip for inviting two convicted IRA terrorists to the Commons just weeks after the Brighton bombing.

Following the 1987 general election, Corbyn was elected secretary of the SCG, with Benn as its chairman. When Benn mounted an

---

* Whilst these salacious details only emerged into the mainstream media as a result of published biographies after Corbyn became leader, they had been in circulation at Westminster for many years. I remember a journalist telling me about the alleged 'cornfield romp' over twenty years ago.

unsuccessful leadership bid against Kinnock in 1988, Corbyn was the leading organiser of his campaign amongst MPs. The resounding defeat of this challenge was a sign that the tide had now firmly turned against the hard left. A number of MPs resigned from the SCG and were rewarded with promotion by Kinnock, whose modernisation of the party had begun to show real results. Corbyn and his SCG colleagues nevertheless continued to oppose changes to the party's policies, with one memorandum circulated by Corbyn pouring scorn on Kinnock's pursuit of 'electability'.

His aversion to the pursuit of a more mainstream policy platform continued after the 1992 election, during the leadership of first John Smith and then Tony Blair. Corbyn became a constant critic of the modernising New Labour project, and his activities at times threatened his position within the party. In September 1996 he invited the leader of Sinn Féin, Gerry Adams, to attend a meeting in Parliament during an active IRA bombing campaign in London, a move that was described by Blair as 'reprehensible'.[6] Corbyn was threatened with expulsion from the Parliamentary Labour Party if the meeting went ahead, and he and Adams decided at the last minute to move the meeting to a location outside Parliament.[*] Had they not done so, Corbyn would have had the whip removed and been prevented from standing as a Labour candidate at the next year's election.

As it was, he remained a thorn in the side of Blair's government, frequently criticising government policy and opposing UK involvement in military action in Iraq and Afghanistan as a member of the Stop the War Coalition. His worldview had not changed since the 1970s, and he remained firmly attached to traditional left-wing causes, railing against

---

[*] The day of the proposed visit is one that sticks in my memory, as it coincided with my first ever visit to the Houses of Parliament as a sixteen-year-old A-Level politics student. Whilst Gerry Adams was denied access to the Palace of Westminster that day, my classmates and I from Havant College enjoyed a full tour.

Western imperialism and NATO, whilst championing the Palestinian cause and being particularly critical of the Israeli government. In 2009 he caused outrage by saying he would be inviting to Parliament his 'friends' from the militant groups Hamas and Hezbollah, a comment that would later come back to cause him particular difficulty after he became leader.

Overall, he was the most rebellious Labour MP of the 1997–2010 Labour government, voting against the whip a total of 428 times. After Labour's return to opposition, he supported Abbott in the leadership election, with Ed Miliband as his second choice. He took over as chair of the Stop the War Coalition in 2011 and was notably opposed to military action against Syria but was less vocally hostile towards the Labour leadership than he had been under Blair.

We then reach 2015 and the extraordinary leadership contest which brought Corbyn to sudden prominence. At the outset, he had no expectation of winning and said he had stood because 'it was my turn' to be the token left winger.[7] In 2007, McDonnell had sought to stand against Gordon Brown but had been unable to secure sufficient nominations; Abbott had stood in 2010 and come last with 7.4 per cent of the vote; and Corbyn was set to follow in their footsteps with another heroically doomed gesture.

This time, however, it was different. As the contest developed, Corbyn's populist interventions seemed to be winning him greater support amongst Labour Party members. A candidacy that had begun as a token effort started to be taken seriously. His rise was an extraordinary phenomenon that has been the subject of much analysis and many articles and books since. In May 2015, before the contest had properly begun, a poll of 1,200 Labour Party members asked them to write in their preference for the next leader. Not a single one suggested Corbyn. On the day he announced his entry into the contest, Ladbrokes put his odds at 100/1, and it was widely expected that he would not secure the nominations required to get onto the ballot. As we have seen, only an appeal to 'widen the debate' saw him pass that hurdle, and his odds tightened to a still distant 25/1. Burnham, meanwhile, was the odds-on favourite to win at 5/6.

There were early signs that the outsider might do better than expected, but most of these were initially dismissed as unreliable. On 12 June, just before nominations closed, the LabourList website had published the results of a readers' survey showing Corbyn in the lead with 47 per cent, well ahead of Burnham on 13 per cent. Then, in a notably prescient blog post on the betting website Betfair, Paul Krishnamurty recommended readers back Corbyn (at odds of 25/1), noting, 'It is no surprise Corbyn struggled to get 35 supporters [from the Parliamentary party], but this has never truly reflected the wider movement, that remains firmly left-wing.' He concluded that:

> At this early stage of a long race, Corbyn has to be the value bet. His core economic message is clear, distinct from the rest and appeals to a wider section of people, particularly political activists, than the mainstream media give credit. It will be no surprise at all to see him top more polls in the next few weeks, if only temporarily, and those odds collapsing into single figures.[8]

Few believed it would happen, even as Corbyn began attracting loud applause for his populist messages during hustings and debates and racking up more nominations from constituency parties. In early July, the union Unite endorsed him, but the decision was widely seen as symbolic, with commentators noting that the front runner, Burnham, would benefit from Corbyn voters' second preferences. Betting odds still predicted Corbyn would finish last. On 15 July, the *New Statesman*'s

Stephen Bush reported that private polling for rival campaign teams showed Corbyn leading the field by more than fifteen points, but this was dismissed by Burnham's spokesperson as '100 per cent rubbish'.[9] As the Corbyn bandwagon gathered pace, following his rebellion against Harman's leadership on benefit cuts, *The Times* published a long profile of 'the outsider who could land the leadership he didn't want' and quoted an unnamed party activist in his Islington North constituency as saying:

> Jeremy is a very very nice, personable chap but his politics are off the f***ing wall. I supported Michael Foot back in the Eighties and that was a disaster. But it is wrong to compare Corbyn with Foot. Michael had had cabinet experience, he could make compromises and deals, he was a liberal intellectual of international standing. Jeremy has none of those credentials. If he wins, it will be much, much worse.[10]

Such fears had begun to be expressed more seriously as the contest went on, particularly after Corbyn lost his temper when pressed on *Channel 4 News* to explain calling Hamas and Hezbollah his 'friends' in the past. In the wake of that appearance, he then pulled out of an interview with the *Jewish Chronicle*. Then on Wednesday 22 July, *The Times* splashed a story on its front page revealing the result of the first public poll of the campaign. On the basis of the YouGov survey of eligible Labour members, Corbyn led on first preference by seventeen points and was set to beat Burnham in the final round. It also found that the new 'registered supporters' of the party, who under Miliband's reforms could sign up for £3 and get a vote in the contest, overwhelmingly backed Corbyn.[11]

The poll confirmed that the race had been transformed, and as a result Corbyn overtook Burnham as the favourite with the betting market. Mainstream Labour MPs regarded the prospect with horror and began plotting how they would oust Corbyn were he to be elected, with one predicting, 'It will be a case of him lasting weeks not months.'[12] Meanwhile, the former ITN political editor John Sergeant offered some advice, drawing on his own experience with the voting public. In 2008, he had become an unexpected star of the BBC's *Strictly Come Dancing*, being kept on the show week after week by the public vote despite being an objectively bad dancer, with people predicting he could even win the show, prompting him to quit. Seeing a parallel with the Labour leadership contest, Sergeant now advised, 'Jeremy should resign because winning, as with me, would be a joke too far.'[13]

Joke or not, Corbyn was now the firm favourite, and when the result was declared on 12 September, he had won by a landslide on the first round, with just short of 60 per cent of the vote. Previous favourite Burnham trailed in a distant second with 19 per cent, just ahead of Cooper on 17 per cent. In a complete reversal of the politics of New Labour, Kendall, generally considered to be the most 'Blairite' candidate, finished last with 4.5 per cent. The political world had been turned upside down. Moderate (and even not-so moderate) Labour MPs were appalled, and mainstream opinion pronounced his election to be a disaster for Labour. *The Times*, in its lead column, gave a comprehensive denunciation of Corbyn's suitability for his new job:

Her Majesty's Opposition has an important constitutional role in holding the government to account. There is no sign that Jeremy Corbyn is suitable for this task or capable of it. In choosing him as its leader the Labour party has therefore pleased itself but done the country a disservice. From all the available evidence, Mr Corbyn will position his party too far to the left of the main course of public opinion to be taken seriously by centrist voters. A party that fails in this way to present itself as a realistic government-in-waiting fails to exert pressure on the actual government of the day. No amount of flag waving and protest rallies are as effective for an opposition as the prospect of power.[14]

The tone and substance of the criticism was reminiscent of that which greeted Michael Foot's election in 1980, and there are certainly some similarities between their tenures. But, as the anonymous activist had noted earlier in the campaign, Corbyn lacked Foot's experience and stature and was much more extreme in his views. Whereas Foot had sought to resist the excesses of the hard left and infiltration of the party by the Militant Tendency, Corbyn had supported that movement and shared its politics.

With this in mind, it is unsurprising that Corbyn was written off from day one as an electoral disaster and that it was considered to be only a matter of time before Labour MPs removed him. What is almost as extraordinary as his ascent to the leadership is that he remained in the job for four and a half years, leading the party at two general elections and coming surprisingly close to actually becoming Prime Minister.

First, however, he played a possibly decisive role in the UK's decision to leave the European Union the following year. The Labour Party was officially in favour of remaining in the EU, a view shared by the overwhelming majority of the parliamentary party and most of its membership in the country. But, as a lifelong Eurosceptic, Corbyn gave an unconvincing and unenthusiastic performance during the campaign, to the frustration of the Remain campaign and many of his colleagues. Some suspected that he privately voted for Brexit himself, and his lack of commitment can certainly be considered a credible factor in the narrow win for Leave.

It was in the aftermath of this second political shock that Labour MPs made their move against Corbyn, with mass resignations from the shadow Cabinet and a vote of no confidence in him by the parliamentary party. Whilst this would have been enough to end the tenure of previous leaders, Corbyn defied his colleagues and claimed his mandate came from the party membership. He then proved the point by defeating a leadership challenge by Owen Smith, securing an even higher share of the vote than he had won the previous year. A total of 313,209 Labour members reaffirmed their support for his leadership.

Public opinion polls, however, told a different story. The Conservatives had held a slim but consistent lead over Labour throughout the first year of Corbyn's leadership, and with Theresa May replacing David Cameron as Prime Minister, this then rose into double figures by the end of 2016. In the spring of 2017, Labour under Corbyn was polling at around 25 per cent, whilst the Conservatives were up in the mid-forties, a lead of up to twenty points. It was in this climate of public opinion that May called an early general election, and the outcome seemed utterly predictable – a landslide Conservative victory and a crushing defeat for Labour, just like 1983.

But once again, things were different this time. In one of the most surprising and dramatic turnarounds of any general election campaign, Labour's share of the vote grew in polls throughout the campaign, as Corbyn mounted a lively insurgent campaign that contrasted with the stilted and awkward performance by May, and a Conservative campaign beset by problems and policy U-turns. On election night Labour gained thirty seats, its share of the vote hitting 40 per cent, ten points higher than in 2015 and only 2.3 points behind the Conservatives. Having lost thirteen seats, May was deprived of her Commons majority and had to rely on a deal with the Democratic Unionist Party (DUP) to remain in power.

It was another extraordinary result. Labour MPs had been preparing to mount another attempt to ditch Corbyn following the expected landslide defeat and were stunned when it failed to materialise. Whilst Labour was still significantly behind the Conservatives in their number of seats in the Commons, the parliamentary arithmetic showed how weak May's grip on power was. Even with the support of the ten DUP members, the Conservatives could only muster 327 votes – one more than the 326 required for an overall majority. Had they lost just a few more seats, those numbers would not have stacked up. In those circumstances, the option of a Corbyn-led minority government was at least a possibility.*

The result bolstered Corbyn's position as leader, and 'Jez-Mania' (as some insisted on calling it) reached its peak in the following weeks, as a jubilant Corbyn was given a rapturous reception at the Glastonbury festival, with the crowd singing his name. In early July 2017, Labour hit 46 per cent in the polls, eight points ahead of the Conservatives. Many of the Labour leader's cheerleaders on the left took to hailing the election as a victory, not a defeat.

This was as good as it would get for Corbyn's leadership. Over the next two years he would come under increasing attack from opponents in his party, particularly over his ambiguous position on Brexit. As the Conservative Party returned to its favourite pastime of tearing itself apart over Europe, Labour's own position was far from clear, and even Corbyn's closest colleagues were divided on strategy. His response to the Salisbury poisonings in 2018, when he seemed unwilling to condemn Russia for its involvement, fuelled anger at him from moderate

---

* The hurdle for Labour was actually higher, as with seven Sinn Féin MPs not taking their seats and the Speaker not voting, the practical 'winning post' for a majority was actually 322 rather than 326. For May to have had no chance of reaching this via a DUP deal would have required the loss of another six or seven seats. Even then, Labour would have had to attract support from every other party in the House to assemble a majority.

Labour MPs. At the same time, there was growing anger over how multiple allegations of antisemitism in the party were being handled by Corbyn, who seemed incapable of accepting the extent of the problem and unwilling to take firm action to root it out.

In February 2019, seven Labour MPs resigned from the party to form a new independent group, with another following soon after. The move had echoes of the SDP breakaway in 1981 but was destined to be even less successful in terms of launching a new party. Nevertheless, it was a strong sign of the despair amongst some Labour MPs over the party's direction under Corbyn. As the year went on and the Brexit crisis deepened, Labour's poll rating fell sharply, along with that of the Conservatives, as support for the Liberal Democrats and the new Brexit Party rose. Amid the political turmoil and May's resignation, it looked at various times as though the government could fall, and once again the prospect of a minority Labour government was not beyond the realms of possibility.

Once Boris Johnson became Prime Minister, his bullish attitude on Brexit restored Conservative fortunes, and the party secured a consistent lead in the polls over Corbyn's Labour. After pushing the constitution to near breaking point with his attempts to 'Get Brexit Done', Johnson called an early general election for December. This time there was no Labour surge during the campaign, and the Conservatives won a large majority of eighty seats.

Corbyn had led Labour to its worst general election result since 1935, losing sixty seats and ending up with just 202 MPs in the Commons. It was the kind of result that his critics had predicted when he became leader and which they had been surprised not to see occur in 2017. As the scale of the defeat became clear overnight, he spoke at his count in Islington North and confirmed he would be standing down, blaming divisions in the country over Brexit for the 'disappointing' result, rather than his own leadership. The following day he repeated the message, saying, 'It's not Corbynism, there's no such thing as Corbynism, the issue was Brexit.'[15] Such comments caused widespread anger amongst his diminished band of MPs, with Rachel Reeves amongst those who confronted him at the following week's meeting of the Parliamentary Labour Party. The problem at the election, she told him, 'was you'.[16]

Unlike his predecessors, Corbyn did not relinquish the leadership immediately, partly because there was no deputy leader to assume the role for the interim (Tom Watson having stood down at the election). His decision to remain in post during the ensuing leadership election was not widely welcomed, and his interventions during the remaining months of his leadership did not endear him to his critics. In his new year message at the beginning of 2020, he made no direct reference to the election defeat and instead delivered a defiant message:

> 2019 has been quite the year for our country and for our Labour movement ... But we have built a movement. We are the resistance to Boris Johnson. We will be campaigning every day. We will be on the front line, both in parliament and on the streets ... And make no mistake, our movement is very strong. We are half a million people and growing. We are in every region and nation of our country. We're not backed by the press barons, by the billionaires or by the millionaires who work for the billionaires. We're backed by you. We are by the many, for the many. 2020 and the years ahead will be tough – no one is saying otherwise. But we're up for the fight, to protect what we hold dear, and to build to win and to transform. The fight continues. There is no other choice.[17]

Whilst this parting shot was met with disdain by many of his colleagues, it perhaps contained the essence of Corbyn – always more comfortable with the rhetoric of resistance and protest than with confronting awkward political realities. His commitment to the 'movement' was always greater than his respect for his party in Parliament, and his mention of fighting 'on the streets' betrayed his lifelong sympathy with direct action as a legitimate alternative to parliamentary representation.

In his radicalism and anti-establishment rhetoric, Corbyn was a most unconventional leader in modern times, but if we cast our minds right back to where we began, we can see he is perhaps not so exceptional. In the late eighteenth century, Charles James Fox was implicated in plotting violent direct action on a number of occasions and certainly had no qualms about appearing on platforms with noted radicals to address protest rallies of thousands of people and whip them up into anger against the government. Admittedly, it is hard to argue that Corbyn was of the same stature as Fox, but it must be said that a shortage of talent or towering intellect has historically been no bar to the leadership for other individuals.

Much harder to dismiss is the ugly stain of antisemitism which came to mark the Labour Party during Corbyn's leadership, and his continuing failure to accept his responsibility for the situation eventually led to him being suspended from the Parliamentary Labour Party less than a year after standing down as leader. He is thus set to end his time in Parliament as he spent so much of it: an isolated backbench figure on the fringes of politics. But his departure from the spotlight should not lead us to forget his real significance.

The election of Jeremy Corbyn as leader of the Labour Party was one of the most surprising events in modern British politics. As we have seen throughout this book, there have been numerous unlikely and obscure candidates who have somehow found themselves leading the opposition. Some have held radical political views and been hostile to the political establishment; and some of them have had a plausible chance of becoming Prime Minister. But the rise of Corbyn was truly an extraordinary phenomenon. It defied all prior expectations and turned a far-left fringe figure with no leadership experience and no real desire for office into the UK's alternative Prime Minister, who then came surprisingly close to reaching Downing Street.

Even without having reached the highest office, Corbyn's leadership had a significant effect. There is a plausible case to be made that it swung the balance in favour of Leave winning the EU referendum and thus led to Brexit. Following that, it was his perceived weakness that persuaded May to call the 2017 general election, whilst his unexpectedly strong performance in the campaign denied her a majority and instigated the turmoil of the next few years, up to and including Boris Johnson's succession to the premiership and his landslide victory in the 2019 general election. Sometimes it is hard to convince people why it matters who the Leader of the Opposition is. After Jeremy Corbyn, it should be obvious.

Epilogue

As both Matt Chorley and I mentioned in our introductory comments, the theme music to the Times Radio feature which inspired this book culminated in Yvonne Fair's epic 'It Should Have Been Me'. The outraged cry of a spurned lover as they watch someone else marrying their ex is a fitting metaphor for political defeat and one with which many a losing candidate should be able to identify.

The other songs in the megamix (and on the Spotify playlist I confess to having put together since for my own entertainment) lean heavily towards the theme of losing: Abba's 'The Winner Takes It All', The Rolling Stones' 'You Can't Always Get What You Want' and, more bluntly, the Beatles' 'I'm a Loser'.

But as I noted at the outset, it is rather crude to reduce our list of forty-four political leaders to the status of losers. If failing to become Prime Minister is the mark of failure, we would have to dismiss the vast majority of politicians in the same way. Most MPs – like the rest of us – are destined not to become Prime Minister. It is hardly an exclusive category.

What marks out the leaders in this book is not that common failure but rather the uncommon position they occupied as the designated alternative Prime Minister. Leader of the Opposition is a unique and peculiar job, whose predominant characteristic is its lack of power. But for those who go on to win an election, it serves as their apprenticeship for office. Their time in opposition is when they make their case, build their support and finally mount their challenge for the top job. This being the case, their attitude to the job is usually one of frustration and impatience. As the great Peter Hennessy once put it, 'Nobody sees it as the peak of their ambition – they can't, can they? It can only be a transit camp, and it's a transit camp to glory – or potential glory – or oblivion.'[1]

This is indeed how most of them have seen it – as a high-stakes contest for the ultimate prize, with failure carrying with it the stigma of being branded a loser. As I know from talking to Neil Kinnock, he continues to cheerfully accept the label of being a 'personal and political failure' for having fought and lost twice.

But, as I have myself protested to him, this cannot be considered the whole story. There is far more to the job of leading the opposition than whether it ends in personal success in the short term. In Kinnock's case, he knew it was a 'two-innings match' from the start and that even after two elections, winning power would have been a challenge. Similarly, William Hague has spoken of having worked the 'night shift' of opposition, attempting to make progress against almost impossible electoral odds. Both had inherited parties shattered by landslide defeats and were left to pick up the pieces. Both began a programme of modernisation of their party structures, which would be picked up and completed by their successors, resulting in ultimate success at the polls.

Whilst Tony Blair and David Cameron were the ones who eventually made the transition from the Leader of the Opposition's office to 10 Downing Street, the contribution made by their predecessors deserves to be acknowledged. The same must be said for the other periods of opposition covered in this book, as a succession of individuals either seized the challenge – or were induced to accept the burden – of leadership. What is most striking about the early leaders is how often it was the latter, as they dutifully submitted to the thankless task, usually after sincere protestations that they had no desire for it.

There is something rather noble (and not in the aristocratic sense) about those who stepped into the breach in this way, knowing that they stood little chance of winning the fruits of victory any time soon. Faced with governments that looked secure in office, they nevertheless braved the political battlefield to keep their party banner flying until such a time as people were more inclined to rally to their side.

For that reason, some of the other songs on my 'Opposition' playlist also add something to our understanding of the role of Leader of the Opposition: Journey's 'Don't Stop Believing', Frank Sinatra's 'High Hopes' and (one of my guilty pleasures, this one) former *X Factor* winner Joe McElderry's version of Miley Cyrus's 'The Climb'. All of these, in their own way, proclaim the noble virtues of the struggle to reach the top, regardless of how long it takes or the fact that inevitably you will sometimes fall short.

That, I believe, is the other crucial side to being a 'failed' leader. Behind the crushing disappointment of ambition thwarted and bitterness at the injustice of what could and should have been, there is an inherent value in what they did. Whether genuine contenders or dutiful placeholders, all of them performed an important democratic function simply by doing the job. Being Leader of the Opposition matters, whether or not it felt like it at the time.

Notes

1. Charles James Fox

1 Cited in L. G. Mitchell, *Charles James Fox* (Oxford University Press, 1992), p2
2 Cited in Ibid., p4
3 Ibid., p8
4 Ibid., p12
5 Henry Wakeman, *Life of Charles James Fox* (W. H. Allen, 1890), p14
6 Cited in Wakeman, p14
7 Cited in Mitchell, p22
8 Ibid., p23
9 Henry Wakeman, Life of Charles James Fox (W. H. Allen, 1890), p54
10 Mitchell, Chapter 2
11 Ibid., p111
12 Charles James Fox, speech on Treason and Sedition Bills, 10 November 1795, in *The Speeches of the Right Honourable Charles James Fox in the House of Commons*, Vol. II (Aylott and Company, 1853), p573
13 Ibid., p572
14 Mitchell, p225
15 'Mr Fox', *The Times*, 15 September 1806, p2
16 *The Times*, Monday 15 September 1806

2. George Ponsonby

1 R. G. Thorne, 'Ponsonby, George (1755–1817), of Corville, Roscrea, co. Tipperary', in *The History of Parliament: The House of Commons 1790–1820*, https://www.historyofparliamentonline.org/volume/1790-1820/member/ponsonby-george-1755-1817
2 James Kelly, 'George Ponsonby', in *Oxford Dictionary of National Biography*, https://www.oxforddnb.com/display/10.1093/ref:odnb/9780198614128.001.0001/odnb-9780198614128-e-22495?rskey=163KZH&result=2
3 'News in Brief', *The Times*, 24 January 1801
4 *The Times*, 5 February 1801
5 Thorne
6 Ibid.
7 Letter from Lord Grenville to the Marquis of Buckingham, in The Duke of Buckingham and Chandos, *Memoirs of the Court and Cabinets of George the Third, from original family documents*, Volume IV (Hurst and Blackett Publishers, 1855), p209

8   HC Debs, 21 January 1808, col. 48
9   Thorne
10 Ibid.
11 *The Times*, 13 May 1812
12 HC Debs, 30 June 1817, col. 1277
13 *The Times*, 1 July 1817
14 *The Times*, 9 July 1817

3. George Tierney

1   HC Debs, 4 June 1841, col. 1188
2   Archibald S. Foord, *His Majesty's Opposition, 1714–1830* (Clarendon Press, 1964), p455
3   *The Times*, 28 May 1798
4   Ibid.
5   R. G. Thorne, 'Tierney, George (1761–1830), of Hertford Street, Grafton Street and Old Burlington Street, Mdx.', in *The History of Parliament: The House of Commons 1790–1820*, https://www.historyofparliamentonline.org/volume/1790-1820/member/tierney-george-1761-1830
6   Ibid.
7   Ibid.
8   *The Times*, 29 January 1830
9   *The Times*, 26 January 1830

4. Henry Petty-Fitzmaurice, 3rd Marquess of Lansdowne

1   Archibald S. Foord, *His Majesty's Opposition, 1714–1830* (Clarendon Press, 1964), p458
2   Grenville, cited in ibid., p452
3   *The Times*, 2 February 1863
4   Ibid.

5. John Spencer, Viscount Althorp

1   Ellis Archer Wasson, 'Spencer, John Charles, Viscount Althorp and third Earl Spencer', in *Oxford Dictionary of National Biography*, https://doi.org/10.1093/ref:odnb/26133
2   Cited in ibid.
3   Letter to Sir James Graham, 17 December 1828, cited in David R. Fisher, 'Spencer, John Charles, Visct. Althorp', *History of Parliament: The House of Commons 1820–1832* (Cambridge University Press, 2009)
4   Letter to Milton, 2 November 1830, cited in ibid.
5   Cited by Sir Llewellyn Woodward, *The Age of Reform, 1815–1870* (Clarendon Press, 1962), p57
6   *The Times*, 3 October 1845

6. Lord George Bentinck

1   HC Debs, 27 February 1846, col. 304
2   Angus Macintyre, 'Bentinck, Lord (William) George Frederic Cavendish-Scott', in *Oxford Dictionary of National Biography*, https://doi.org/10.1093/ref:odnb/2157
3   HC Debs, 27 February 1846, col. 304
4   Ibid., col. 349
5   HC Debs, 17 December 1846, col. 1381
6   Letter to Croker, 26 December 1847, cited in Louis J. Jennings, *The Croker Papers* (John Murray, 1884), p157
7   Ibid.
8   *The Times*, 23 September 1848
9   Benjamin Disraeli, *Lord George Bentinck: A Political Biography* (Colburn and co., 1852), p2
10 'Biography of Lord George Bentinck', *The Times*, 23 September 1848

NOTES

7. Charles Manners, Marquess of Granby

1 Angus Hawkins, *The Forgotten Prime Minister: The 14th Earl of Derby: Volume I: Ascent, 1799–1851* (Oxford Scholarship, 2009), p341
2 Ibid., p341
3 Robert Blake, *Disraeli*, (Faber & Faber, 2012)
4 *The Times*, 5 March 1888

8. John Charles Herries

1 *The Times*, 29 August 1827
2 Angus Hawkins, *The Forgotten Prime Minister: The 14th Earl of Derby: Volume I: Ascent, 1799–1851* (Oxford Scholarship, 2009), pp352–3

9. Granville Leveson-Gower, 2nd Earl Granville

1 Edmond Fitzmaurice, *The Life of Granville George Leveson Gower, Second Earl Granville*, Volume I (Longmans, Green and Co., 1905), p311
2 Ibid., p304
3 Ibid., p339
4 HL Debs, 11 July 1870, col. 3
5 *The Times*, 14 May 1885
6 Muriel E. Chamberlain, 'Gower, Granville George Leveson, second Earl Granville', in *Oxford Dictionary of National Biography*, https://doi.org/10.1093/ref:odnb/16543
7 *The Times*, 1 April 1891

10. James Harris, 3rd Earl of Malmesbury

1 Earl of Malmesbury, *Memoirs of an Ex-Minister*, Volume I (Longmans, Green and Co., 1884), p33
2 Ibid., pp133–4
3 Ibid., pp40–41
4 Ibid., pp316–17
5 Ibid., p41
6 Ibid., p318
7 *The Times*, 18 May 1889
8 Ibid.
9 Ibid.

11. Hugh Cairns, 1st Baron Cairns

1 *The Times*, 15 May 1858
2 Earl of Malmesbury, *Memoirs of an Ex-Minister*, Volume II (Longmans, Green and Co., 1884), p378
3 Ibid., p285
4 Circular from Lord Cairns to the House of Lords, 24 July 1869, reproduced in ibid., p410
5 David Steele, 'Cairns, Hugh McCalmont, first Earl Cairns', in *Oxford Dictionary of National Biography*, https://doi.org/10.1093/ref:odnb/4346
6 *The Times*, 9 February 1870
7 *The Times*, 3 April 1885

12. Charles Gordon-Lennox, 6th Duke of Richmond

1 Robert Blake, *Disraeli* (Methuen, 1969), p516
2 'Death of the Duke of Richmond', *The Times*, 28 September 1903
3 'Death of the Duke of Richmond', *The Times*, 28 September 1903
4 HL Debs, 17 June 1872, col. 1841

5   Cited in John Vincent (ed.), *A selection from the diaries of Edward Henry Stanley, 15th Earl of Derby (1826–93), between March 1869 and September 1878* (Royal Historical Society, 1994), p184
6   F. M. L. Thompson, 'Lennox, Charles Henry Gordon-, sixth duke of Richmond, sixth duke of Lennox, and first duke of Gordon', in *Oxford Dictionary of National Biography*, https://doi.org/10.1093/ref:odnb/33468

13. Spencer Cavendish, Marquess of Hartington

1   Harcourt to Hill, 1874, cited in A. G. Gardiner, *The Life of Sir William Harcourt* (London, 1923), p282
2   Cited in John P. Rossi: 'The Selection of Lord Hartington as Liberal Leader in the House of Commons, February 1875', *Proceedings of the American Philosophical Society* (volume 119, number 4, 1975), p309
3   Ibid., p310
4   'The Choice of a Liberal Leader', *The Times*, 28 January 1875
5   'The Leadership of the Liberal Party', *The Times*, 4 February 1875
6   Ibid.
7   'The Duke of Devonshire', *The Times*, 25 March 1908

14. Sir Stafford Northcote

1   Cited in David Steele 'A New Style and Content: 1880–1885 and 1886', in Stuart Ball and Anthony Seldon, *Recovering Power: The Conservatives in Opposition since 1867* (Palgrave Macmillan, 2005), p55
2   'Sudden Death of the Earl of Iddesleigh', *The Times*, 13 January 1887
3   Professor Peter Hennessy, Founder's Day address, Hawarden Castle, 8 July 1999

15. Sir Michael Hicks Beach

1   *The Times*, 9 June 1885
2   'Death of Lord St Aldwyn', *The Times*, 1 May 1916

16. John Wodehouse, 1st Earl of Kimberley

1   *The Times*, 18 September 1865
2   *The Times*, 21 May 1866
3   'Political Notes', *The Times*, 15 April 1891
4   'The Meeting of Parliament', *The Times*, 19 January 1897
5   'Death of Lord Kimberley', *The Times*, 9 April 1902

17. Sir William Harcourt

1   *The Times*, 25 June 1895
2   HC Debs, 24 June 1895, cols. 1747–8
3   *Diary of Lewis Harcourt*, 23 January 1883 (Oxford, Bodleian Libraries, MS. Harcourt 352)
4   *The Times*, 27 January 1882
5   A. G. Gardiner, *The Life of Sir William Harcourt*, Volume II (George H. Doran Company, 1923), p207
6   Patrick Jackson (ed.), *'Loulou': Selected Extracts from the Journals of Lewis Harcourt* (Fairleigh Dickinson University Press, 2006), p264
7   'Death of Sir William Harcourt', *The Times*, 3 October 1904
8   Roy Jenkins, 'From Gladstone to Asquith: The Late Victorian Pattern of Liberal Leadership', *History Today* (1964), vol. 14, no. 7, pp445–52, pp446–7

18. John Spencer, 5th Earl Spencer

1   'Ireland', *The Times*, 25 December 1868

2 'Manifesto by Lord Spencer', *The Times*, 10 February 1905
3 'Ireland', *The Times*, 11 February 1905
4 Cited in Peter Gordon, 'Spencer, John Poyntz, fifth Earl Spencer', in *Oxford Dictionary of National Biography*, https://doi.org/10.1093/ref:odnb/36209

19. George Robinson, 1st Marquess of Ripon

1 Philip Ziegler, *Melbourne: A Biography of William Lamb, 2nd Viscount Melbourne* (Atheneum, 1982), p96
2 Cited in Anthony F. Denholm, 'Robinson, George Frederick Samuel, first marquess of Ripon', in *Oxford Dictionary of National Biography*, https://doi.org/10.1093/ref:odnb/35792
3 'The Eighty Club and Lord Ripon', *The Times*, 25 November 1908
4 Ibid.

20. Henry Petty-Fitzmaurice, 5th Marquess of Lansdowne

1 Jowett to Lansdowne, 27 April 1872', in Evelyn Abbott and Lewis Campbell, *The Life and Letters of Benjamin Jowett, MA* (John Murray, 1897), p45
2 'Review of Parliament: The Historic Debate', *The Times*, 23 November 1909
3 Ibid.
4 'Parliament Bill Passed', *The Times*, 11 August 1911
5 Baron Newton, *Lord Lansdowne: A Biography* (Macmillan & Co., 1929), p440

21. Joseph Chamberlain

1 'The Chamberlain celebration in Birmingham', *The Times*, 10 July 1906
2 Ibid.
3 'Death of Mr Chamberlain', *The Times*, 4 July 1914

22. Edward Carson

1 Geoffrey Lewis, *Carson: The Man Who Divided Ireland* (Bloomsbury Academic, 2006), p41
2 'Central Criminal Court, April 4', *The Times*, 5 April 1895
3 Joseph Bristow, *Oscar Wilde on Trial: The Criminal Proceedings, from Arrest to Imprisonment* (Yale University Press, 2023), p408
4 Lewis, p103
5 'Sir Edward Carson at Belfast', *The Times*, 18 July 1913
6 'Political Notes', *The Times*, 22 October 1915
7 'Statue of Lord Carson', *The Times*, 10 July 1933

23. William Adamson

1 Cited in David Torrance, *The Scottish Secretaries* (Birlinn Ltd, 2006), p103
2 'The General Election', *The Times*, 15 December 1910
3 'Political Notes – New Labour Chairman elected', *The Times*, 25 October 1917
4 HC Debs, 13 February 1918, col. 144
5 'Labour as Official Opposition', *The Times*, 8 January 1919
6 Ibid.
7 Ibid.
8 'The New House', *The Times*, 5 February 1919
9 Ibid.
10 HC Debs, 11 February 1919, cols. 62–3
11 'Mr William Adamson', *The Times*, 24 February 1936
12 Entry for 14 January 1919 in Margaret Cole (ed.), *Beatrice Webb, Diaries 1912–1924* (Longman, 1952), p330; Emanuel Shinwell, *The Labour Story* (Macdonald, 1963), pp111–12
13 'Mr William Adamson', *The Times*, 24 February 1936

24. Sir Donald Maclean

1 'Sir Donald Maclean', *The Times*, 16 June 1932
2 Roland Philipps, *A Spy Named Orphan: The Enigma of Donald Maclean* (Bodley Head, 2018)
3 'Free Liberals and their Leader', *The Times*, 27 April 1920
4 'The New Parliament', *The Times*, 24 January 1919
5 'A Challenge to Labour', *The Times*, 29 January 1919
6 'To-Day's Welcome To Mr Asquith', *The Times*, 1 March 1920
7 'Free Liberals and their Leader', *The Times*, 27 April 1920

25. Arthur Henderson

1 'Election Intelligence', *The Times*, 27 July 1903
2 *The Times*, 27 July 1903
3 'The Session Opens', *The Times*, 9 September 1931
4 'A Shattering Blow', *The Times*, 29 October 1931
5 Ibid.
6 'Getting to Work', *The Times*, 4 November 1931

26. George Lansbury

1 A. J. P. Taylor, *English History 1914–1945* (Oxford University Press, 1965), p142
2 'House of Commons', *The Times*, 26 June 1912
3 'Incitement to Crime', *The Times*, 5 May 1913
4 Cited in E. S. Turner, *Dear Old Blighty* (Faber and Faber, 2012)
5 'Mr Lansbury and The King', *The Times*, 7 January 1924
6 Cited in John Shepherd, 'A Life on the Left: George Lansbury (1859–1940): A Case Study in Recent Labour Biography', *Labour History* (2004) vol. 87, pp147–65
7 Cited in Richard Heller, 'East Fulham Revisited', *Journal of Contemporary History* (1971), vol. 6, no. 3, pp172–96, p185
8 HC Debs, 3 September 1939, col. 299

27. James Maxton

1 'House of Commons', *The Times*, 22 May 1940
2 HC Debs, 21 May 1940, col. 30
3 'Obituary – Mr James Maxton MP', *The Times*, 24 July 1946

28. Hastings Lees-Smith

1 HC Debs, 13 May 1940, col. 1502
2 Ibid., col. 1504
3 Clement Attlee, *As It Happened* (William Heinemann Ltd, 1954), p116
4 HC Debs, 13 May 1940, col. 1502
5 'The Opposition Front Bench', *The Times*, 23 May 1940
6 HC Debs, 12 April 1937, col. 738
7 HC Debs, 19 December 1941, col. 2250

29. Frederick Pethick-Lawrence

1 'Parliamentary Recess: Provisional Arrangement for Reassembly', *The Times*, 20 December 1941
2 'Labour Spokesman in the Commons', *The Times*, 22 January 1942
3 'Mr Churchill's Defeat', *The Times*, 7 December 1923
4 'Mobilizing Foreign Capital – Mr Pethick-Lawrence's Letter', *The Times*, 29 August 1931
5 Cited in Brian Harrison, 'Lawrence, Frederick William Pethick-, Baron Pethick-Lawrence', in *Oxford Dictionary of National Biography*, https://doi.org/10.1093/ref:odnb/35491
6 HC Debs, 29 May 1940, col. 571

30. Arthur Greenwood

1 '"We Shall March with France" Mr Greenwood on the Delay', *The Times*, 4 September 1939
2 HC Debs, 2 September 1939, cols. 282–3
3 'Mr Greenwood attacked in street', *The Times*, 3 July 1942
4 HC Debs, 22 February 1944, col. 704
5 HC Debs, 17 March 1944, col. 555
6 Francis Beckett, *Clem Attlee* (Politico's, 2000), p270
7 Ibid., p270.
8 HC Debs, 15 June 1954, col. 1749

31. Herbert Morrison

1 Peter Mandelson, *The Third Man* (HarperCollins, 2010), p44
2 Cited in Francis Beckett, *Clem Attlee* (Politico's, 2000), p150
3 Cited in Beckett, p197
4 Ibid., p199
5 'Three Nominated for Labour Leadership', *The Times*, 9 December 1955

32. Hugh Gaitskell

1 Philip M. Williams, *Hugh Gaitskell – A Political Biography* (Jonathan Cape, 1979), p19
2 Cited in D. E. Butler and Richard Rose, *The British General Election of 1959* (Macmillan and Co., 1960), pp32–3
3 'Mr Gaitskell To Fight "To Save Party"', *The Times*, 6 October 1960
4 Hugh Gaitskell, speech to the Labour Party conference, 5 October 1960
5 Hugh Gaitskell, speech to the Labour Party conference, 3 October 1962
6 'Mr Gaitskell's Condition Worse', *The Times*, 16 January 1963
7 'Condition of Mr Gaitskell worsens', *The Times*, 17 January 1963
8 Morris Cargill, *Jamaica Farewell* (Lyle Stuart, 1978), p196
9 Ibid., p197

33. George Brown

1 Tony Benn, *The Benn Diaries 1940–1990* (Arrow Books, 1996), p95
2 Ben Pimlott, *Harold Wilson* (HarperCollins, 1992), p255
3 George Wigg, *George Wigg* (Michael Joseph, 1972), p258
4 'Mr Brown Quits Then Returns', *The Times*, 21 July 1966
5 'The Case for George Brown', *The Times*, 14 January 1967
6 Cited in Pimlott (1992), pp498–9
7 Cited in ibid., p497
8 'An Honest Man's Warning', *The Times*, 4 March 1976

34. Robert Carr

1 Edward Heath, *The Course of My Life* (Hodder & Stoughton, 1998), pp534–5
2 David Wood, 'Mr Heath steps down as leader after 11 vote defeat by Mrs Thatcher', *The Times*, 5 February 1975

35. Michael Foot

1 Michael Horsnell, 'The Times Diary', *The Times*, 9 November 1981
2 Chris Smyth, '"Mr Foot, what an awfully nice coat"', *The Times*, 4 March 2010
3 HC Debs, 20 November 1985, col. 286
4 Michael Foot, 'Putting Parliament at Stake', *The Times*, 23 May 1975
5 'Mr Foot wins Labour leadership by margin of 10 votes', *The Times*, 11 November 1980
6 'An Unmitigated Folly', *The Times*, 11 November 1980

36. Neil Kinnock

1 Neil Kinnock, speech to the Welsh Labour Party conference, 15 May 1987
2 Martin Westlake, *Kinnock: The Biography* (Little Brown, 2001), p78
3 Ibid., p105
4 Neil Kinnock, speech to the Labour Party conference, 1 October 1985
5 Julian Haviland, 'Kinnock speech a masterpiece, say moderates', *The Times*, 2 October 1985
6 Neil Kinnock, 'Leading the Opposition', in Nigel Fletcher (ed.), *How to be in Opposition* (Biteback, 2011), p131

37. John Smith

1 HC Debs, 12 May 1994, col. 430
2 Ibid., col. 431
3 Cited in Robert Taylor, 'Smith, John', in *Oxford Dictionary of National Biography*, https://doi.org/10.1093/ref:odnb/55724
4 Cited in Mark Stuart, *John Smith – A Life*, (Politico's, 2005), p136
5 HC Debs, 24 September 1992, col. 22
6 HC Debs, 12 May 1994, col. 431

38. Margaret Beckett

1 Margaret Beckett, speaking on *The Reunion*, (BBC Radio 4, 14 September 2014)
2 Ibid.
3 Judy Goodwin, 'All I remember is the isolation', *The Times*, 30 May 1992
4 Ibid.
5 Mark Stuart, *John Smith: A Life* (Politico's, 2005), p173
6 'Margaret Beckett', *The Times*, 16 April 1992
7 'Beckett calls for poverty census', *The Times*, 29 May 1992
8 Jill Sherman, 'Beckett issues new challenge to Blair', *The Times*, 11 June 1994
9 Peter Riddell and Philip Webster, '"One of my women colleagues said to me: They buried you with John"', *The Times*, 21 June 1994
10 Philip Webster, '"As he promoted me I replied in one word, with four letters"', *The Times*, 28 June 2006
11 Michael White, 'Labour's New Leader: Bruised Beckett will be looked after', *The Guardian*, 22 June 1994

39. William Hague

1 Fred Emery, 'Conference Notebook', *The Times*, 13 October 1977
2 David Sanderson, 'William Hague tells Cheltenham: Teenage speech cast me as a "freak for life"', *The Times*, 14 October 2022
3 Cited in D. R. Thorpe (ed.), *Who's In, Who's Out: The Journals of Kenneth Rose*, Volume I (Weidenfeld & Nicolson, 2018), pp551–2
4 William Hague, speech to the Conservative Party conference, 12 October 1977
5 Jo-Anne Nadler, *William Hague – In His Own Right* (Politico's, 2000), p49
6 Ibid., p49
7 Ibid., p77
8 'What was in Norman Lamont's Budget Box?', *BBC News*, 26 November 1998
9 *A Night To Remember* (ITN Factual, directed by Don Jordan), Channel Four, 18 April 1998
10 William Hague, speaking on *Reflections with Peter Hennessy* (BBC Radio 4, 17 August 2017)
11 Sanderson

40. Iain Duncan Smith

1 Nicholas Watt, 'Tebbit sours contest with gay smear as Portillo prepares bid', *The Guardian*, 12 June 2001

2   Matthew Parris, 'Victory, but not in front of the children', *The Times*, 14 September 2001
3   Matthew Parris, 'Emotional wisdom meets the challenge of tragedy', *The Times*, 15 September 2001
4   Lucy Ward, 'Duncan Smith's public service vision', *The Guardian*, 11 October 2001
5   Melissa Kite, 'Shadow Cabinet "packed with Eurosceptics"', *The Times*, 19 September 2001
6   Iain Duncan Smith, speech to the Conservative Party conference, 10 October 2002
7   'Full text: Iain Duncan Smith's statement', *The Guardian*, 5 November 2002
8   Tom Baldwin, 'Blood in the air as party weighs up the succession', *The Times*, 24 October 2003
9   Iain Duncan Smith, 'Back me: I'm ready to address my leadership's shortcomings', *The Times*, 29 October 2003
10 Iain Duncan Smith, 'The Parliamentary party has spoken', *The Times*, 30 October 2003

41. Michael Howard

1   Colin Brown, 'Tories complain over Paxman interview', *The Independent*, 26 November 2004
2   Michael Prescott, 'Howard damned as "dangerous" by his minister', *Sunday Times*, 11 May 1997
3   Steerpike, 'Sixty highlights from sixty years of PMQs', *The Spectator*, 19 July 2021

42. Harriet Harman

1   Harriet Harman, speaking on *Reflections with Peter Hennessy* (BBC Radio 4, 24 August 2017)
2   Ibid.
3   Alice Thompson and Rachel Sylvester, 'We must be united whoever leads the party, says Harman', *The Times*, 12 September 2015

43. Ed Miliband

1   Harriet Harman, *A Woman's Work* (Penguin, 2017)
2   Medhi Hasan and James Macintyre, *Ed: The Milibands and the Making of a Labour Leader* (Biteback, 2011), p49
3   Ed Miliband, speech to the Labour Party conference, 28 September 2010
4   'Ed Miliband: politics was an abnormal rite of passage but it shaped me', *The Times*, 10 June 2010
5   Harman, p150
6   Ann Treneman, 'He may look like a geek poster boy but he believes he is the party's only hope', *The Times*, 4 September 2010

44. Jeremy Corbyn

1   Alex Nunns, *The Candidate* (OR Books, 2018)
2   Sam Coates, 'Labour puts left-winger in the final four for leadership', *The Times*, 16 June 2015
3   Ibid.
4   Tom Bower, *Dangerous Hero: Corbyn's Ruthless Plot for Power* (William Collins, 2019), p3
5   Ibid., p51
6   Philip Webster, Nicholas Watt and James Landale, 'Blair threatens to expel MP over Adams visit', *The Times*, 26 September 1996; James Landale, 'Corbyn and Benn still face party disciplinary action', *The Times*, 27 September 1996
7   Simon Hattenstone, 'Jeremy Corbyn: "I don't do personal"', *The Guardian*, 17 June 2015
8   Paul Krishnamurty, 'Next Labour Leader Betting: Corbyn will liven up a dull race and could surprise', betting.betfair.com, 15 June 2015
9   Ashley Cowburn, 'Shock poll puts Corbyn on course to lead Labour', *The Times*, 16 July 2015
10 Sean O'Neill and Laura Pitel, 'Corbyn, the outsider who could land the leadership he didn't want', *The Times*, 18 July 2015
11 Sam Coates, 'Labour war as Corbyn closes in on leadership', *The Times*, 22 July 2015
12 Sam Coates, 'Week when party turmoil became toxic', *The Times*, 25 July 2015
13 Patrick Kidd, 'TMS: Watch Corbyn cross the floor', *The Times*, 25 July 2015

14 'Shadow Politics', *The Times*, 14 September 2015

15 Henry Zeffman, 'Go now, Corbyn urged after worst defeat since 1935', *The Times*, 14 December 2019

16 Henry Zeffman, Francis Elliott and Oliver Wright, 'Mary Creagh and furious Labour MPs slam Corbyn for election defeat', *The Times*, 18 December 2019

17 'Jeremy Corbyn's New Year message: We're the resistance to Boris Johnson', *Sky News*, 30 December 2019

Epilogue
___

1 Peter Hennessy interviewed by Michael Cockerell for *How to Be Leader of the Opposition* (BBC Television), BBC Two, 19 June 1999

Acknowledgements

Does anyone ever read the acknowledgements pages of a book like this? I was once told they're just a courtesy and that unless they're expecting to be mentioned, readers will just skip it. Personally, I find them a bit of a treat – something akin to a literary Oscars speech. Which is somewhat appropriate for this book, because in all the weeks of doing the Leaders of the Opposition slot on Times Radio, I had to make sure I got through everything I wanted to say before the news music started playing in the background, which always felt like the orchestra striking up at an awards show to tell you to wrap up. I like to think I got quite good at it.

So, to begin, I must thank Matt Chorley for inviting me to do the show in the first place and for encouraging me to write the book as a follow-up. I've known Matt since he interviewed me over a decade ago in connection with the first book I edited on political opposition, so there is neat symmetry that he has played a crucial part in inspiring this one. His whole team at Times Radio were also great to work with – producers Lewis, Chloe, Andrew and all the studio staff. Thanks too, to all the listeners who told me they enjoyed the series. I will never forget getting a round of applause from them in the audience of the Bloomsbury Theatre when Matt gave me a shout-out from the stage during his excellent stand-up show. My ego still hasn't deflated.

Once I'd decided to embark on the book, James Stephens and Olivia Beattie at Biteback were very encouraging and supportive, and I am particularly indebted to my diligent editor, Cat Allon. As well as making sense of my prose, she has rigorously fact-checked and queried the historical content, so if any errors remain it's almost certainly because I've failed to match her high standards. We are also grateful to *The Times* for granting the necessary permissions to quote extracts from their archive. The whole team at Biteback have turned this book around amazingly quickly – I had the first meeting about it in February, wasn't able to start writing it in earnest until the start of April, and chapters have since been flying back and forth until shortly before going to press in August.

During the writing period, I was on a bit of a treadmill to churn out the chapters and turned into something of a recluse, shutting myself away in my study with my books and my online time machine of archives for hours on end. I therefore owe huge thanks to my lovely husband Kieran Richardson, for tolerating my working through weekends and evenings and for putting up with me more generally. I should apologise to him and other friends and colleagues, who found me rather stressed at times as I juggled this project with other commitments.

Finally, I have dedicated this book to my parents, who gave me the best start in life anyone could wish for, encouraged me in my interests and have given me more love and support than I can ever repay. A few words in a book are inadequate to record my gratitude, but I take satisfaction from thinking that my heartfelt thanks will now be on the public record and will hopefully remain on bookshelves and in various libraries for years to come.

And with that, I hear the orchestra starting to play…

Index

Abbott, Diane 309–10, 312
Aberdeen, Earl of 40, 43, 67
Adam, William 8, 99
Adams, Gerry 311
Adamson, William xv
    early life and career 156–7
    early political career 157
    as Leader of Opposition 158–61, 164–6
Addington, Henry 32, 60
Alexandra, Queen 148
Ali, Tariq 300
Althorp, Viscount *see* Spencer, John
American War of Independence 7
Argyll, Duke of 98
Asquith, H. H. 135, 140, 141, 151, 154, 157–8, 165–6
Attlee, Clement 181, 183, 185, 189, 191, 192, 196, 199, 201, 202, 204, 205–6, 208, 209, 210–11, 217

Baldwin, Stanley 172
Bale, Tim 308
Balfour, Arthur 102, 132, 135, 139, 140, 147–8
Balls, Ed 302, 303
Barnes, George 170
Beaverbrook, Lord 234–5
Beckett, Leo 259
Beckett, Margaret xv
    as Leader of the Opposition 250, 257–8, 261–3, 291
    as deputy leader 255, 260–61
    early life and career 258–9
    early political career 259–61

    in Blair government 263
    and Jeremy Corbyn 307
Bedford, Duke of 23
Belardinelli, Alex 307–8
Bellingham, John 66
Benn, Tony 237, 239, 246, 248, 252, 259, 260, 300, 303, 310–11
Bennett, Alan 12
Bentinck, Lord George
    early life and career 48–9
    and Corn Laws 50–51
    as Leader of the Opposition 52–3, 54, 56
    death of 53–4
Bercow, John 278
Bevan, Nye 211–12, 216, 217, 234, 235–6, 242
Bevin, Ernest 181, 210, 211, 224
Birmingham, Lavinia 42, 43
Blair, Tony 251, 254–5, 258, 262, 263, 272, 277, 287, 289, 293, 294, 302, 324
Blake, Robert 56, 88
Bolingbroke, Viscount 24
Bonar Law, Andrew 142, 158, 160
Brexit 316, 318, 319
Brittan, Leon 268, 284, 286
Brown, George xv
    as Leader of the Opposition 223–4, 225
    early life and career 224
    early political career 224–5
    in Wilson government 225–8
    death of 228
    and Neil Kinnock 244
Brown, Gordon 183–4, 254–5, 258, 294, 295, 301–3, 312

Burke, Edmund 5, 13
Burke, T. H. 120
Burnham, Andy 307, 313, 314
Bush, Stephen 313–14
Butler, Lady Mary 20

Cairns, Hugh (Baron Cairns) 78
    early life and career 80–81
    role in government 81–2
    as Leader of the Opposition 82–5
    retirement 85–6, 88, 89
    death of 86–7
Cairns, Rosanna 81
Cairns, William 80–81
Callaghan, James 224, 237–8, 245, 252
Cameron, David 273, 290, 296, 317, 324
Campbell-Bannerman, Sir Henry 132, 133
Canning, George 35, 39, 44, 49, 60, 61
Cargill, Morris 214, 221
Carr, Robert xvi 229–31
Carrington, Lord 265
Carson, Sir Edward
    as Leader of the Opposition 150–51, 153–4
    early life and career 151–2
    and Home Rule 152–5
    in Lloyd George government 154
    death of 155
Cash, Bill 278
Castle, Barbara 223, 225, 234, 235, 237
Cavendish, Elizabeth 20
Cavendish, Frederick 100–101, 130
Cavendish, Spencer
    as Leader of the Opposition 69–71,
        98–101, 102–3
    notoriety of 95–6
    early life and career 96–7
    early political career 97
    in Gladstone and Salisbury governments
        101–2
    death of 102
Cavendish, William 96
Chamberlain, Austen 274
Chamberlain, Joseph xi
    and John Spencer 132
    70th birthday celebrations 143–4
    early life and career 144–5
    in government 145–7
    as Leader of the Opposition 148
    legacy of 148–9
    and Harriet Harman 292
Chamberlain, Neville 199, 209, 235
Chapman, Jane 309

Charles I, King 2
Charles II, King 2, 89
Charlotte, Queen 17
Chelmsford, Lord 82
Churchill, Lord Randolph 70, 107, 112, 114
Churchill, Winston 132, 185, 186, 188, 195, 201,
    202, 204, 210
Clandestine Marriages Act (1753) 4–5
Clarendon, Lord 69
Clarke, Kenneth 271, 276–7, 284
Clause IV (of Labour Party constitution) 219, 255
Clynes, J. R. 161, 171
Coe, Sebastian 271
Cook, A. J. 185
Cook, Robin 254
Cooper, Yvette 307, 315
Corbyn, Jeremy xi
    and George Lansbury 182
    and Harriet Harman 296
    wins 2015 leadership election 306–8, 312–15
    early life and career 308–10
    early political career 310–12
    as Leader of the Opposition 315–22
Corn Laws 40, 50–51, 56, 75
Craigie, Jill 235, 236
Creagh, Mary 307
Cripps, John 234
Cripps, Stafford 216, 234
Croker, John Wilson 52
Crooks, Will 169–70
Crosland, Anthony 223
Crossman, Richard 235
Curzon, Lord 142

Dalton, Hugh 216, 225
Davis, David 289
Derby, Lord 40, 49, 57, 63, 67, 68, 77, 81, 82, 85, 89
Devonshire, Duke of 33
Disraeli, Benjamin 51, 52, 53–4, 56–7, 58, 62–3,
    77, 78, 82, 85, 89, 91–2, 106–7, 199, 130
Douglas-Home, Robin 286
Douglas-Home, Sholto 286
Dowden, Oliver 289
Dromey, Jack 292
Duncan, Alan 86, 269
Duncan Smith, Iain
    as Leader of the Opposition 274, 276–80,
        288–9
    early life and career 275
    early political career 275–6
    later political career 280
    and Michael Howard 288

Duncannon, Lord 30
Duty of the Age, The (Robinson) 134

Eden, Anthony 214, 217, 230
Edward VII, King 93, 96
Elizabeth, Queen Mother 233
European Economic Community/European
    Common Market 220, 236, 237, 252, 285–6
Exchange Rate Mechanism (ERM) 256

Fair, Yvonne ix, xvi
Fawcett, Millicent 198
Field, Frank 294
Fitzwilliam, Earl 21
Fleming, Annie 213, 214, 218
Fleming, Ian 213, 214
Fletcher, Nigel x
Foord, Archibald S. 19, 29–30, 37
Foot, Dingle 234
Foot, Isaac 233
Foot, Michael
    on Hugh Gaitskell 216
    as Leader of the Opposition 232–3,
        238–40, 316
    early life and career 233–5
    early political career 235–6
    in Wilson government 236–7
    in Callaghan government 237–8
    and Neil Kinnock 242–3, 245–6
    and John Smith 252
    and Margaret Beckett 260
Forster, William E. 98, 99
Forth, Eric 278
Fowler, Norman 284, 286, 287
Fox, Charles James
    as Leader of the Opposition xv, 10–15
    statue of 1–2
    early life of 2–4
    early political career 4–9
    and George III 6–7, 12–13, 16, 17–18
    as Foreign Secretary 8–9
    in Fox–North Coalition 9–10
    and Regency Crisis 12–13
    reaction to French Revolution 13–15
    support for freedom of speech 14–15
    leaves Parliament 15
    returns as Foreign Secretary 15–16
    death of 16–17
    and George Tierney 32
    and Charles Gordon-Lennox 89
    and Jeremy Corbyn 321
Fox, Henry 2–3, 6

Fox, Sir Stephen 2
French Revolution 13–15

Gaitskell, Hugh
    as Leader of the Opposition 211–12,
        213–14, 217–20
    death of 214–15, 220–22, 250–51
    early life and career 215–16
    early political career 216
    as Chancellor of the Exchequer 216–17
    and George Brown 225
George III, King 6–7, 9–10, 12–13, 14, 16, 17–18,
    25, 122
George IV, King 9, 12–13, 17–18, 20–21, 25,
    45, 134
George V, King 148, 171
Gladstone, William 66, 69, 71, 97–8, 100,
    101–2, 104, 107, 111, 112–13, 118, 119, 123, 125,
    126, 129, 130, 135, 138–9, 145–6
Goderich, Viscount 35, 39, 43, 60, 61, 133, 134
Gordon-Lennox, Charles
    as Leader of the Opposition 85, 88, 89–91
    early life and career 88–9
    early political career 89
    as Lord President of the Council 91–2
    in Lord Salisbury government 92
    retirement and death 93
    legacy of 93–4
Gould, Brian 254, 255
Granby, Marquess of *see* Manners, Charles
Granville, Earl of *see* Leveson-Gower,
    Granville
Great Reform Act (1832) 46
Greenwood, Arthur
    political career 197, 199–204, 208, 210
    early life and career 200–201
    as Leader of the Opposition 202–4
    death of 204
Grenville, Lord 15–16, 23, 25, 32, 38, 60
Grey, Earl 19, 23, 25, 30, 31, 34, 35, 37, 38, 39,
    42, 45, 46
Guiccioli, Teresa 74
Guillemard, Laurence 125–6
Guilty Men (Foot *et al.*) 235
Gummer, John 284

Hague, Charles 266
Hague, Nigel 266
Hague, William xi
    at 1977 Conservative Party conference
        264–5
    early life and career 265–8

Hague, William *cont.*
  early political career 268–70
  as Leader of the Opposition 271–2
  later political career 272–3
  and Iain Duncan Smith 276
Halifax, Viscount 201
Harcourt, Lewis 124
Harcourt, Sir William
  on William Gladstone 97–8
  as Leader of the Opposition 121–2, 126–7
  early life and career 122–3
  as Home Secretary 123–5
  as Chancellor of the Exchequer 125–6
  death of 127
Hardie, Kier 168, 170
Hardinge, Lord 89
Hardwicke, Lord 2–3
Harman, Harriet xv
  as Leader of the Opposition 291, 295, 296
  early life and career 292–3
  political career 293–6
  and Ed Miliband 297–8
Harris, James
  early life and career 73–4
  early political career 74–9
  as Foreign Secretary 75–7, 78–9
  as Leader of the Opposition 77–8, 89
  death of 78
  and Hugh Cairns 82
Hart, Judith 259
Hartington, Marquess of *see* Cavendish, Spencer
Hastings, Warren 11
Hattersley, Roy 245, 246
Healy, Denis 238–9, 252
Heath, Edward xvi, 229–31
Hecht, Bernat 282–3
Hecht, Hilda 282
Henderson, Arthur
  and William Adamson 157
  early life and career 168–9
  early political career 169–70
  in Asquith and Lloyd George
    governments 170–71
  as Foreign Secretary 171
  as Leader of the Opposition 171–2
  later political career 173
  death of 173
  and Frederick Pethick-Lawrence 195
Hennessy, Peter 109, 324
Herbert, Sidney 76
Herries, Charles 59

Herries, John Charles
  early life and career 59–60
  early political career 60–62
  as Leader of the Opposition 62–4
  death of 63
Herries, Mary 59
Hewitt, Patricia 293
Hicks Beach, Sir Michael
  as Leader of the Opposition 111–12, 113,
    114–15
  early life and career 112
  in Disraeli government 112
  in opposition 112–13
  in Salisbury government 113–14
  death of 114
Hitler, Adolf 182, 201
Howard, Michael
  and William Hague 271
  interview with Jeremy Paxman 281–2
  early life and career 282–5
  early political career 285–9
  as Leader of the Opposition 289–90
Howard, Pamela 283
Howard, Peter 235
Howard, Sandra 286
Howe, Geoffrey 264, 268
Hudson, Hugh 248
Huskisson, William 61

If John Smith Had Lived (TV programme) 251
In Place of Fear (Foot) 242

Jamaica Farewell (Cargill) 214
Jay, Douglas 216
Jenkins, Roy 239
Johnson, Alan 304
Johnson, Boris 319
Johnson, Walter 232–3
Joseph, Sir Keith 265
Jowett, Benjamin 138

Kaufman, Gerald 233
Kendall, Liz 307, 315
Kennedy, John F. 215
Keppel, Admiral 7–8
Ker, John 49
de Kérouaille, Louise 2
Khan, Sadiq 307
Khrushchev, Nikita 220
Kimberley, Earl of *see* Wodehouse, John
Kingsley Wood, Howard 196
Kinnock, Glenys 243, 248

Kinnock, Neil
  as Leader of the Opposition 241–2, 246–9
  early life and career 242, 243
  early political career 242–6
  and John Smith 252–3, 254
  and Harriet Harman 293
Kerchever Arnold, Thomas 117
Kozak, Marion 298, 299–300
Krishnamurty, Paul 313

Lamborn, Harry 293
Lammy, David 307
Lamont, Norman 269, 284, 288
Lansbury, Angela 175
Lansbury, Anne 176
Lansbury, George
  as Leader of the Opposition 173, 176,
    180–81
  descriptions of 175–6
  early life and career 176
  political career 176–80, 182
  in MacDonald government 180
  death of 182
Lansdowne, Marquess of see Petty-
  Fitzmaurice, Henry
Laski, Harold 299
Lees-Smith, Hastings
  as Leader of the Opposition 188–90, 192,
    193, 196
  early life and career 190
  political career 190–92
  and Frederick Pethick-Lawrence 195
Lennox, Caroline 2, 3, 89
Lennox, Charles 89
Lestor, Joan 259
Leveson-Gower, Granville
  offices held 65–6
  early life and career 66
  early political career 66–8
  as Leader of the Opposition 68–72
  in Gladstone government 69, 71
  death of 71
  and Hugh Cairns 83, 84
  and Charles Gordon-Lennox 90–91
  and John Wodehouse 119
Lewington, Charles 270
Lewis, Derek 281, 288
Lincoln, Lord 76
Liverpool, Lord 26, 49, 60
Livingston, Ken 309
Lloyd George, David 140, 142, 148, 154, 157–8,
  164, 170

Longford, Lord 292
Lonsdale, Lord 75

Maastricht Treaty 255, 275
MacDonald, Ramsay 161, 170, 171–2, 184, 191,
  195–6, 216, 233
McDonnell, John 306, 312
Maclean, Donald
  and William Adamson 159, 160, 164–6
  father of Soviet spy 162–3
  early life and career 163
  early political career 163–4
  as Leader of the Opposition 164–7
Maclean Jr., Donald 162–3
Maclean, Gwendolen 163
Maclean, John 163
Macleod, Iain 284
Macmillan, Harold 215, 218, 230, 265
Madness of George III, The (Bennett) 12
Magee, Patrick 310
Major, John 248, 250, 256, 270, 286, 287
Malmesbury, Earl of see Harris, James
Manchester, Duchess of 98
Mandelson, Peter 206, 207, 248, 294
Manners, Charles 55–8
Manners, John 56
Marr, Andrew 251
Marsden, Gordon 306
Marx, Eleanor 176
Marx, Karl 299
Maudling, Reginald 230, 231
Maxton, James xv
  Gordon Brown's thesis on 183–4
  early life and career 184
  early political career 184–5
  as Leader of the Opposition 185–7, 189, 193
May, Theresa 149, 317
Mayhew, Patrick 286
Melbourne, Viscount 40, 46, 47, 62
Memoirs of an Ex-Minister (Harris) 78
Miliband, David 298, 299–300, 302, 303
Miliband, Ed
  as Leader of the Opposition 295–6, 303–5
  early life and career 297–8, 299–302
  early political career 301–3
Miliband, Ralph 298–9
Militant Tendency 240, 247, 316
Ministry of All the Talents 16, 22, 32, 38
Morrison, Herbert
  political career 201, 205–13
  and leadership of Labour Party 201,
    205–6, 208, 210–12

Morrison, Herbert *cont.*
  early life and career 207
  death of 212
Mosley, Sir Oswald 284, 308
Mountbatten, Earl 197
Mussolini, Benito 182
My Quest for Peace (Lansbury) 182

Napoleon III, Emperor 74, 76–7
Nightingale, Florence 135
North, Lord 5, 6, 7, 8–10
Northcote, Sir Stafford
  as Leader of the Opposition 104, 107, 111
  early life and career 105
  as Chancellor of the Exchequer 105–7
  civil service reform 106, 109, 110
  as Foreign Secretary 107–8
  death of 108–9

Osborne, George 290
O'Toole, Peter 175
Owen, Daid 239
Owen, Frank 235

Palmerston, Lord 40, 43, 67–8, 69, 74, 76, 97, 117
Pankhurst, Emmeline 194, 195
Parliamentary Socialism: A Study in the Politics of Labour (Miliband) 299
Parris, Matthew 277, 286
Paxman, Jeremy 281
Peel, Robert 43, 50, 51, 62
Perceval, Spencer 25–6, 27, 60, 66
Peterloo massacre 34, 44
Pethick, Emmeline 194–5, 197–8
Pethick-Lawrence, Frederick
  as Leader of the Opposition 193–4, 196–7
  early life and career 194–5
  political career 195–6, 197–8
  death of 197
Petty, John 38
Petty-Fitzmaurice, Henry (3rd Marquess of Lansdowne)
  and George Ponsonby 24, 25
  early life of 37–8
  in Parliament 38–9
  as Leader of the Opposition 39, 40
  as possible Prime Minister 39–40
  death of 41
  and 1830 general election 45
Petty-Fitzmaurice, Henry (5th Marquess of Lansdowne)

early life and career 137–8
in Gladstone and Salisbury governments 138–9
as Leader of the Opposition 139–42
in Asquith government 142
death of 142
Phipps, Colonel 35
Pitt the Younger, William 10, 11, 15, 20, 22, 31–2, 43, 60
Ponsonby, George xi
  as Leader of the Opposition 19–20, 23–7
  early life and career 20
  in Irish Parliament 20–21
  enters UK Parliament 21–3
  and George Tierney 23, 26, 32–3
  illness and death 26–8
Ponsonby, John 20
Ponsonby, Thomas 23
Portillo, Michael 271, 276
Portland, Duke of 9, 20, 21
Postgate, Oliver 176
Powell, Enoch 231
Prescott, John 262, 294

Rawnsley, Andrew 297–8
Redwood, John 270
Reeves, Rachel 320
Regency Crisis (1788–9) 12–13
Reynolds, Joshua 1
Richmond, Duke of *see* Gordon–Lennox, Charles
Ripon, Marquess of *see* Robinson, George
Robinson, George
  early life and career 133–4
  in government 135–6
  as Leader of the Opposition 136
  death of 136
Rockingham, Marquess of 9
Rodgers, Bill 239
Roosevelt, Franklin D. 182
Rosebery, Earl of 71, 119–20, 121, 126
Rossi, John P. 98
Rothschild, Nathan Mayer 60
Russell, Lord John 40, 52, 67, 68, 117
Rutland, Duke of 56

St John-Stevas, Norman 265
Salisbury, Lord 82, 85, 86, 92, 102, 107, 108, 111, 113–14, 135, 139, 147, 152
Scargill, Arthur 246–7, 260
Sergeant, John 315
Shelburne, Earl of 9, 38

Shinwell, Emmanuel 161
Short, Edward 236, 238
Smith, Andrew 306
Smith, John
    death of 250–51, 256, 257
    early life and career 251
    early political career 251–4
    as Leader of the Opposition 254–6
    and Harriet Harman 293
Smith, Owen 317
Snowden, Philip 216
Spencer, Esther 43
Spencer, Frederick 128
Spencer, George 42
Spencer, John (5th Earl Spencer)
    early life and career 128–9
    in Gladstone government 129–30
    support for Home Rule 130–31
    as Leader of the Opposition 131–2
Spencer, John (Viscount Althorp)
    as Leader of the Opposition 42, 44–7
    early life and career 42–3
    early political career 43–4
Stanley, Lord 29, 50, 51, 56, 57, 75, 85
Straw, Jack 255

tariff reform 102, 147–8
Taverne, Dick 259
Taylor, A. J. P. 175
Taylor, Peter 175
Tebbit, Norman 275, 276
Thatcher, Margaret 230, 231, 232, 238, 248, 253, 264, 287
Tierney, George
    and George Ponsonby 23, 26, 32–3
    on role of opposition 29
    as Leader of the Opposition 30, 33–6
    early life and career 30
    enters Parliament 30–31
    duel with Pitt 31–2
    and Charles Fox 32
    death of 35–6
Timothy, Nick 149
Trevelyan, Sir Charles 106
Truss, Liz xiii

Vane, Colonel 169
Vansittart, Nicholas 60
Varley, Eric 252
Venables Vernon, Edward 122
Victoria, Queen 40, 68, 93, 102, 122, 130
Villiers, Charles 100

Wakeman, Henry Offley 7
Walker, Patrick Gordon 226
Walpole, Robert ix, xiv, 5
Watson, Tom 320
Webb, Beatrice 161, 177
Wellington, Duke of 35, 39, 44, 45, 46, 60, 61, 89
Weston, Kim ix
Wheeler, George 81
Whelan, Charlie 302
Whitbread, Samuel 19, 24–5
Whitty, Larry 257
Widdecombe, Ann 281–2, 288
Wilde, Oscar 151–2
Wilkinson, Ellen 209
William IV, King 46
Williams, Shirley 238, 239
Wilson, Harold 216, 222, 223–4, 225–6, 227–8, 236, 244, 252
Wodehouse, Anne 116
Wodehouse, John
    early life and career 116–17
    in Gladstone and Palmerston governments 117–18
    as Leader of the Opposition 119–20
    death of 120